1993

SUBJECTIVITY, IDENTITY, AND THE BODY

SUBJECTIVITY, IDENTITY, AND THE BODY

Women's Autobiographical Practices
in the Twentieth Century

SIDONIE SMITH

INDIANA UNIVERSITY PRESS

Bloomington and Indianapolis

The paper used in this publication meets the minimum requirements of American National Standard for Information Sciences—Permanence of Paper for Printed Library Materials, ANSI Z39.48-1984.

Manufactured in the United States of America

Library of Congress Cataloging-in-Publication Data

Smith, Sidonie.
    Subjectivity, identity, and the body : women's autobiographical practices in the twentieth century / Sidonie Smith.
        p.   cm.
    Includes bibliographical references and index.
    ISBN 0-253-35286-X (alk. paper). — ISBN 0-253-20789-4 (pbk.)
    1. Autobiography—Women authors.   2. Women's studies—Biographical methods.   3. Biography—20th century.   I. Title.
CT25.S6   1993
920.72'09'04—dc20   92-25022

1 2 3 4 5   97 96 95 94 93

to Janet,
whose voice I can still hear

"I" am not "I," I *am* not, I am not *one*. As for *woman,* try and find out."

Luce Irigaray, *This Sex Which Is Not One*

She was not ready to understand her dream. She had no idea that everyone we dream about we are.

Michelle Cliff, *Abeng*

To accept one's past—one's history—is not the same thing as drowning in it; it is learning how to use it.

James Baldwin, *The Fire Next Time*

Despite our desperate, eternal attempt to separate, contain, and mend, categories always leak.

Trinh T. Minh-ha, *Woman Native Other*

CONTENTS

ACKNOWLEDGMENTS

Since completing *A Poetics of Women's Autobiography* five years ago, I have come to know many of the people working on autobiographical practices. This broad network of colleagues and friends, developed through my involvement in the new MLA Division of Autobiography, Biography, and Life Writing and through my collaboration with Julia Watson on the anthology entitled *De/Colonizing the Subject: The Politics of Gender in Women's Autobiography,* has become increasingly important to me. I look to the presentations, essays, and books by these friends and colleagues for stimulation, insights, and critical strategies. I think especially of Françoise Lionnet, Caren Kaplan, William L. Andrews, Carole Boyce Davies, Shirley Neuman, Margo Culley, Bella Brodzki, Leigh Gilmore, Rebecca Hogan, Shirley Geok-lin Lim, Barbara Harlow, and Hertha Wong. And of course I think of Julia, whose incisive readings, inquiring mind, and personal support I have found continually sustaining. We have worked well together.

I thank the graduate students with whom I have worked through feminist theories over the last several years. Their eagerness to engage in the debates and their perceptive readings of possibilities and liabilities inherent in various points of departure for theory have led me to become a much more careful reader of my own work as well as the work of others.

I thank also Peter Wagner, Provost of the State University of New York at Binghamton, for his generosity in providing me with a year's research leave when I left my administrative position. Without that year, I would not have been able to combine disparate articles and unpublished materials into a unified study. It was a wonderful year for writing.

Finally, I thank my family, Greg and Tony. They are always there for me with jokes and love.

An abbreviated version of chapters 1 and 2 appeared as "Resisting the Gaze of Embodiment: Women's Autobiography in the Nineteenth Century," in *Fea(s)ts of Memory: The Auto-*

biographical Writings of American Women, ed. Margo Culley (Madison: The University of Wisconsin Press; © 1992 by the Board of Regents of The University of Wisconsin System). A slightly expanded version of chapter 3 appeared as "Self, Subject, and Resistance: Marginality and Twentieth-Century Autobiographical Practice," in *Tulsa Studies in Woman's Literature* 9 (Spring 1990): 11–24. A version of chapter 8 appeared as "The Autobiographical Manifesto: Identities, Temporalities, Politics," in *Prose Studies* 14 (September 1991): 186-212. I thank all three editors for permission to reprint.

I also thank the following for permission to quote material:

All quotes from *Borderlands/La Frontera: The New Mestiza,* © 1987 by Gloria Anzaldúa. Reprinted by permission of Aunt Lute Books (415) 558-8116.

To the University of Chicago for permission to quote from Hélène Cixous, "The Laugh of the Medusa," *Signs* (Summer 1976).

To the Estate of Gertrude Stein per Calman A. Levin for permission to quote from *The Autobiography of Alice B. Toklas.*

SUBJECTIVITY,
IDENTITY,
AND THE BODY

I

THE UNIVERSAL SUBJECT, FEMALE EMBODIMENT, AND THE CONSOLIDATION OF AUTOBIOGRAPHY

> I have shown myself such as I was. . . . I have unveiled my inmost self such as You Yourself have seen it. Eternal Being. . . .
>
> Jean-Jacques Rousseau, *Les Confessions*
>
> Although it may be impossible, in the end, to escape the hegemony of patriarchal structures, none the less, by unveiling the prejudices at work in our cultural artefacts, we impugn the universality of the man-made models provided to us, and allow for the possibility of sidestepping and subverting their power.
>
> Nelly Furman, "The Politics of Language"

As she peruses a recent novel, the narrator ("Mary") of Virginia Woolf's *A Room of One's Own*[1] bemoans the textual imperiousness of the autobiographical "I" marking the text of "man." "But after reading a chapter or two," the narrator complains,

> a shadow seemed to lie across the page. It was a straight dark bar, a shadow shaped something like the letter "I." One began dodging

this way and that to catch a glimpse of the landscape behind it.
Whether that was indeed a tree or a woman walking I was not quite
sure. Back one was always hailed to the letter "I." One began to be
tired of "I." Not but what this "I" was a most respectable "I";
honest and logical; as hard as a nut, and polished for centuries by
good teaching and good feeding. I respect and admire that "I" from
the bottom of my heart. But—here I turned a page or two, looking
for something or other—the worst of it is that in the shadow of the
letter "I" all is shapeless as mist.[2]

Through this tongue-in-cheek critique, Woolf points to the occlud-
ing vision of that "hard nut" of universal selfhood. Bored with the
text, she speculates about the source of that boredom: "But why
was I bored? Partly because of the dominance of the letter 'I' and
the aridity, which, like the giant beech tree, it casts within its shade.
Nothing will grow there. And partly for a more obscure reason.
There seemed to be some obstacle, some impediment of Mr. A's
mind which blocked the fountain of creative energy and shored it
within narrow limits" (104). Perhaps, then, the bar needs to be
crossed in some fundamental way.

This "I" is, of course, what autobiography is about since autobiography has been the story of the "I," that "bar" that dramatically marks the white page, at least the story of that bar up to some
moment before the metaphorical crossing of the bar. But that bar is
itself a sign of death-in-life. Casting aridity within its shade, it
blocks out creativity like a sunscreen. The bar thus becomes barren, sans imagination and fecundity. And so, for Woolf, the bar
that serves metaphorically as site of the universal subject and its
normative masculinity, requires barring. It must be crossed, perhaps double-crossed, before it can signal the trace of female subjectivity in an autobiographical text.

Now I want to shift texts and authors for a moment to that
strange tale of enframed silence. In "The Blank Page" (a short story
that has become an oft-invoked text in feminist analytical practice)
Isak Dinesen elaborates a poetics of women's textual and sexual
silences. The Spanish convent functions truly as a house of repute.
Along its corridors, perused by all who pass through, hang the
enframed wedding night sheets of aristocratic marriages, marked
by the blood of defloration (sign of reputation). The Rorschach-like
bloodstain, signifying simultaneously the presence and absence of
virginity, certifies the aristocratic daughter's fulfillment of her des-

tiny and the fragile material basis upon which the aristocratic house rests. These very sheets maintain the genealogy of the landed families, testifying as they do to patriarchal values fulfilled, to female sexuality penetrated, appropriated, and framed. Accompanying the sheet is the princess's name. Both name and stain interchangeably mark female identity and destiny. As the narrator of another Dinesen story, "Sorrow-Acre," tells us, the bodies of women hold up the houses of the aristocracy like the caryatids supported ancient temples.

Here blood serves as the metonymic marker of "woman." The sheets on the walls are tapestries, self-portraits, representations of women's lives, lives lived in thrall to, lives reduced to female anatomy. Signs of emptiness (in the womb), the bloodstained sheets paradoxically signal the presence of female self-narrative, or to be more exact, proto-narrative. Signatures merely of cultural expectations, the frames carry in them the repetitive autobiographies of the princesses. But, of course, the princesses have not written their stories, their bodies have expelled them. Hanging on the walls of the convent, the autobiographical sheets tell the same story, row after row, wall after wall, frame after frame—until the blank page of one autobiographical sheet breaks the narrative pattern in its silence, in its refusal to be framed in the same way. In this one frame the sheet remains white, disturbingly, provocatively barren of that metonymic marker of female identity, elusively silent about one princess's wedding night. Out of this silence erupts women's autobiographical storytelling since the possibilities of storytelling proliferate with the absence of the body's mark. The frame, in its wordlessness, its bloodlessness, its disembodiment, risks another story. Female sexuality and textuality herein defy the inherited frame of an essentialized embodiment. In this blank space/page woman's autobiographical fabrication becomes possible. As the old crone, the docent of the convent, tells her listeners: "Look at this page, and recognize the wisdom of my grandmother and of all storytelling women!"[3]

These two disparate texts, written by different women in the early twentieth century, raise explicitly and implicitly a set of interlocking issues with which this study is concerned. The one points to the history of the universal subject and the hard nut of its normative (masculine) individuality. It speaks as well of the tyranny of the arid "I," which obscures through a gray and shapeless mist everything colorful that lies within its vision. And it implicitly issues a challenge to the woman who, in entering the textual space of that "I," would appropriate the position of the autobiographical subject. For there may be as many costs as benefits to surrendering to the "I" that she finds installed there. And there are certainly histories of the subject to be negotiated in that "I" space, histories that make trouble for her as she takes up that autobiographical "I." Those histories may press her to silence or they may encourage her to cross, crisscross, doublecross that "I" in order to move from silence into self-narrative. They certainly force her, in Valerie Walkerdine's words, to "struggle to become [a] subject" as she simultaneously "resist[s] *provided subjectivities* in relation to the regulative power of modern social apparatuses."[4]

The other narrative speaks of the cultural inscription of the female body and of one woman's resistance to the tyranny of biological essentialism and by implication of the complex relationship of embodiment to disembodiment. It speaks of a different "experientially based"[5] history of the body that breaks the old frames, the old discourses of identity. It also speaks of the institutional power of "official" frames governing self-portraiture and of a "law of genre"[6] that constitutes officially sanctioned autobiographical subjects. Here the subject of unauthorized, perhaps unspeakable, experiences (there is, after all, no blood on the sheet) troubles the official history written on the convent wall by "talking back"[7] to those who read the gallery of sheets. This autobiographical story may seem to be in the same kind of frame as the other personal narratives, but by virtue of its difference it serves to critique the official frame-up. In its resistance it becomes a hybrid form.

My fascination with the complex ways in which histories of the subject, discourses of identity, cultural inscriptions of the body, and laws of genre coalesce in the autobiographical "I" has prompted the following study of women's autobiographical practices spanning the last half of the nineteenth century and the twentieth century. I attempt here no history of Euroamerican autobiographical practices throughout the last one hundred years. I want to use this occasion to probe the ways in which specific writers, through specific autobiographical engagements, reveal their troubles with the old "I" at the same time that they make trouble with that generic "I," in both senses of the word. Before turning to these readings, however, I want to map out in this introductory chapter abbreviated histories of the universal subject and of the embodied subject. These histories are meant to suggest given subjectivities available to the autobiographer, subjectivities that were taken up in complicity and/or resistance.

The Universal Subject

Terry Eagleton notes that "certain meanings are elevated by social ideologies to a privileged position, or made the centres around which other meanings are forced to turn."[8] The meaning of western selfhood was one such meaning of privilege in the late eighteenth and nineteenth centuries, and it secured its privileges by means of specific historical phenomena, that is, by means of philosophical, economic, political, theological, scientific, and literary influences. The inaugural moment of the West's romance with selfhood lay in the dawn of the Renaissance, during which time the notion of the "individual" emerged, a universal human subject[9] who is marked individually.[10] Subsequently pressed through the mills of eighteenth-century enlightenment, early nineteenth-century romanticism, expanding bourgeois capitalism, and Victorian optimism, the individual came by the mid-nineteenth century to be conceptualized as a "fixed, extralinguistic" entity consciously pursuing its unique destiny.[11]

From this ideological perspective, every self, as J. Hillis Miller remarks, "has its own sharp configuration, different from all others. Each is present to itself and to other such spiritual entities as force, as presence."[12] The "sharp configuration" to which Miller alludes suggests the certitudes of well-defined, stable, impermeable boundaries around a singular, unified, and atomic core, the unequivocal delineation of inside and outside. Separated from that which is external to it, the self as *isolato* constantly asserts its place outside, beside, aside from other clearly configured selves.

Consequently, this unitary self strives to be an "unencumbered subject."[13] Its refusal of encumbrance derives from a culturally specific orientation of the individual to the social. Throughout the seventeenth and eighteenth centuries, suggests Francis Barker, "the modern subject is constructed as the bearer of naturalism, the

facticity of things and their weightless transcription in discourse"
and as such "is contrasted to an outer world which, although
'social,' becomes for it a kind of nature." As a result of this
alienation of the self from its constitutive affiliations to the outer
world, "it [becomes] possible to speak with some certainty of
society—the associative name we give to lived isolation—when it
has been effectively desocialized, its humane production elided by
the separation from it of the constitution of the human subject."[14]
Independent of forces external to it, the self is neither constituted
by, nor coextensive with, its class identifications, social roles, or
private attachments. Social and communal roles with their elaborate masks of meaning may be inevitabilities. But however integumentary, they do not entirely absorb the essential self, whose
internal integrity lies elsewhere in a discrete core, abstracted from
society. Encroachments, disturbances, occasional detours, they do
not determine but rather remain tangential to the central drama of
an unembedded selfhood.

Unique, unitary, unencumbered, the self escapes all forms of
embodiment. Barker attributes this profound change in consciousness in the eighteenth century not only to the disassociation of the
self from interdependency with the outer world. He notes also that,
with the move toward "the newly interiorated subjectivity," the
body itself as a mere object is disassociated from mind or conscious
being and situated elsewhere: "Neither wholly present, nor wholly
absent, the body is confined, ignored, exscribed from discourse,
and yet remains at the edge of visibility, troubling the space from
which it has been banished."[15] The banishment or splitting off to
the margins of the conscious self of what now becomes a "supplementary body" invites on the one hand a neutralization of the body
through a self-censoring that functions to contain, control, and
co-opt the body's "dangerous passions." For a Descartes, the body
so restrained, so drained of its chaotic and grotesque potential,
serves as a vessel for the soul. Yet, since the body always persists in
that elsewhere at the horizon of experience and meaning, it can
never be "jettisoned entirely," nor can it be wholly contained.[16] On
the other hand, this banishment of the body and its desires to the
borders of consciousness through the ideological enshrinement of
what M. M. Bakhtin calls the "classical" body and the consequent
objectification of the body encourages the process whereby others

whose bodies are identified as culturally "grotesque" become more fully body.[17]

Despite myriad specificities or contingencies of geography, history, culture, economic circumstances, etc., this self is conceived to be persistently rational. As such it is an ahistorical or transcendent phenomenon and remains autonomous and free. From this autonomous site the self comes to identify, classify, and know the world in a monologic engagement that establishes individual consciousness as the center and origin of meaning.[18] Disjoined from the body, the self becomes a governing consciousness synonymous, as Stanley Corngold contends, with the "Cartesian subject, the *res cogitans,* a substantial self identified uniformly with the thinking subject and cited in 'philosophies of consciousness,' where it is erected into the foundation of an epistemology."[19] Its predominant mode of epistemological engagement with the world is through the agency of reason; and its powers encompass the authority to theorize, generalize, and thereby appropriate the knowable as well as the ability to transcend the contingencies of "desire, affectivity, and the body," those constraining particularities of human existence.[20] While emotional life is not denied the self, it remains publicly suspect: Linked as it is to the only partially repressed body, it is subordinated to and by reason.

With the body subordinated, the enlightenment self pursues, according to Jane Flax, "a form of reason capable of privileged insight into its own processes and into the 'laws of nature.' "[21] Reflecting on its essential nature, abstracting its teleological motion, delineating and defining coherent boundaries of experience, the self thereby presumes the possibility of self-knowledge. Through this lens, the self can turn toward the world and fix upon it, through a reason that "transcends all situation, context, and perspective," a universalizing vision characterized as impartial.[22] The very words used to describe the rational practices of autonomous selfhood suggest the degree to which vision as truth or enlightenment predominates. "The notion of truth involved here," writes Candace D. Lang in her discussion of romantic personhood, "remains a fundamentally Platonic one, that of an abstract eternal essence to be glimpsed in a dazzling vision or a brilliant insight; which is to say that seeing (what is hidden behind a veil of appearance) remains the only valid mode of knowing."[23] As subjectivity metamorphoses into objectivity and impartiality, the self assumes its privileged status as the origin of meaning, knowledge, truth. "The Cartesian ego founding modern philosophy," writes Iris Marion Young, "realizes the totalizing project. This *cogito* itself expresses the idea of pure identity as the reflective self-presence of consciousness to itself. Launched from this point of transcendental subjectivity, thought now more boldly than ever seeks to comprehend all entities in unity with itself and in a unified system with each other."[24] What has come to be called the humanist credo of the universal subject presumes individual participation in an "eternal human nature,"[25] and an identification with a common ontology—what we call rational thinking. The primacy of reason and self-consciousness, separated off from the contingencies of that most personal entity, the body and its irrational desires, and from the vagaries of tradition, promotes the belief that, since everyone shares this common source, one individual can share, understand, and identify with another. All "I"s are ontologically identical, rational beings—but all "I"s are also unique. This is the stuff of myth, imperious and contradictory.

Imperial interpreter, provocateur of totalization, the essential self is likewise a "free" agent, exercising self-determination over meaning, personal destiny, and desire. Neither powerless nor passive, it assumes and celebrates agency. Its movement through time/history is purposeful, consistent, coherent, hence teleological. And since, as Terry Eagleton notes, thinking teleologically "is a way of ordering and ranking meanings in a hierarchy of significance, creating a pecking order among them in the light of an ultimate purpose,"[26] the teleological drift of selfhood concedes nothing to indeterminacy, to ambiguity, or to heterogeneity. Such purposiveness leads to the silencing of that which is contingent, chaotic, tangential to a true self.

Politically, the enlightenment self is aggressively individualistic in its desires and liberal in its philosophical perspective. The French Revolution with its cry for liberty, equality, fraternity; the philosophical systems of Locke and Rousseau with their emphasis on empiricism and the experience of the individual's senses as originary loci of knowledge; the self-absorption of Romanticism and its preoccupation with subjective experience; the economic and political shift from aristocratic to bourgeois power; the progressive tendencies of Darwinism, particularly social Darwinism; the consolidation of Protestant ideology with its emphasis on the accessibility of God to individual prayer and intercession: all these phenomena coalesced to privilege the self-determining individuality of desire and destiny. Thus every person could autograph history, could mark the times. "Individual effort," notes Mary Poovey, "became the mark of past accomplishments and the guarantor of future success; this was the era of the 'self-made man,' when aristocratic privilege could finally be challenged on a wide scale by individuals possessed of talent, opportunity, and the capacity for hard work."[27] Yet the individual self could endure as a concept of human beingness only if, despite the specificities of individual experience, despite the multiplication of differences among people, the legend continued to bear universal marks. This self has to move freely toward its cultural positioning as universal subject[28] but retain a threshold of particulars.

It also has to establish a self-regulating stance, a prerequisite to entry into the domain of the subject of democratic liberalism. Peter Stallybrass and Allon White have elaborated the complex lineaments of the identity formation of this new "democratic" subject in the eighteenth century. It required the consolidation of "a 'neutral,' 'middling,' 'democratic,' 'rational' subject" who "appeared to be contentless, a point of judgement and rational evaluation which was purely formal and perspectival." In fact, they go on to argue, this subject was "constituted through and through by the clamour of particular voices to which it tried to be universally superior. It is on this account that the very blandness and transparency of bourgeois reason is in fact nothing other than the critical negation of a social 'colourfulness,' of a heterogeneous diversity of specific contents, upon which it is, nonetheless, completely dependent."[29] In return for this evacuation of "color" that results from the processes of self-regulation, the democratic self can claim equal access to the universally human.

Yet within this claim there is implicit a hierarchy wherein what is and is not appropriate, at any given juncture, to the universal subject gets staked out. Founded on exclusionary practices, this democratic self positions on its border all that is termed the "colorful," that is, that which becomes identified culturally as other, exotic, unruly, irrational, uncivilized, regional, or paradoxically unnatural. Since the "low" does not participate in this privileged selfhood, it is the "low" that constitutes the "high"—the colorful, the neutral. Or to invoke the theoretical insights of Julia Kristeva and of Iris Marion Young,[30] the realms of the universal subject and the socially abject mutually constitute one another. To secure the universality of the self, cultural practices set various limits, and those limits are normative limits of race, gender, sexuality, and class identifications. A scrupulous classification of the shades of difference establishes clear boundaries around the neutral self. That which is expelled through classification becomes the socially abject, a cultural gesture that installs itself psychologically in the founding identifications of the universal subject.[31]

And here we rejoin the discussion of the disembodiment of the universal subject. Since the body is what Judith Butler describes as "a region of *cultural* unruliness and disorder,"[32] it serves, in its alignments of anatomical parts, as the margin joining/separating one subject from the other, one sex from the other, one race from another, the sane from the mad, the whole from the unhealthy, and so on. It functions as a sorting mechanism whereby the culturally dominant and the culturally marginalized are assigned their "proper" places in the body politic. This politics of the body as border/limit determines the complex relationship of individuals to their bodies, to the bodies of others, to fantasies of the founding subject, and to the body politic. Drawing all these alignments together in her review of Kristeva's notion of the abject and Young's use of Kristeva to understand forms of oppression, Butler suggests that "the repudiation of bodies for their sex, sexuality, and/or color is an 'expulsion' followed by a 'repulsion' that founds and consolidates culturally hegemonic identities along sex/race/ sexuality axes of differentiation."[33] Consolidation of dominant notions of the universal subject requires the consolidation of the essentialized identities of others as the abject, with the effect that "the body rendered as Other—the body repressed or denied and, then, projected reemerges for this [hegemonic] 'I' as the view of others as essentially body."[34] Thus certain people, those positioned peripherally to the dominant group, those claiming and/or assigned marginalized identities, find themselves partitioned in their bodies and culturally embodied.

The Subjectivity of Embodiment

This history of the universal subject thereby underwrites a history of the female subject, for the architecture of the universal subject rests upon and supports the founding identifications of those that are the nonuniversal, the colorful, among whom is "woman."[35] "Technologies of gender," to use Teresa de Lauretis's phrase,[36] hypostatize an ideology of sexually marked selfhood in the nineteenth century that rigidly construes and partitions masculine and feminine spheres of desire, fate, and identity. To woman is attributed another kind of selfhood, an essential selfhood, but not the selfhood of the universal human/male subject. And so, what does she know of universal selfhood or selfhood know of her?

Discourses of the universal subject assume reciprocities of self and soul, and they assign the "tremulous private body" to marginal status at the periphery of consciousness. Such peripheralization allows the greatest possible space in which self and soul can commingle, free of biologically determined influences. But since female identity inheres in woman's embodiment as procreator and nurturer, the female subject inhabits mostly that colorful margin; or rather, a colorful marginalization of embodiment fills her self and soul. The dynamics of such partitioning reveal the degree to which, as Butler argues,

> masculine disembodiment is only possible on the condition that women occupy their bodies as their essential and enslaving identities. . . . By defining women as 'Other,' men are able through the shortcut of definition to dispose of their bodies, to make themselves other than their bodies—a symbol potentially of human decay and transience, of limitation generally—and to make their bodies other than themselves. From this belief that the body is Other, it is not a far leap to the conclusion that others *are* their bodies, while the masculine 'I' is the noncorporeal soul. The body rendered as Other—the body repressed or denied and, then, projected—reemerges for this 'I' as the view of others as essentially body. Hence, women become the Other; they come to embody corporeality itself. This redundancy becomes their essence.[37]

For woman, "anatomy is destiny," a deterministic proclamation attributable to both Napoleon and Freud, those male giants who towered over the beginning and end of the century with equally fateful albeit different kinds of swagger. Anatomy becomes the irreducible granite at the core of woman's being. This, then, becomes her essence, and, paradoxically, her route to nonessentiality, as Diana Fuss argues when she critiques this fundamentally Aristotelian conception of woman: "On the one hand, woman is asserted to have an essence which defines her as woman and yet, on the other hand, woman is relegated to the status of matter and can have no access to essence." So as Fuss concludes, "it is the essence of woman to have no essence."[38]

Embodiment is a complicated phenomenon, marking woman with congeries of meaning. If the topography of the universal subject locates man's selfhood somewhere between the ears, it locates woman's selfhood between her thighs. The material and symbolic boundary of the female body becomes the hymen—that physical screen whose presence or absence signals so much. "In contrast to males," reflects Roberta Rubenstein, "females have a physical marker of virginity in the membrane of the hymen; upon its rupture countless women's fates have been decided."[39] Gender ideologies assign so much meaning to that rupture because they identify that thin skin signed by blood as the irreducible material core of woman's selfhood. Border of both integrity and violation, that skin defines an inside/outside boundary wholly other from that of the universal subject. For that place is inside the body where, paradoxically, inside and outside meet. The discrete and clear boundaries drawn around the universal subject inevitably blur or disappear altogether in such vague space. There is no isolable core of selfhood there for woman, for in the act of heterosexual intercourse, the female body is penetrated by the body of the other and in the experience of pregnancy, that other that is part of the subject takes up greater and greater space inside until it is suddenly expelled. Inside is outside; outside inside. The cultural notion of autonomous individuality is totally confused, since, as Susan Bordo has suggested, pregnancy is an "embodiment that houses otherness in the self."[40]

Discourses of embodiment also mark woman as an encumbered self, identified almost entirely by the social roles concomitant with her biological destiny. Affiliated physically, socially, psychologically in relationships to others, "her individuality [is] sacrificed to the 'constitutive definitions' of her identity as member of a family, as someone's daughter, someone's wife and someone's mother."[41] The unified self disperses, radiating outward until its fragments dissipate altogether into social and communal masks. Thus woman's destiny cannot be self-determined, and her agency cannot be exercised. At best she can only wait, a fate acknowledged by the narrator of Henry James's *Portrait of a Lady:* "Most women did with themselves nothing at all; they waited, in attitudes more or less gracefully passive, for a man to come that way and furnish them with a destiny."[42] Since the cultural construction of pregnancy made of the womb a receptacle awaiting the activation of the sperm, her very body passively awaited its destiny.[43]

Furthermore, by the nineteenth century, the very soul of woman surrenders to embodiment, signaling a radical shift away from the salvational equality found in an earlier Christianity. Augustine and Aquinas, whatever their differences, both held the soul to be neutral ground and as such unsexed. While woman's subordinate status in creation and her less-than-fully human "moral apparatus" may have prohibited her full participation in the earthly life, such inequality did not characterize the relationship of her soul to man's soul and thus did not preclude her sharing equal access to grace.[44] Throughout the seventeenth and eighteenth centuries, however, a newly sexualized female soul gradually displaced the theologically unsexed soul of the Medieval period and the Renaissance. "The gradual processes of secularisation and theological revision," argues Denise Riley, "were accompanied by an increasing sexualisation which crowded out the autonomous soul—while at the same time a particularly feminised conception of Nature began to develop."[45] As a result, Riley contends, "the associations of 'women' with the natural were magnified to a point of mutual implication." "Femininity" gradually fills the soul until, by the beginning of the nineteenth century, "no neutral enclave of the person remains unfilled and unoccupied by [it]."[46]

In various philosophical and religious discourses, the sexualization of woman's mind influences her intellectual capacities. In thrall to her body and to the affections and behavior associated with her encumbrances, woman remains "naturally" less rational than man.

Rather than working logically, her mind works through another kind of logic, which becomes a marginalized logic. Her way of knowing and interpreting is less abstract, less integrative, less transcendent, less impartial, and less self-conscious than the interpretive mode of the universal subject. Inhabiting domesticating space (a space located closer to nature and necessity, a space of immanence and immediacy), she exhibits the less authoritative "feminine" mode of engagement with the world, one characterized as intuitive, irrational, particularistic, and practical.[47] Consequently, woman seems unable to theorize, to draw generalizations, a limitation Hannah More elaborated in the late eighteenth century:

> [Women] seem not to possess in equal measure the faculty of comparing, combining, analysing, and separating these ideas; that deep and patient thinking which goes to the bottom of a subject; nor that power of arrangement which knows how to link a thousand connected ideas in one dependent train, without losing sight of the original idea out of which the rest grow, and on which they all hang.[48]

Effectively woman goes incognito before the Cartesian *cogito* as self-consciousness evades her.

The epistemological projects of men and women are consequently differentiated as masculine (those of the universal subject) or feminine, a differentiation delineated by Horace Mann in his 1853 treatise on the "Powers and Duties of Woman":

> Between the sexes, then, I hold there are innate and connate distinctions, which nature never loses sight of, unless occasionally in the production of a monster or a *lusus*. They are not alike, but there is a mutuality of superiority. As a general law, the man surpasses the woman in stature, in physical strength, and in those groups or combinations of the intellectual faculties where causality plays a part; but the woman surpasses the man in beauty, in taste, in grace, in faith, in affection, in purity. His better nature tends more to science and wisdom; hers, to love and the sympathies. He delights more in the worldly uses of truth; she, more in its immortal beauty; or, as Swedenborg somewhere oddly expresses it: "Man was created to be the understanding of truth, and woman the affection of good."[49]

Mann's attestation of mutual superiority notwithstanding, such differentiation of man's and woman's ways of knowing reinforced an already effective hierarchy that privileged the masculine mode as more radically severed from nature and thus the more perfect human achievement. Woman's mode, conceived as more natural and less fully human and mature because speechless, inarticulate, unanalytical, unreflective, disqualifies her for public life and the arena of cultural discourse. As George Eliot trenchantly acknowledged, "Women have not to prove that they can be emotional, and rhapsodic, and spiritualistic; every one believes that already. They have to prove that they are capable of accurate thought, severe study, and continuous self-command."[50]

At a distinct disadvantage, woman so defined cannot fully know or reflect upon herself. She harbors no unified, atomic, Adamic core to be discovered and represented. There are no masks to uncover because paradoxically there are only masks, only roles and communal expectations. She cannot find herself as universal man does in his romantic journey inward to the core of his being, except through those social roles already defined for her, the very masks romantic man would define, penetrate, and discard. And if she claims her own equal powers of self-conscious reasoning, she implicates herself in postures of carnivalesque monstrosity. As Lynn Sukenick notes, "Not only has this capacity been regarded as not innate in women, it has been seen by some—by those who posit an opposition between mind and 'sheer being'—as a distinct threat to woman's 'basic' nature": woman functions best as a "receptacle of feeling" or a "nonreflective bios."[51] Effectively, the woman who would reason like universal man becomes unwomanly, a kind of monstrous creature or *lusus naturae*. Thus nineteenth-century representations of the intellectual woman oftentimes turn on the disalignment of her bodily parts, as if to suggest that the very exercise of the intellect pulls natural phenomena into grotesque postures.

The surrender of woman's reason to embodiment also contaminates her relationship to the word. Allying her speech with the seductive Eve and the serpent and with the forces of cultural unruliness, gender ideologies of the early nineteenth century reaffirmed the association of the hole in woman's face with the contaminations of sex. In America and Europe generally women could not preach publicly; nor could they recite poetry before mixed groups of people without compromising their reputation; nor could they participate in formal education (at least until later in the century in America when a limited number of colleges allowed women to matriculate). Moreover, in her appropriate sphere or out of it, she could use certain kinds of discourses but not others, according to cultural rules of female propriety—for instance, the languages of sentiment, of piety, of "true womanhood." The wrong words in the wrong mouths articulated in the wrong places would confuse social relations and provided subjectivities.

Framed through embodiment, the "proper" woman remains subject to man's authority and theorizing because, if unmanned and misaligned, she will subvert the body politic. To the extent that woman represses the body, erasing her sexual desire and individual identity while embracing encumbering identities in service to family, community, and country, she positions herself as a proper lady who surmounts her negative identification with the body through selflessness.[52] To the degree that woman contests such roles and postures by pursuing her own desire and independence from men, she becomes a cultural grotesque. For the identification of female selfhood with the body is nowhere more dramatic than in the fear of woman that saturates nineteenth-century culture: "As the soul of the woman shrinks and is made gender-specific," suggests Riley, "so vice swells in her body; not, of course, with any novelty, except that, crucially, the territorial powers of the body are at the same time enlarged."[53] The "fallen" woman who succumbs to her "true nature" to become sexual, narcissistic, and venal, self-absorbed and self-promoting, acts too much the woman, thereby reaffirming what Mary Poovey calls "the fundamental paradox that pervades all discussions of women" in the eighteenth and nineteenth centuries: "At the heart of the explicit description of 'feminine,' Angelic women, superior to all physical appetite, resides the 'female' sexuality that was automatically assumed to be the defining characteristic of female nature."[54] Thus even as her body is revealed to be aesthetically beautiful, it is corrupt and grotesque. Here there is no line between the beautiful and the grotesque; they are mutually attested. Because "the tremulous private body" always threatens to "overflood its walls" and return from the margins, it threatens to disrupt the central places of consciousness and power.[55]

And here the discourses of race, class, and gender interpenetrate as working-class women and women of the "darker" races are assigned an embodiment unreprieved by the angelic. The discourse of the embodied woman is a discourse constitutive of the subjectivity of bourgeois women, those "angels in houses." Just as the universal subject takes his shape through multiple discourses of identities and differences, discourses of race, class, and sexuality among them, so those angels take shape through the discourses of various kinds of contaminated women, those even more "colorful" others who are denied the possibility of escaping the drag of the body.

The Subject of Autobiography

These histories of universal subjectivity and embodied subjectivity determine the narrative practices that people in the century take up as well as the provided subjectivities made available through those narratives. For instance, a certain ideology of language accompanies the notion of universal selfhood. The self so understood is both prelinguistic and extralinguistic. Constituted neither in nor by language, it exists prior to and independent of language, which is conceived as transparent and mimetic. Emboldened by this correspondence between words and world, emboldened also by what Stephen Heath calls the "confidence of knowledge," the self names, configures, and controls a world, which in turn assures the self of its epistemological probity.[56] The life of the self becomes one such instantly accessible world, accessible to representation, "the sorting out of identity and difference," the naming, forming, and controlling of interpretations.[57] Thus life can be represented, and that representation,[58] like the self controlling it, is coherent, unified, univocal, what Jane Gallop calls "well-defined and firm."[59] Both self and representation are as bold, indivisible, and unitary as the "I" that marks the space of selfhood on the page of autobiography.

Western autobiographical practices flourished because there seemed to be a self to represent, a unique and unified story to tell that bore common ground with the reader, a mimetic medium for self-representation that guaranteed the epistemological correspondence between narrative and lived life, a self-consciousness capable of discovering, uncovering, recapturing that hard core at the center.[60] All these certitudes of traditional autobiography follow, as Lang suggests, upon "the conviction that 'I,' the speaking subject, has a single, stable referent." They also follow from what she describes as "the development of the concept of the author as the sole authority, or single individual responsible for (and therefore expressed through) his writings."[61] Given these epistemological certitudes, the century assumed the efficacy of pursuing and representing the "truth" of selfhood, an orientation captured in Rousseau's confident and proleptic assertion: "I have shown myself such as I was. . . . I have unveiled my inmost self such as You Yourself have seen it. Eternal Being. . . ."[62] Indeed, selfhood and autobiography mutually implied one another.

Typically the pursuit of selfhood develops in two directions. The self may move consecutively through stages of growth, expanding the horizons of self and boundaries of experience through accretion, but always carrying forward through new growth that globe of an irreducible, unified core. This direction we might call horizontal. Or the self may proceed vertically, delving downward into itself to find the irreducible core, stripping away mask after mask of false selves in search of that hard core at the center, that pure, unique or true self. Launched on a romantic journey, the self steams into the interior of itself, through lake after lake, layer after layer of circumstance to an unencumbered center of quiet water, pure being or essence. Either engagement leads to certain teleological itineraries—the unfolding of the mind toward greater knowledge, or the unfolding of personal history toward some progressive goal, two synonymous and bourgeois creations—individual career and progress in the public aisle.

And so, autobiography consolidated its status as one of the West's master discourses, a discourse that has served to power and define centers, margins, boundaries, and grounds of action in the West. As Felicity A. Nussbaum provocatively argues in her exploration of ideologies of genre, bourgeois subjectivity, and gender in the eighteenth century,[63] autobiographical practices helped consolidate bourgeois subjects who understood themselves to be individuals, rational, free, autonomous, and "middling"; in turn those practices reflected the historical forces that pressed persons into certain kinds of subjectivities. Autobiographies told of public and professional achievements, of individual triumphs in strenuous adventures. They chronicled private journeys of the soul toward God. They chronicled stages of intellectual development, the evolution of consciousness. They charted a progressive narrative of individual destiny, from origin through environment and education to achievement.[64] Even in the countertendencies of a resistant romanticism, the interior drama of an alternative mode of absorbing the world, through intuition and emotion rather than a dogmatic reason, privatized the progression of the unique self, that core of true self-consciousness characteristic of the universal human subject. In whatever form, the primacy of personal memory displaced that of communal memory. Or perhaps, communal memory played itself out as the interiorized drama of the individual: personal saga represented communal saga rather than vice versa. Ultimately, the narrative itinerary of traditional autobiography reinscribed official histories of the universal subject.

Offering an official account for the community, the subject of traditional autobiography marshaled the vagaries of his unique history under the banner of the universal subject. Through this practice he reaffirmed, reproduced, and celebrated the agentive autonomy and disembodiment of the universal subject, valorizing individuality and separateness while erasing personal and communal interdependencies. As he did so he reenacted the erasure of the feminine that facilitates male entrance into the public realm of words, power, and meaning. Woman, mother, and the feminine functioned in the text of traditional autobiography to signal the place of lost innocence, the forces of desire pressing upon the individual, or the source of salvation. They were part of "the mess and clutter"[65] of the nonidentical that the autobiographer had to clear out as he struggled toward self-identity and the narrative of a coherent past. And so autobiography provided a discursive arena in which individuals worked to coordinate the colorfulness of their specific experiences with the bland neutrality of a universal selfhood.[66] In effect traditional autobiography became a way of accommodating and containing colorfulness. Or to return to Virginia Woolf's descriptive rhetoric, it became one of the means by which the "I" asserted itself as "honest and logical; as hard as a nut, and polished for centuries by good teaching and good feeding."

Traditional autobiography, perhaps more than any other genre, may have held out the hope of a unified vision of the universal subject. But other things happened on the way to self writing. Stallybrass and White suggest of the universal bourgeois subject that its itinerary of suppressing "the low and distracting voices within (its attempts to 'come clean' about its identity) only exacerbated its duality, the sense, sometimes appalling, sometimes exhilarating, of being an outsider to itself."[67] And so traditional autobiography also implicated those who entered its arena in the inevitabilities of split subjectivity, the tensions of self-alienation. The self may not be sole, or unitary, nor the itinerary of progress convincing. In pursuit of the unifying vision of itself through a narrative of public achievement or emerging self-consciousness, the autobiographical subject became entangled in webs of contradictory discourses of identification. As a result the autobiographer could never exercise complete control, or sovereign authority, over the kind of subject he presented to the public. The "I" may not have been that hard a nut to crack. And so we might ask of the traditional autobiographical text, where is the colorful, the nonidentical, the carnivalesque? In the repressed body of and in the text? In the figures of the abject that people the text? In the hint of aberrant practices, those narrative possibilities that are rejected by the text? In those moments where the discourses of the universal human subject lapse? In the leakages that sap the power of self-unification? These are fascinating possibilities for reading Western autobiography.

But such questions are not mine in this study.

Reading Subjectivity, Identity, and the Body

I want to explore how the excluded and colorful have used autobiography as a means of "talking back." For the official histories of the subject remain vulnerable to the destabilizing strategies of the "others" who have been only inexactly excluded, all those who have been identified with the carnivalesque or grotesque. As Susan Stanford Friedman suggests, they enter precisely because they experience "alienation from the historically imposed image of the self"[68] culturally assigned them. With their entry there is mess and clutter all around.

When these subjects enter the scene of autobiographical writing, they engage dialogically[69] with the cacophonous voices of cultural discourses, what Bakhtin calls productive and unpredictable heteroglossia. These discourses affect various technologies of subjectivity by means of which autobiographical subjects secure themselves, dislodge themselves, or refashion themselves, discourses of the universal and the embodied subject primary among them. But the hegemonic discourses of the universal subject and the embodied subject are never, to paraphrase Toril Moi on patriarchal ideology, "homogeneous and all-encompassing in [their] effects."[70] While ideologies such as gender ideologies rigidly script identities and differences according to apparently "natural" or "God-given" distinctions, these cultural scripts of difference remain vulnerable to contradictions from within and contesting social dialects from without that fracture their coherence and dispute their privileges. There are always those points at which the dominant culture and its discourses of identity do not work "neatly and efficiently" since "phantoms always lurk, messing up."[71] Hegemonic discourses can also be tested through and displaced by nonhegemonic discourses, or what might be called unofficial knowledges. In their messy heterogeneity, discourses can be both stiflingly congruent and productively cacophonous. Altogether discourses are many, their temporal consonances and dissonances variable, their impacts often unpredictable.

Moreover, coming out of a complex experientially based history (a history of specifics of gender, race, class, nationality, religion, ethnicity) to engage official histories of the subject, the autobiographical subject speaks not from one overdetermined position within the webs of discourse. Each autobiographical subject becomes what Lee Quinby labels "multiply designated," severally situated within diverse, sometimes congruous, often competing, even contradictory discursive fields.[72] This multiplication of speaking positions increases "the possibility of resistance through a recognition of the *simultaneous* non-unity and non-consistency of subject-positions."[73]

Technologies of subjectivity play through autobiographical subjects with differential effects and perceived potentials. Autobiographical subjects play with them in different and deferring ways, proceeding through the entanglements of the web, choosing some directions, choosing against others. And they carry with them through these negotiations the specificities of their material circumstances, their degrees of self-consciousness about cultural determination, the temporalities of their bodies. Heteronomous subjects, they each participate actively as "agents," since, as Paul Smith argues, "a person is not simply the *actor* who follows ideological scripts, but is also an *agent* who reads them in order to insert him/herself into them—or not."[74]

Confronting the mess and clutter of the many unofficial, "inauthentic," and nonidentical subjectivities available to them as well as the invitation to identification with official histories of the universal subject, women find narrative and rhetorical strategies through which to negotiate the laws of genre and the calls to provided subjectivities. Not merely passive subjects of official autobiographical discourse, they become agents of resisting memory and creative misprision.

The following readings take up these issues through a series of interlocking questions with which I will conclude this introduction. The first set of questions look to the relationship of subjectivity to identity in autobiographical practice. What kind of subject speaks throughout the autobiographical text? How does the writer manipulate the "I" so as to fill it, not with the prescriptive history of female essentialism, but with her own experientially based history? How does she redefine for herself the identity contents of the "I"? How is a fluctuant subjectivity channeled into representation, and thus into identities that are secured by narrative representations? What identities are embraced and what identities refused through specific autobiographical practices? What are the ideological and narrative tensions between subjectivity and the identities culturally assigned to the autobiographical subject? What is the relationship between collective social identities and the autobiographical subject?

When a specific woman approaches the scene of writing and the autobiographical "I," she not only engages the discourses of subjectivity through which the universal human subject has been culturally secured; she also engages the complexities of her cultural assignment to an absorbing embodiment. And so the autobiographical subject carries a history of the body with her as she negotiates the autobiographical "I," for autobiographical practice is one of those cultural occasions when the history of the body intersects the deployment of subjectivity. I see a set of questions conjoining subjectivity and this history. Whose history of the body is being written? What specific body does the autobiographical subject claim in her text? How and where does the autobiographical speaker reveal or conceal, give or withhold[75] (or both) her identity or body, and for what purposes? Does the body drop away as a location of autobiographical identity, or does the speaker insist on its founding identification? What are the implications for subjectivity of the body's positioning? How is the body the performative boundary between inner and outer, the subject and the world? What regulatory actions of the body politic impinge on the deployment of the autobiographical body? How are other bodies arranged in the text? Is the body a source of subversive practice, a potentially emancipatory vehicle for autobiographical practice, or a source of repression and suppressed narrative?

Finally, at the scene of writing, each woman struggles with inherited autobiographical narratives constitutive of the official histories of the subject. When does she take up the sanctities of official narratives and when set them aside? How far does she accommodate inherited forms, the official and officious calls to a specific subjectivity, and how far does she stretch the form to fill her own needs and desires? What are the pressure points she puts on traditional autobiography as it presses her into a specific kind of autobiographical subject? Where exactly does she discover the narrative elasticities and subversive possibilities of the genre? What narrative counterpractices does she import into the text? What formal experiments or out-law practices does she pursue? And how do those experiments enable her to evade narrative fixture in official scripts of the universal subject or the embodied subject?

II

ELIZABETH CADY STANTON, HARRIET JACOBS, AND RESISTANCES TO "TRUE WOMANHOOD"

People are beginning to inquire how far public sentiment should sanction or tolerate these unsexed women, who would step out from the true sphere of the mother, the wife, and the daughter, and taking upon themselves the duties and the business of men, stalk into the public gaze, and, by engaging in the politics, the rough controversies and trafficking of the world, upheave existing institutions, and overrun all the social relations of life.

"Woman's Rights in the Legislature,"
The Albany Register (March 7, 1854)

Living as we did—on the edge—we developed a particular way of seeing reality. We looked both from the outside in and from the inside out. We focused our attention on the center as well as the margin. We understood both.

bell hooks, *Feminist Theory: From Margin to Center*

Had she maintained the posture of that embodied subject and refused the autobiographical "I," the nineteenth-century woman would have remained silenced, unwritten and unread. Her life would have remained one of the cultural unspokens. Yet just as some women did not stay in their appointed place but trespassed upon the grounds of the universal subject, so some women did not stay in their appointed narrative silence but trespassed upon the grounds of the autobiographical "I." The century's preoccupation with autobiographical writing, as well as the increase in book production and the increase in levels of literacy, provided diverse, if sometimes uncomfortable, occasions for the excluded, white middle-class women, working-class women and men, and women and men of color to constitute themselves as subjects of history, to use autobiography to assert their participation in the culture's celebration of the universal subject with its ideology of human possibility, desire, and meaning. And so, despite the cultural discourses that suppressed female subjectivity and denied to woman the metaphysical selfhood prerequisite to entry into the culture's master narratives, actual women wrote autobiographies in increasing numbers, especially middle-class women, but also working-class women, as Regenia Gagnier has recently elaborated,[1] and escaped slaves.

The autobiographer brought with her a varied and complex repertoire of provided subjectivities that influenced her negotiations of the autobiographical "I." She also confronted a complex nexus of issues revolving around the relationship of embodiment to subjectivity. How could she boldly enter the autobiographical "I" when, to escape the drag of her body and the potential for evil associated with it, she had to renounce self-assertion through a posture of self-sacrifice to others, to children, family, husband, to God? Distanced from any essential core outside of embodiment and its encumbrances, how could she discover a unified, monadic self with which to fill the writing space of the "I"? How could she structure a teleological narrative outside the defining points in a woman's life, those defining points of a biological destiny, without assuming the subject position of a *lusus naturae*? Responding to these dilemmas she had to simultaneously turn down the level of the body to assume the subject position of man and also turn up the level of the body to assure the reader that her body was aligned as a woman's body should be aligned socially within the matrix of reproduction and nurturing. To do neither was to write something "scandalous" or grotesque,[2] to write, that is, against the law of genre. Thus the autobiographical project fastened the autobiographical subject to her body as it unloosed her from it.

In this chapter I consider two autobiographical occasions in the nineteenth century, the occasion of the famous and very public advocate of women's rights, Elizabeth Cady Stanton, and the occasion of the escaped slave, Harriet Jacobs, in order to explore how women with radically different experientially based histories[3] negotiated the generic territory of the autobiographical "I." How did these women trespass upon the grounds of the universal subject? What history of the body did they bring to the body of the text? What resistances did they mount to the laws of genre? Radically different, the trespasses, the histories, and the resistances are not unrelated to one another.

While Stanton pays lip service to the history of female embodiment and to domestic femininity, she subversively redefines the domestic as a place not of peace and solicitude but of drudgery and violence. As boldly, she appropriates the speaking position of the republican subject, un-manning that subject and undermining the grounds of its exclusions. But reading Jacobs's slave narrative after Stanton's more traditional autobiography also exposes the privileged nature of Stanton's autobiographical practice by specifying the ideological bases upon which the architecture of "true womanhood" rested. Explicitly, it elaborates the vexed relationship of "race" to the ideology of gender inherent in universal and embodied conceptions of selfhood. For the universal subject, which casts its shadow across everything that falls in its shadow line, is not only engendered as masculine but racialized as normatively white.

Reading "Elizabeth Cady Stanton"

Elizabeth Cady Stanton announces in the preface to *Eighty Years and More, 1815–1897* that this story of her life is actually one of two stories: "The story of my private life as the wife of an earnest reformer, as an enthusiastic housekeeper, proud of my skill in every department of domestic economy, and as the mother of seven children, may amuse and benefit the reader. The incidents of my public career as a leader in the most momentous reform yet launched upon the world—the emancipation of woman—will be found in 'The History of Woman Suffrage.' "[4] The public achievements of instrumental selfhood Stanton assigns to an elsewhere distant from her autobiographical project, thereby banishing to the margins of her "woman's" text of domesticity the story of agency and autonomy. Even there, in that elsewhere, the title of the volume suggests that individual achievement is displaced by self-less or impersonal history: her centripetal role disperses into a communal rather than personal story of the suffrage movement. Refusing to make unwomanly or monstrous claims for publicity, Stanton signals at the gateway to her narrative her resistance to self-promotion. Even her purposes in writing *Eighty Years* are conventionally "feminine" ones: she gives herself to others through a story that may amuse and edify her reader.

Splitting both story and subjectivity into the separate spheres of private ("feminine") and public ("masculine") activity, as well as into separate narrative spheres of history and autobiography, Stanton gestures, on the threshold of her text, to the commonplaces[5] of bourgeois gender arrangements in the nineteenth century. And yet this is simultaneously a threshold of commonplace transgression. Her claims for herself as an empowered subject in that elsewhere of the public sphere are grand and dramatic rather than self-effacing: she alludes to herself as a "leader" in "the most momentous reform yet launched upon the world." And, as we will see, her agenda in her autobiographical text becomes increasingly subversive of the doctrine of separate spheres. Stanton does not want to stay in her separate sphere, or in her separate "woman's" autobiographical narrative.

Initially Stanton appears to embrace the cultural identity of bourgeois woman. To counter any reading as a *lusus naturae,* a self-asserting but monstrous woman, she positions herself squarely inside the enclosure of domestic space, the territory of embodied selfhood and true womanhood. As she traces her childhood, youth, courtship, and marriage through the opening chapters of the text, she attends to the script of female embodiment, those defining moments of the female life cycle. Moreover, she uses the languages assigned women in their separate sphere. For instance, she wraps the commonplaces of story of courtship in the language and figures of sentimental fiction. "When walking slowly through a beautiful grove," she writes of her husband, "he laid his hand on the horn of the saddle and, to my surprise, made one of those charming revelations of human feeling which brave knights have always found eloquent words to utter, and to which fair ladies have always listened with mingled emotions of pleasure and astonishment" (60). Representing herself as the desirable and decorous heroine of romance, Stanton invokes the idealized script of young womanhood and heterosexual union. The language of sentimentality continues to surface throughout the text as she invests commentary about motherhood in similarly sentimental garb. Talking of young women whose singing is much admired, she announces: "One has since married, and is now pouring out her richest melodies in the opera of lullaby in her own nursery" (414).

Throughout the descriptions of her various journeys to promote the suffrage cause, Stanton deploys the language of martyrdom and tireless self-sacrifice as she emphasizes the physical discomforts and tribulations of her demanding activities. At other times she speaks as the experienced grandmother, practical, authoritative, aggressive in her concern for the welfare of children. In the discourse of housewifery, the older woman offers advice on such domestic concerns as healthy ventilation, stoves, child-rearing practices. Everywhere she invokes the language of cleanliness and healthiness, as if to clean up her story, clean up the body, and assure her reader of a spotless integrity. And as Estelle Jelinek suggests, even as she represents herself as an exceptional woman, Stanton uses the language of sisterhood to assert her identification with a broad range of women, even the lonely, isolated, impoverished plainswoman.[6] Through all these discourses appropriate to the true woman, Stanton mutes her presentation of herself as "individual," as the universal subject.

Most critically, the outspoken woman mutes the autonomy and agency inherent in her decision to engage in political activism by sustaining the subject position of the true woman—sensitive to suffering, eager to sacrifice herself to others, willing to serve as the vessel for another's will. "My experience at the World's Antislavery Convention," she writes, "all I had read of the legal status of women, and the oppression I saw everywhere, together swept across my soul, intensified now by many personal experiences. It seemed as if *all the elements had conspired to impel me* to some onward step" (148, emphasis mine). Resisting even the appearance of indelicate self-assertion, Stanton invests the story of her purposeful life quest with the conventions of the "romance of the calling."

In doing so she displays what Carolyn G. Heilbrun, in discussing the autobiographies of public women of the late nineteenth century in America, suggests is the etiology of bourgeois woman's public activism: "The only script for women's life insisted that work discover and pursue them, like the conventional romantic lover."[7] Work becomes the lover who secures her position as desirable fiancée and devoted wife.

However often Stanton invokes the languages and assumes the subject positions appropriate to the true woman, she cannot screen out her self-presentation as American individualist. Stanton's representation of herself as wife, mother, and true woman persistently recedes into the background of the text.[8] The narrative of embodied selfhood ends fairly early when the roles have been fulfilled, when the courtship and romance culminate in marriage and childbearing. Henry Stanton appears in the early pages and then disappears almost entirely once he has married her and fathered several children. Stanton erases him so effectively that the reader is not really clear whether he has died when she concludes her narrative. Nor do her children assume much prominence in the text. They are noted when she talks about the early trials of marriage and housekeeping, but then they too disappear until the end when they reappear, woven in and out of the text, given as much narrative space as the hundreds of other friends she visits. It is as if she has efficiently dispatched the cultural call to what Nancy K. Miller and Rachel Blau DuPlessis have called the "female plot" of nineteenth-century fiction. "By female plot," argues Miller, "I mean quite simply that organization of narrative event which delimits a heroine's psychological, moral, and social development within a sexual fate"; that is, "her obligatory insertion within the institutions which in society and in fiction name her—marriage, for example."[9]

This dispatch is useful and necessary, however. The shadow existence of both husband and children in the text serves the function of legitimizing Stanton's excessive quest narrative. Since her cultural authority and readability depend upon her fulfillment of that generic contract whereby she presents herself as true woman, husband and children establish her identity and credibility as a narrating subject. No virgin spinster (like Susan B. Anthony) Stanton assures her reader that female embodiment has operated in culturally respectable and expected ways. All bodily parts having worked properly and effectively, all domestic spaces having been cleaned up, this bourgeois woman has fulfilled her destiny. Having positioned herself toward the body in this way, Stanton achieves at least two effects. She diffuses the lurking threat of the monstrous body that always threatens to return from the margins of woman's text to "upheave existing institutions, and overrun all the social relations of life," as the anonymous author of the *Albany Register* warns. Second, she provides herself with a strategic counter: She can use brief, fleeting references to husband and children to reinforce her legitimacy again and again in a text that quickly begins to contest the institution of marriage itself, to seek the release of the female body from its patriarchal bondage, and to celebrate female quest outside marriage.

For the preface and sentimental posturings notwithstanding, the thrust of Stanton's narrative undoes the cultural mystification of the home as sanctuary for the true woman, and contests the sanctity of marriage and even the motherhood Stanton would promote. To the roles of wife and mother and their attendant responsibilities she traces her profound dissatisfaction with the fate of bourgeois women and the constraints of female embodiment. Her domestic life in Seneca Falls she presents as drudgery, isolating, hard, dulling. Parenting she constantly assesses as constricting, brutalizing. Describing her experience as a young mother, she writes:

> I now fully understood the practical difficulties most women had to contend with in the isolated household, and the impossibility of woman's best development if in contact, the chief part of her life, with servants and children. . . . The general discontent I felt with woman's portion as wife, mother, housekeeper, physician, and spiritual guide, the chaotic conditions into which everything fell without her constant supervision, and the wearied, anxious look of the majority of women impressed me with a strong feeling that some active measures should be taken to remedy the wrongs of society in general, and of women in particular. (147–48)

Throughout her text she interjects commentary on the pettiness, tyranny, and brutality of men and their victimization of women, emotional, physical, political, economic. Marriage for women is a kind of legal bondage since they can be left penniless, ruined financially and socially, by profligate husbands. For Stanton, a bourgeois family dependent on the denial of legal and educational rights to women does not promise stability for women; it threatens drudgery, victimization, infantilization. Thus she deploys the discourse of liberal humanism against those who advocate separate spheres and the spiritual superiority of women over men.

In an implicit critique of heterosexual social arrangements, Stanton locates mutual understanding and comradeship in her relationship with Susan B. Anthony (and with women generally) rather than in her relationship with men, whether husband or father. Pointedly she dedicates her narrative not to husband or children but to Anthony, "my steadfast friend for half a century." Woman-to-woman bonding supersedes woman-to-man bonding as Anthony textually displaces Henry Stanton as source of inspiration. In offering a brief biography of Anthony, Stanton draws upon a rhetoric that celebrates the complementarity of the sexes traditionally identified with marriage partners:

> So entirely one are we that, in all our associations, ever side by side on the same platform, not one feeling of envy or jealousy has ever shadowed our lives. . . . To the world we always seem to agree and uniformly reflect each other. Like husband and wife, each has the feeling that we must have no differences in public. . . . So closely interwoven have been our lives, our purposes, and experiences that, separated, we have a feeling of incompleteness—united, such strength of self-assertion that no ordinary obstacles, difficulties, or dangers ever appear to us insurmountable. (166, 184)

Stanton spends considerable narrative time weaving Anthony's presence into the text, testifying to the priority of female friendship over wifehood and motherhood.

And whatever lip service she might give to the centrality of the home for women, the text constantly displays a kind of homelessness, albeit a privileged homelessness not occasioned by poverty but by choice. Stanton describes her travels across the West, back and forth to Europe, from one home to another, one friend to another, one public speaking engagement to another. In her mobile existence even the home to which she returns constantly shifts from place to place. Home is stripped of stability. And if the home is decommissioned, then the doctrine of separate spheres loses its topographical anchorage. Thus the narrative homelessness undermines the doctrine of woman's influence that derives from her location in her separate sphere.

For a "woman's narrative" that purports to be about the stable roles of wife, mother, and housekeeper, this one incessantly frays, breaks apart, disappears, and reassembles into another story of developmental selfhood, a story that is sketchy, not prominently linear but suggestively so. Through the barest shell of an alternative teleology, Stanton locates the originary moments of her developmental selfhood. First she recalls her experience at the death of her brother when her father refuses to acknowledge her as the substitute son she would be. Then she describes her experience in her father's law office listening to the wives, mothers, and widows who find themselves powerless economically. From there she proceeds to track her involvement in first the abolitionist and then the suffrage movements with their various and complex stages of political activism.

Charting the course of her education and public involvement, Stanton reifies the liberal humanism and individualism that serve as cornerstones of the ideology of the universal subject in the nineteenth century. Effectively, she figures herself as a kind of unembodied, "self-made man," fiercely rational, intellectually keen, independent, agentive, mobile, fearless, outspoken, tenacious, combative. In fact, she revels in usurping man's position. Again and again she describes her engagements with men, in the process claiming her place alongside them, even claiming a superiority of position. For instance, she confidently denounces the advice of the doctors attending her after her first delivery and describes how ineffective they were, how she assumed their place, determining her own solution to the problem of the baby's health. She also creates a militant identity for herself. Recalling how she sparred with various clergy, she dismisses them as reactionary conservatives, arguing her own position on the Bible and on biblical interpretation. Toward the conclusion of the text she discusses her very rewriting of the Bible itself (as *The Woman's Bible*), a gesture through which she appropriates the founding text of her culture and turns it to her own purposes. For it is the Bible that is invoked to sanction the "natural" (rather than cultural) inferiority of woman, her secondary status in marriage, and her assignment to the private sphere. Finally, Stanton's autobiographical narrative becomes one more ground on which she fights men for the authority to establish the boundaries of the voting subject. As she boldly and adroitly takes up one male-identified discourse after another (biblical, legal, and political exegesis among them), Stanton begins to unman the gender ideology underwriting the universal subject and the true woman.

Textually, Stanton enacts her pledge to her father—"I will try to be all my brother was" (21)—by assuming the position of son, figuring herself as pseudo-lawyer, reformer, politician, interpreter. In what she claims to be a personal and domestic narrative, Stanton stakes her claim to an empowered metaphysical selfhood for herself and for bourgeois women generally. Resisting the position of the true woman, which allows her only a vague influence, she emphasizes in the text her exercise of "direct power": "A direct power over one's own person and property, an individual opinion to be counted, on all questions of public interest, are better than indirect influence, be that ever so far reaching" (376).[10] Stanton travels from domesticated territory, out of the shadow of influence, to the territory of direct action, analysis, speech, and individual quest.

In this way Stanton unsexes herself, uncouples her subjectivity from embodiment. In this way she legitimates her desire (and the desire of bourgeois women in the suffrage movement) to achieve equal political rights with men, to achieve the status of voting subject alongside men. She clears a space for herself within the ideological territory, the cultural pageantry of the republican/ democratic subject whose identity is founded upon legal, educational, and franchisal equality.[11] Performing out of gender, out-manning man, so to speak, Stanton at once honors his difference and her identification of promissory sameness. In a sense, then, Stanton's autobiographical project begins to extricate the tentacles of gender identity from the universal subject as she works to unsex the democratic subject. But even if her strategy unsexes the discourse of the universal subject, it does not dismantle it. What she wants to do is expand its boundaries to include bourgeois women,[12] to add the history of feminist individualism[13] to the history of the universal subject. Yet she would keep the universal subject for her class. After all, with all those bourgeois women leaving the family for the territories of the universal subject, who is left to do the work of the family but domestic servants, including ex-slave women.

The Subject of the Slave Narrative

In a certain way, what remains unspoken in Elizabeth Cady Stanton's narrative is the plight of the black woman, as slave and ex-slave and as domestic servant. Stanton acknowledged the aims of the abolitionist and reconstructionist cause to broaden the boundaries of the republican subject to incorporate the black male. She chose to give priority to another argument for extension of the boundaries. She wanted equal access to that territory of the universal subject for white women. But in this triangulated schema whereby one either calls for bringing white women into the space of the universal (male) subject or the black man into the space of the universal (white) subject, the missing subject of both arguments is the black woman, whom Barbara Johnson describes as "the other of the other."[14] Yet if the black female subject is an unspeakable in Stanton's narrative, she is not silent in the century. And so I turn now to Harriet Jacobs's slave narrative published in 1861, some thirty-seven years earlier than Stanton's autobiography.

Exploring the significance of the cultural notion of race in recent western history, Henry Louis Gates, Jr., notes that there existed in the mid-nineteenth-century environment a "shared assumption among intellectuals that race was a 'thing,' an ineffaceable quantity, which irresistibly determined the shape and contour of thought and feeling as surely as it did the shape and contour of human anatomy."[15] Consequently, the identifying marker of race, continues Gates, served as "a trope of ultimate, irreducible difference between cultures, linguistic groups, or adherents of specific belief systems which—more often than not—also have fundamentally opposed economic interests" (5). Encoding the figuration of the Other, race cast difference in fixed, essentialist terms (of skin color, anatomy, physiognomy, intelligence, ideas, traditions).

The ideology of race supporting the system of slavery in the southern states (like the ideology of race supporting European colonial expansion in Africa, Asia, and South America) fixed "Africans" on the bottom rung of what Gates calls the "minutely calibrated" evolutionary ladder. Blending with vestigial remnants of an earlier discursive ladder, the Renaissance's great chain of being, the century's "scientific" discourses—of Darwinism, social Darwinism, medical anthropology, ethnography—established a hierarchy of races ranging from the "atavistic" to the "civilized." In the position of hierarchical ordination, white, western culture stood at the apex of evolutionary achievement, far removed from the Africans, identified with primitive impulses, ideas, social institutions, religious practices, with uninhibited sexual practices.[16] The very humanity of Africans remained problematic. For without a written language, Africans appeared deficient in memory, mature reason, vision, and, critically, history. Since the century inherited from the Enlightenment its privileging of reason as the fundamental cornerstone supporting the architecture of universal selfhood, and since the century privileged knowledge of the arts and sciences as the highest achievement of reason and writing as the evidentiary scene of reason, absence of written language signified absence of full humanity.[17] Indeed, Africans were accorded fractional humanity, signified by their status as three-fifths of a human being in the discussions of the "founding fathers." Fixed in their essential racial difference, they were denied metaphysical selfhood and relegated instead to an inescapable embodiment as the system's beast of burden.

To write the self into history thus served as an oppositional gesture, at once humanizing and individualizing the Africans through recourse to the very "technology of reason" that would dehumanize them.[18] Slave narratives contested the claims of slavery's advocates that Africans were primitive, uneducable, outside history and culture. As Frederick Douglass acknowledged in the preface to his narrative, "Not only is slavery on trial, but unfortunately, the enslaved people are also on trial. It is alleged, that they are, naturally, inferior; that they are *so low* on the scale of humanity, and so utterly stupid, that they are unconscious of their wrongs, and do not apprehend their rights."[19] The narratives established the legitimacy of the Africans' desire for full political, economic, and intellectual participation in the life of the nation. Further, writing autobiography, ex-slaves appropriated a western generic contract promoting the primacy of individual selfhood and proclaimed that selfhood publicly. "Text created author," Gates argues, "and black authors, it was hoped, would create, or re-create, the image of the race in European discourse. . . . The recording of an authentic black voice—a voice of deliverance from the deafening discursive silence which an enlightened Europe cited to prove the absence of the African's humanity—was the millennial instrument of transformation through which the African would become the European, the slave become the ex-slave, brute animal become the human being" (11–12). Combining personal histories with a cultural history of the slave system, the narratives became powerful weapons in the abolitionist cause, especially after 1831 when the crusade gained momentum through widespread organization. Widely read and circulated throughout the northern states, they were written to enlighten potential supporters of the antislavery crusade about the horrors of the "peculiar institution" that would reduce human beings to such degradation.[20] As Frederick Douglass wrote to his editor: "Any facts, either from slaves, slaveholders, or by-standers calculated to enlighten the public mind, by revealing the true nature, character, and tendency of the slave system, are in order, and can scarcely be innocently withheld."[21] Personalizing the story of slavery, the diverse materials incorporated in slave narratives accumulated to convey an immediate rather than abstract portrait of systematic dehumanization and evil and thus to strike "right to the hearts of men."[22]

And yet as William L. Andrews argues, the white readers of slave narratives did not necessarily privilege the individuality of the narrator. Rather, "American aesthetic standards of the time made a black narrative that exposed the institutional facts of slavery preferable to one that expressed the subjective views of an individual slave." As a result, the narrator entered a scene of writing that, like the scene of slavery itself, required the erasure of individual history and of self: "To follow this agenda was to alienate oneself from one's past and to banish oneself in the most fundamental ways from one's own autobiography. Yet speaking too revealingly of the individual self, particularly if this did not correspond to white notions of the facts of black experience or the nature of the Negro, risked alienating white sponsors and readers, too." Andrews suggests that the most sophisticated of the slave narratives reveal a complex resistance to this contradictory set of personal and public expectations. In various ways, he argues, these narrators "resisted the fragmenting nature of objective autobiography, which demanded that a black narrator achieve credence by objectifying himself and passivizing his voice."[23] Harriet Jacobs's narrative is one such text.

"The Other of the Other"

Making herself into a "talking book" entitled *Incidents in the Life of a Slave Girl, Written by Herself,* Jacobs engaged the mythology of race in order to give voice to herself and face to her people through alternative myths of empowerment.[24] In the process she struggled to break the chains of slavery by breaking the chain of being that would relegate her as an African to the lowest rung of the ladder and by intervening in the constraints of generic expectations that would reappropriate her life in normativizing narrative. Engaging the conventions of self-mastery and authority, she staked her claim in the territory of the human. The black woman, however, had a far more complex struggle for selfhood on her hands than either the white woman or the black man. Doubly the site of western culture's totalizing representations, doubly embodied as African and woman, doubly colonized in the territory of rape and enforced concubinage, the slave woman confronted conflated destinies, discourses, and identifications. Marginalized vis-à-vis both universal and embodied white selfhoods, Jacobs travels arduously toward both territories as she narrates a paradigmatic tale of spiritual and rhetorical as well as physical journeys from bondage to "freedom." On the way, she engages in what Mae Gwendolyn Henderson describes as "contestorial dialogue with the hegemonic dominant and subdominant or 'ambiguously (non)hegemonic' discourses."[25]

Unwilling to accept the conditions of slavery, "Linda Brent" (the name of Jacobs's masked protagonist) determines to escape her circumstances. Eluding her master, she hides in her grandmother's attic for seven years and then flees north to New York where she finds work, regains her children, and achieves freedom.[26] At the center of Jacobs's escape story is Brent's will, her determination to figure life on her own terms. If, according to Abdul R. JanMohamed, "it is through the construction of the minority subject that the dominant culture can elicit the individual's own help in his/her oppression,"[27] Brent's agency functions as the sign of her resistance to her social construction as "slave," subject always to another's will. Describing her struggle with her master, Dr. Flint, Brent anticipates this agency through metaphors of warfare, that quintessential masculine activity: "The war of my life had begun; and though one of God's most powerless creatures, I resolved never to be conquered."[28] Through this hand-to-hand combat, Brent literally and figuratively wrests agency from the master as her prerogative, beating the master at his own game, outwitting and outmanning "the man." He cannot make her accept the identity of the slave, subject to and of his will, and so he cannot, as Dana D. Nelson notes, make her reflect back to him his identity as master. Furthermore, in choosing Mr. Sands over Dr. Flint, Nelson claims Brent plays "master against master, king against king."[29] In other words, she troubles the social arrangements among the masters.

The narrative presents Brent as an avatar of the "self-made man," bent on achieving freedom by means of iron will, intelligence, courage, and perseverance as well as moral purposefulness. Both story and text affirm her individuality despite her qualified achievement in the North and her continuing struggle "to affirm," as Elizabeth Fox-Genovese notes, "the self in a hostile, or indifferent, environment."[30] This achievement of freedom and humanity in the face of overwhelming obstacles links Jacobs's narrative to those of other escaped slaves. But her identity as a woman and her cultural positioning as "the other of the other" distinguish her from the majority of those slave narrators who were men. For unlike the male slave narrator, Jacobs has to confront not only Brent's estrangement from universal selfhood, but also and synchronously her estrangement from "true [white] womanhood" and its sentimental narrative frames.

The ideology of true womanhood, elaborated by feminist historians looking at the nineteenth century, assigned to the true woman what Barbara Welter has described as "four cardinal virtues—piety, purity, submissiveness and domesticity."[31] But that assignment implied another assignment—one directed at unprivileged women, women of color and working-class women. Hazel V. Carby argues that while the establishment of "what constituted a woman and womanhood" may have brought "coherence and order to the contradictory material circumstances of the lives of women," it did so by "balancing opposing definitions of womanhood and motherhood [for white and black women], each dependent on the other for its existence."[32] For instance, the fragile physique characteristic of the true woman contrasted markedly to the bodily strength desirable in the black female slave.[33] Any effort by an ex-slave woman to establish her consonance with true womanhood involved a crossing over from one definitional territory (that of the subjected female slave) to another's definitional territory, a crossing over to a place whose boundaries depended on keeping black women in their place.[34] And the challenge to the slave narrator compounded the problematics of representation. The fierce purposefulness of a slave woman's efforts to escape her bondage and to establish her full humanity, so central to the narrative purpose of the genre of slave narratives, violated the code of submissiveness so central to true womanhood. In various ways Jacobs as narrator assumes certain postures antithetical to the postures of the true woman—her willfulness noted above, her not always suppressed anger, her independent critique of both southern and northern society, and her revelation of sexual concubinage.

Inevitably, black and white women experienced differing relationships with their bodies. A white woman exercised some control over her body. Despite the discourse labeling her naturally lustful, despite the implicit fear of her sexuality evidenced in the most elaborate defenses of her goodness and purity, she could achieve some modicum of power by resisting the temptations of the flesh and keeping her body clean, chaste. By maintaining her virginity and her reputation, she could secure marriage and with it social legitimacy within the closures of domesticity. After marriage she could fulfill her duty by bearing legitimate children for the patrilineage. Or she could maintain her virginity and serve her family as dutiful daughter or her cause as selfless evangelist. Enshrined in her separate sphere, she could secure a certain cultural status and currency (literally and figuratively).

While neither male nor female slaves had control over their own bodies, the female slave suffered physical violation beyond what the male slave suffered, a reality to which Jacobs painfully alludes: "When they told me my new-born babe was a girl, my heart was heavier than it had ever been before. Slavery is terrible for men; but it is far more terrible for women. Superadded to the burden common to all, *they* have wrongs, and sufferings, and mortifications peculiarly their own" (77). Within that "peculiar institution" the fate of woman was itself "peculiar." If in the various discourses of embodied selfhood the white woman always carried the potential for illicit and disruptive sexuality, she was promised, to the degree that she erased the stains of sexuality, the cultural consolations of true womanhood. The black slave lived in that crawlspace of sexual lasciviousness by virtue of the mark that was her skin color. Her African body condemned her to an inescapable essentialism because, in the mythology of race, it served as her defining characteristic, the very sign of her unrepressed and unrepressible sexuality, her licentiousness and insatiability. From the less authoritative discourse of the chain of being to the more scientifically respectable discourse of medical pathology, black female sexuality became synonymous with abnormal sexual appetite.[35] Effectively, her body stood as an invitation to white male desire. And so the white master satisfied his prurient sexual desire and his desire for human capital on the female slave's body in one act. In this way her body functioned as the vessel for reproducing "chattel" for the system (since children followed the mother) and for shielding the "proper," sexually repressed white woman from the uninhibited sexual desires of the white man, both strategies for maintaining colonial relationships of power. As bell hooks notes, "Rape as both right and rite of the white male dominating group was a cultural norm. Rape was also an apt metaphor for European imperialist colonizations of Africa and North America."[36] The black female body served the slave system as both the ground upon which the patriarch satisfied his desire and the metaphorical ground upon which the slave owner asserted his cultural authority over the black male. And so, as Nelson notes, the system "served to negate her entitlement to her own 'womanhood' as that concept was culturally constructed."[37]

Despite apparently intractable cultural obstacles separating the slave woman from a venerable embodiment, Jacobs seeks to establish in her narrative some relationship (albeit ultimately contestatory as I will argue later) to true womanhood by situating Brent inside shared boundaries with white women, women like Elizabeth Cady Stanton. In response to the great irony of her situation—"the more enormous the crimes committed against her, the less receptive people are to hearing about them, especially from the victim herself"—Jacobs seeks, according to Andrews, to "forestall the wrong kind of reading of her book" by constituting in her text a "woman-identified reader" and "remodeling" through the text the kind of enlightened community that would "offer a truly familial kind of fellowship."[38] To this end Brent speaks directly to white middle-class northern women, comfortable in their identity and status as true women. Speaking as a woman to other women whose sympathy, understanding, and action she would enlist in the antislavery crusade, she asks that they identify with her sufferings as a woman who shares their concerns for home and children. This desire to gain common ground with her reader through a kind of identity politics determines the emphases in the narrative on the struggle to achieve control over her body and the related struggle to establish a home for the children of that body.

In tracing the former struggle, however, Jacobs reveals not only her determination to escape sexual exploitation but also her surrender to concubinage, confessing that in resisting her master's will she entered deliberately into liaison with another white man by whom she bore two children. Thus the narrator must position herself as the "fallen" woman whose very utterances, because unspeakable, threaten the sanctity of that protected space of true womanhood. The reality of this threat is acknowledged by Lydia Maria Child in her introduction:

> I am well aware that many will accuse me of indecorum for presenting these pages to the public; for the experiences of this intelligent and much injured woman belong to a class which some call delicate subjects, and others indelicate. This peculiar phase of Slavery has generally been kept veiled; but the public ought to be made acquainted with its monstrous features, and I willingly take the responsibility of presenting them with the veil withdrawn. I do this for the sake of my sisters in bondage, who are suffering wrongs so foul, that our ears are too delicate to listen to them. (3–4)

There is no room for Jacobs's experience as a black woman inside the borders of true womanhood. In fact, as Valerie Smith argues, Child herself seemed to understand here the incompatibility of maintaining decorous rhetorical and narrative habits and unveiling the reality of a system that positioned slave women in enforced concubinage, the incompatibility between decorum and veracity. Since silence surrounds the indecorous subject matter and marginalized speaking position of the narrator—"It would have been more pleasant to me to have been silent about my own history"

(2)—Jacobs/Brent risks rejection by her reader in order to tell the story of her fall from virginity into concubinage, in order to insist on the legitimacy of the experientially based history of her body. Moreover, the establishment of her veracity, by both Child and Jacobs, forestalls the escapist tendencies in a reader who by not looking directly at the situation might retreat into what Smith calls "insensitivity and self-involvement."[39]

The narrative strategies Jacobs/Brent uses to stake her claim as a black woman to a place within the community of true women are fascinating and provocative. In tracing her struggle for physical self-determination she appeals rhetorically to her audience by appropriating the very language and narrative conventions of popular fiction, most particularly invoking (and rewriting) the tale of seduction.[40] Presenting herself as a resisting victim of Dr. Flint's sexual aggression, Brent figures a story about the forced loss of innocence and the long, anguished struggle to achieve bodily integrity in the face of unremitting emotional and physical abuse. Chronicling her experiences in slavery and out, she stresses the emotional and physical consequences of her decision to resist sexual victimization, the superhuman self-sacrifice necessary. She suffers separation from her children. Harassed, exhausted, feverish, infected, contorted by the seven-year enclosure in her grandmother's attic, her body bears the marks of the master's brutality, the horrible price of "virtue."

Jacobs also appeals to white women as mothers by creating Brent as the heroic mother whose steel purpose is to achieve freedom and a home for her children and by figuring her story in the rhetoric of domestic fiction with its celebration of the domestic virtues. Presenting herself in "the most valued 'feminine' role" of the century, she emphasizes how hard-fought the achievement must be for the female slave, precisely because motherhood posed significant problems for the black woman caught in a system that intervened ruthlessly and purposefully in family relationships,[41] a system that denied motherhood to the slave woman. Amassing detailed accounts of the difficulties of motherhood in slavery, Jacobs insists on Brent's total commitment to her children to the point of self-sacrifice: "My friends feared I should become a cripple for life; and I was so weary of my long imprisonment that, had it not been for the hope of serving my children, I should have been thankful to die;

but, for their sakes, I was willing to bear on" (127). Moreover, Jacobs surrounds Brent's struggle as a mother with the struggle of her larger family, a family whose members—grandmother, father, mother, aunts, uncles—she figures as powerful, physically resilient, spiritually hearty, loving, courageous, loyal. She thereby places herself in a noble family lineage, a lineage embodying the highest values of a civilized society, a lineage characterized by spiritual, moral, and social heroism despite the degrading circumstances of slavery. And even as she concludes with an acknowledgment that she can never achieve that separate sphere available to white women, she maintains the legitimacy of her desire for equal access: "I still long for a hearthstone of my own, however humble," she concludes, "I wish it for my children's sake far more than for my own" (201).

Finally, Brent assumes the narrative posture of the true woman who sacrifices herself and her privacy to others by telling her tale for the benefit of her people and their cause, as she earlier sacrifices herself and her comfort for her children and their freedom. As Andrews suggests, she sacrifices her very privacy in order to enlighten and to benefit her readers: "Jacobs approaches her woman-identified reader with a personal history of secrets whose revelation, she hopes, will initiate that reader into the community of confidence and support that nineteenth-century women needed in order to speak out above a whisper against their oppression."[42] Jacobs recognizes that only by speaking the unspeakable can she hope to bring the history of the slave woman's body before the body politic.

Escaping Discursive Territories

Significantly, as Valerie Smith notes, both Brent as protagonist and Jacobs as autobiographical narrator wrest individuality and freedom through incremental stages of willed change, each stage of which brings temporary enclosure in a "loophole of retreat."[43] Everywhere the narrator confronts her own vulnerability in a system of bondage that requires and exacerbates vulnerability. Yet within the enclosures of physical (sexual and racial) and discursive (literary) victimization, Brent (the running woman) and Jacobs (the writing woman) devise and implement strategies of resistance. It is Jacobs's enclosure in literary discourses and the strategies of evasion she develops to manipulate within such discursive loopholes to which I want to turn now. As Smith reminds us, loopholes are both constraining spaces and points of escape. As narrator, Jacobs is both caught inside narrative conventions and skillful in finding a point of escape from their constraints.

The closing reference to her failed effort to gain her own home underscores the grim reality of Jacobs's/Brent's status as exile in her own country and in the country of ideal (white) womanhood. Ex-slaves, however much they celebrated their freedom, remained second-class citizens, remained strangers in their own land, variously homeless. Pointedly, Brent is not even free to claim the legitimacy of her experience for herself. Rather she is dependent upon the testimony of Lydia Maria Child, the white abolitionist whose necessary authorization of Jacobs's text points to the ex-slave's reinscription within certain appropriative structures.[44] Moreover, she is dependent upon Child for the editing and marketing of her narrative. As Alice A. Deck suggests, Child's imprint upon the narrative is multiple.[45] Child herself wrote to Jacobs that she "transpos[ed] sentences and pages, so as to bring the story into continuous *order,* and the remarks into *appropriate* places"; she requested that Jacobs send her more materials about "the outrages committed on the colored people, in Nat Turner's time," thus emphasizing dramatic details even when they were not a part of Jacobs's personal story; she deleted a last chapter on John Brown because "it does not naturally come into your story and the MS is already too long."[46] As other ex-slave narrators, Jacobs finds her narrative and her self-representation subject to a certain amount of white paternalism.[47] Yet despite this editorial colonization, the narrative maintains the fierce integrity of an oppositional vision.

Literally as well as figuratively homeless, Jacobs/Brent speaks from a position very different than the one Elizabeth Cady Stanton achieves at the conclusion of her narrative. The reality of her homelessness exposes the bourgeois luxury of the mobility of women like Stanton. Unlike Stanton, she stands in the speaking position of the "deterritorialized," to use the current phrase of Gilles Deleuze and Felix Guattari.[48] From her specific position of homelessness, Jacobs can see both inside and outside white culture, inside and outside true womanhood and its supporting ideology, for she has what bell hooks calls a kind of doubled sight. This doubled sight characterizes Jacobs's stance toward the cultural discourses she invokes to gain credibility for the truth of her tale: those of the seduction novel, domestic fiction, the more common male slave narrative, biblical tropes, picaresque narratives, and the spiritual narrative of the movement of the soul toward salvation and freedom. Since these loci of authority are white and/or male identified, she engages them from her oppositional position, often uncomfortably. Negotiating the intersections of multivalent discourses, Jacobs effectively troubles all these centering rhetorics simultaneously. Her deterritorialized vision leads her to probe, unconsciously and consciously, certain loopholes in those conventions.

Jacobs/Brent challenges the very notions of American freedom, democracy, and equality, and in doing so contests the presence of the agency and autonomy associated with American notions of bourgeois individuality. For instance, in a passage cited for its unveiled, assertive voice,[49] Brent comments on the fact that her freedom has been bought for her by a white woman:

> So I was *sold* at last! A human being *sold* in the free city of New York! The bill of sale is on record, and future generations will learn from it that women were articles of traffic in New York, late in the nineteenth century of the Christian religion. It may hereafter prove a useful document to antiquaries, who are seeking to measure the progress of civilization in the United States. I well know the value of that bit of paper; but much as I love freedom I do not like to look upon it. I am deeply grateful to the generous friend who procured it, but I despise the miscreant who demanded payment for what never rightfully belonged to him or his. (200)

Assuming the authoritative stance of a biblical prophet, Brent defiantly, unsentimentally, scorns the hypocrisy of the nation and its founding documents. Moreover, as Nelson argues, Mrs. Bruce's purchase of Brent's freedom establishes yet another system of inequality, one in which the charitable and philanthropic white woman exacts another kind of servitude from the black woman,[50] a relationship of inequality recognized by the narrator.

From the perspective of the homeless, Jacobs interrogates even as she imitates the ideology of true womanhood, revealing its inherent racial nature. As Carby argues: "*Incidents* demystified a convention that appeared as the obvious, commonsense rules of behavior and revealed the concept of true womanhood to be an ideology, not a lived set of social relations as she exposed its inherent contradictions and inapplicability to her life."[51] For instance, Jacobs incorporates in the narrative of her struggles with Dr. Flint the contradictions of the rules of behavior governing the institution of true womanhood. In promising Brent her own home and his enduring affection, Flint invites the slave woman to participate in the institution of true womanhood,[52] but the invitation is a perverse lure since what stands behind it is the whole apparatus of enforcement in the slave system. The assumption behind his behavior is that she is all body and her body is his to violate. Jacobs uses his mockery of the ideal of true womanhood to emphasize the differential relationship of women to that ideal in their lived circumstances.

She also undermines the corporate ideal of the true woman as sympathetic sister by differentiating among specific groups of women in terms of their response to their sisters in bondage. On the one hand, she suggests that certain white southern women transcend the privileges of their class and status in identifying with her plight and flight, giving her shelter and support. She challenges thereby the totalized vision of white southern women as proslavery. On the other, she condemns the complacency and indifference of northern women, even those associated with the abolitionist cause, revealing her perception of the absence of sisterly concern[53] among them by quoting from the Bible: "Rise up, ye women that are at ease! Hear my voice, ye careless daughters! Give ear unto my speech" (Isaiah xxxii, 9). Or she manifests, albeit mutedly, a certain bitterness toward her northern reader in her comparisons of their life to hers.

But more directly, Jacobs unmasks the ideology of true womanhood as a fiction in her characterization of southern women who collude in the degradation of other women and deny the primacy of conjugal bonds. "The qualities of delicacy of constitution and heightened sensitivity, attributes of the Southern lady," notes Carby, "appear as a corrupt and superficial veneer that covers an underlying strength and power in cruelty and brutality."[54] In contrast to the ruthless and uncivilized familial relationships of whites, she creates a world of nurturing, supportive black women, a world of strong black relationships. Incorporating episodes that make of white men sexual profligates and moral pigmies, that make of white women uncaring, jealous, petty tyrants, this slave narrator provides a contrast of cultures that reverses ideological notions of civilized and uncivilized, hierarchized as white and black.

Contrary to the conventional figuration and fate of the antagonist of the seduction tale, Jacobs presents her seducer not as any kind of Byronic figure whose power is attractive and redeemable if lethal but rather as a dehumanized pervert, brutalizing and bestial.[55] Turning the tables on the ideology supporting the slave system, Jacobs renders the white man as less than fully human and assigns him a position low on the chain of being. Moreover, she presents herself not as the passive victim but as the iron-willed antagonist who fights her master's victimization with bravado. And she voids the narrative of the threat of seduction. The fate of the female body is the profound unspeakable of the seduction tale—unspeakable but always thinkable. When Jacobs takes as her point of departure the body already taken, already raped, she forces her reader to begin on the other side of the convention and to consider how the heroine can survive. As Yellin notes, "Jacobs's narrator . . . asserts that—even when young and a slave—she was an effective moral agent" who "takes full responsibility for her actions." And the narrator further differentiates between a selfhood synonymous simply with bodily chastity and a selfhood emanating from self-esteem and integrity as she "abandon[s] her attempt to avoid sexual involvements in an effort to assert her autonomy as a human being."[56] For instance, she makes a careful distinction between being forcibly raped by her master and choosing her lover: "It seems less degrading to give one's self, than to submit to compulsion" (55).

Ironically, Jacobs inverts the tale of seduction: the passive victim chooses her lover, chooses her fall. Moreover, and obviously, her tale of seduction and captivity does not end conventionally in Richardsonian fashion, with either marriage or death. It is impossible to make marriage the reward for virtue after the fact of children, especially in this case where marriage to the father of her children would be illegal. This reality surrounding the narrative demystifies the conventions of sentimental fiction by rendering them class specific. Nor can death serve her purposes. As Smith suggests, Jacobs "replac[es] the self-indulgent mythification of death with the more practical solution of freedom."[57] Jacobs understands that sentimentality will not do as a response to the brutalities of slavery since it functions ideologically to maintain the status quo. Of more effect is the celebration of freedom, and the assertion of an alternative moral vision that challenges the simplistic notions of morality associated with true womanhood, a morality that would erase the specificities of the slave woman's experience. "Still, in looking back, calmly, on the events of my life," she reflects, "I feel that the slave woman ought not to be judged by the same standard as others" (56). Later, when she describes how Brent reveals the truth of her past to her daughter Ellen and wins Ellen's acceptance, Jacobs reveals her own narrative priorities: she cares more for a daughter's forgiveness than for the reader's (and larger culture's) forgiveness. Jacobs places slavery on trial rather than Brent's social deviancy.[58] For these reasons, argues Yellin, Jacobs might be calling for "a new definition of female morality grounded in her own sexual experience in a brutal and corrupt patriarchal racist society."[59] Such a notion of morality would not be founded solely upon woman's physical/hymenal purity but on more complicated, contextual grounds. Such morality would be morality historicized rather than essentialized. Thus Jacobs uses the history of her body to effect a misprision of the very seduction narrative that founded bourgeois notions of separate spheres and to rewrite the history of morality.[60]

Jacobs/Brent rewrites the fiction of domesticity by calling for direct political action and intervention rather than the more limited influence of domesticated feminism being promoted by certain white feminists of the period. As a homeless woman she sees the self-satisfied complacencies of a feminism that would limit its concerns to reform and celebration of that separate sphere and elevation of a sisterly sympathy when political, economic, and social forces limited the availability of that sphere to white middle-class women and its security to only certain bodies.[61] For one, sympathy as an arena for communication across division often, according to Nelson, "assumes *sameness* in a way that can prevent an understanding of the very real, material *differences* that structure human experience in a society based upon unequal distribution of power."[62] As Brent's story makes inescapably clear, the experiences of motherhood are radically different for different women, and so the grounds of action for social change cannot be projected from any homogeneous point of origin. Moreover, she reveals the inevitable failures and insufficiencies of influence. She has no influence on Flint, nor does Flint's wife. While she may have some influence on Sands, legally he remains her master.

Jacobs's narrative provides a critique of certain kinds of domestic spaces and, as noted above, the familial subjects inhabiting such spaces. It was a concept of home challenged also by those feminists of the period with whom she worked and corresponded, Lydia Maria Child and Amy Post. "The publication of Jacobs's autobiography," suggests Andrews, "constituted a double opportunity, for as woman and slave, Jacobs dramatized the feminist analysis of the parallel slavery of race and sex. . . . From the feminist point of view, which labeled true womanhood white slavery and submissive wifehood prostitution, Jacobs's multiply marginal identity qualified her amply as one of the most truly representative women of her time."[63] Yet Jacobs's narrative does not seek to undo the centrality of any home. The persistence with which she claims the necessity of home suggests the degree of difference between the black domestic servant who writes and the white women who encourage her. Jacobs constantly has to make a home out of homelessness. To make home, or what bell hooks calls "homeplace," is an act of resistance to slavery and to the ideology of African inferiority. Moreover, when she constitutes herself narratively as a self-sacrificing mother, she promotes no idealized version of domesticity and "mother worship." She makes that motherhood the political expression of choice and willfulness, as opposed to "the perfect embodiment of a woman's 'natural' role." In this insistence Jacobs reveals what hooks describes as "the remarkable re-visioning of both woman's role and the idea of 'home' that black women consciously exercised in practice" as a means to "racial uplift."[64] For the homeless mother, home cannot be so easily dismissed, as it is by Stanton, as a place of empowerment and a site of resistance, nor can it be dismissed as a place where a woman can exercise bodily integrity and autonomy.

Jacobs also rewrites the conventions of the male slave narrative, which assumes the representative privilege of the male slave's experience of bondage and escape. Unlike Frederick Douglass, who in his several narratives acknowledges neither the woman who helped him escape (and who later became his wife) nor other networks assisting him as he fled, Jacobs eschews the representation of herself as the isolato, self-contained in her rebellion, figuring herself instead as dependent always on the support of family and friends, particularly her grandmother.[65] Moreover, the rhetoric of the male slave narratives worked to equate the achievement of freedom with the achievement of manhood without then elaborating what this achievement would portend for the female slave. "The slave narrative," writes Smith, "often extols the hero's stalwart individuality. And the narratives of male slaves often link the escape to freedom to the act of physically subduing the master."[66] As a woman Jacobs may outwit her master; she never physically subdues him. The achievement of manhood also implied the achievement of heroic stature, a posture of intellectual acumen and self-control, "most often," according to Sherley Anne Williams, "the means by which the black male hero also assumes the mantle of the 'patriarch' " within a black community.[67] Jacobs assumes heroic stature, but that stature is not the stature of the patriarch. After all, at the conclusion of the narrative she is neither self-employed artisan nor great public orator. She is, as Andrews reminds us, a domestic servant, a woman whose very servitude supports the privileged domesticity of white women by keeping that domain clean and tidy. Gaining self-control meant different things for male and female ex-slaves, precisely because of the differential vulnerabilities of male and female bodies.

Unchaining the Subject in Chains

Through all these rewritings, Jacob contests the notion of selfhood's fixedness. "I was born a slave; but I never knew it till six years of happy childhood had passed away (3)," she writes in opening her narrative. Early in the narrative Jacobs introduces the distinction between an essentialized or fixed idea of selfhood founded on the status of the body and a culturally and historically marked notion of selfhood.[68] By doing so she challenges the mythology of racial identity as an essential phenomenon. Providing character, nobility, full humanity to her black family and complex humanity to herself, she deconstructs the stereotypes of black identity spawned in the ideology of race. Refusing to be figured as the sexually unrepressed primitive black woman whose body constitutes her identity, refusing to be figured as the "mammy" of white children, refusing to be figured as morally and spiritually bankrupt, refusing therefore to be figured as less than fully human, she destabilizes colonial notions of the African.

Moreover, Jacobs foregrounds not only the intertextualities of self-representation but also the discursive staging of identity. Her discourse resists the finalizing impact of the history in the text. The mutual constitution of reader and narrator marks the text and its self-representational project as simultaneously fluid and contextual. Novelistic passages introduce the dialogic nature of self-representation, the indeterminacies of role-playing and multiple voicings.[69] Lifewriting becomes the site of subjectivity, now understood as discursive, contextual, communicative. Thus Jacobs's narrative testifies to the ambiguities of any core of irreducible, essentialist selfhood founded upon the body's contribution to an identity politics. Moreover, the female body persists in circulating through the text, discursively unsubdued, a gap that Smith suggests works to reveal the inadequacy of the sentimental genre to account for female desire entirely.

The narrative of Harriet Jacobs reveals a timely uneasiness with discourses of the universal subject and female embodiment. From her position of homelessness, Jacobs interrogates in far more complex ways than does Stanton conventional pieties of woman's embodied selfhood in the nineteenth century as well as conventional empowerments of metaphysical selfhood. As an escaped slave she insisted on herself as a writing subject "capable," as Craig Werner notes, "of participating in the discourses—literary and political—that shape the lives of that self and the community from which it cannot be separated."[70] She could see more clearly the inherent contradictions in and the ultimate constructedness of the essentialist ideology of true womanhood and its specular relationship to the universal subject because she had to factor in other differences and identifications and because as a slave she had "an enforced awareness that the self cannot be taken for granted, . . . that the self is contingent, an ever-shifting social construct."[71] Out of the friction generated as she engages competing and contradictory discourses that never quite fit the parameters of her historically specific experience in slavery, Jacobs experiments with the narrative discourses available to her for self-representation. What Henderson calls "a multiple *dialogic of differences*"[72] operates to both accommodate and diffuse identification between narrator and reader, between personal experiences and discursive meanings. Jacobs simultaneously speaks in heteroglossic tongues and unspeaks inherited tongues. Hers is a particularly provocative narrative, one which adumbrates those disturbances of the territorial boundaries of both universal and embodied selfhood characterizing autobiographies written by women in the twentieth century. In fact, this outsider's text serves as a harbinger of what have become variously radical challenges to the old narratives of the universal subject.

III

TURNING THE CENTURY ON THE SUBJECT

> Language, for the individual consciousness, lies on the borderline between oneself and the other. The word in language is half someone else's. It becomes "one's own" only when the speaker populates it with his own intention, his own accent, when he appropriates the word, adapting it to his own semantic and expressive intention. Prior to this moment of appropriation, the word does not exist in a neutral and impersonal language (it is not, after all, out of a dictionary that the speaker gets his words!), but rather it exists in other people's mouths, in other people's contexts, serving other people's intentions: it is from there that one must take the word, and make it one's own.
>
> Mikhail Bakhtin, "Discourse in the Novel"

> "I" is only a convenient term for somebody who has no real being.
>
> Virginia Woolf, *A Room of One's Own*

Cloaked in the garb of the natural, the common sensical, the fundamentally human, the metaphysical or universal subject appeared unassailable as the century turned. Yet as manifold discursive technologies consolidated selfhood's privileges, radical forces began to open up fissures along its ontological borders. Those forces promoting the new orientation toward self that would erupt after World War I were actually coalescing throughout the nineteenth century, for there was a dark side to the nineteenth century's embracement of evolutionary progress and its attendant celebration of an optimistic individualism. The very liberation of thought from the straitjacket of religious fundamentalism lead to an expansiveness of possibility. And with expansiveness came the loss of belief, the death of God, the confrontation with the relativity of culture itself. The other side of science's advancement was the disturbing linkage of man to ape that emerged from Darwin's evolutionary scheme. The other side of the wealth created by industrialization was the massification and dehumanization of large segments of the working-class poor. The other side of global expansionism was the destabilization of old social arrangements. The other side of capitalism's triumphant celebration of individualism was what Candace D. Lang describes as the "suppress[ion of] the individual, as well as authentic artistic expression, as the work of art became a mass-produced commodity."[1] The other side of the century's creativity was the madness and excess of romantic self-absorption. The other side of the romantic glorification of nature was the flight of God from its framing beauty and the residue of crass mechanism serving as its law. The other side of its ideology of separate spheres for men and women was the increasing unwillingness of women to remain in their place. The other side of the ideology of race that separated and hierarchized peoples according to physical characteristics was the increasing unwillingness of subject peoples to accept their inferior status. In fact, the instabilities of the late nineteenth and early twentieth centuries constitute what Sandra M. Gilbert and Susan Gubar have described as "the shredding fabric of patriarchal authority."[2]

If various threads of the old patriarchal fabric were beginning to unravel, what then of the universal subject and the ideology of individualism woven through it? Candace Lang argues that by the end of the nineteenth century, "romanticism . . . is characterized by a somewhat mournful preoccupation with the self and a gloomy nostalgia for a lost golden age of individuality and unmediated self-expression."[3] And John Dewey, in an essay entitled "The Public and Its Problems," recognized the paradoxical relationship between the fixation on self and its destabilization: "The theory of the individual possessed of desires and claims . . . was framed at just the time when the individual was counting for far less in the direction of social affairs, at a time when mechanical forces and vast impersonal organizations were determining the frame of things."[4] Preoccupation with the metaphysical self as sovereign locus of knowledge coincided with the cultural disempowerment of other originary loci of meaning such as religion and history. And yet an increasing sense of alienation contracted that locus of selfhood into a fast dwindling space of knowledge, and even that space began to drift beyond the horizon. Sundry forces colluded in contesting the solidity of the isolable and unified core of any self, along with the impermeability of its boundaries, the confidence of its progressive development, the authority and legitimacy of its totalizing self-consciousness, the very agency of the old universal subject. As James Olney remarks, "agonizing questions of identity, self-definition, self-existence, or self-deception" began to challenge any comfortable, unselfconscious investment in metaphysical selfhood.[5] It is as if the dominant culture caught up with the very instabilities of identity and self-knowledge that the institution of slavery and escape to the North forced upon Harriet Jacobs.

Radical challenges to the notion of a unified and unitary core of selfhood wrenched the ideology of the universal subject out of its ontological, teleological, and topographical boundaries. The essential self encountered possibly its first disturbances in the Marxian analysis of class consciousness and the insertion of a determinative link between individual consciousness and larger economic forces. Individuals lost their autonomy and agency as they became subjected to, and thus perversely manipulated subjects of, economic structures and relationships. Then the theories of Freud served to destabilize the notion of the rational self by reconfiguring it, altering and expanding the notion of the self by insinuating the presence of forces beyond conscious control and thereby introducing a subversive unconscious, potentially threatening the apparently calm and stable surfaces of consciousness. Freud also disputed the notion of language as a neutral tool for human manipulation. And theories of linguists such as Saussure further problematized language, stripping what was formerly conceptualized as a medium of self-expression of its transparency, its mimetic privileges. No longer does the subject employ language to its own purposes. For the subject is now more spoken by language than speaker of language, more product of discursive regimes than explorer of any reified self-essence. So the problematic relationship of language to that which it purports to represent, the problematic relationship of any "I" to self-narrative, eroded the certainties of authorial intentionality.[6] Self-estrangement and self-fragmentation now become more characteristic of the universal subject than self-discovery and self-knowledge.

If, according to Edward Said, the increasing sophistication of the study of linguistics generated the "disturbance taking place at the *interior* of thought," the development of ethnology initiated "a disturbance . . . having to do with the subject's *exteriority* to thought."[7] Certainly the burgeoning interest in anthropological research brought westerners in contact with cultures whose ideologies of selfhood challenged the homogeneity of the theory of any universal subject and reinforced the link between the framing of human thought and language and the culture in which that framing takes place. Moreover, new notions of time destabilized the solidities of chronology, relativizing those external and internal temporalities of history and memory. National liberation movements toppled the old colonial relationships and their interdependencies of identity. And since midcentury, Lacanian psychoanalysis and Derridean deconstruction have furthered the already energetic dismantling of metaphysical conceptions of self-presence, authority, authenticity, truth. For both Lacan and Derrida the "self" is a fiction, an illusion constituted in discourse, a hypothetical place or space of storytelling. The true self, or core of metaphysical selfhood, can never be discovered, unmasked, revealed because there is nothing at the core. The self has no origin, no history, since both origin and history are, like the self, fictions. Moreover, since the self is split and fragmented, it can no longer be conceptualized as unitary. At any given moment the self is different from itself at any other given moment. As Virginia Woolf would remark, "'I' is only a convenient term for somebody who has no real being."[8]

Shattered by collisions of all kinds, the old center of Cartesian selfhood, to paraphrase Yeats, could not hold. And so, asks Said, "of what comfort is a kind of geological descent into identity from level to lower level of identity, if no one point can be said confidently to *be* irreducible, beginning identity? Of what philosophical use is it to be an individual if one's mind and language, the structure of one's primary classifications of reality, are functions of a transpersonal mind so organized as to make individual subjectivity just one function among others?"[9] Site of fractures, splittings, maskings, dislocations, vulnerabilities, absences, and subjections of all kinds, the architecture of selfhood seems to have collapsed into a pile of twentieth-century rubble. The self and its "I"/mark on the page become the sign of the not-one, as if now only a dot-matrix printer, with its minutely calibrated interruptions, can sign for it. With the metaphysical self problematized, the very grounds of representation soften, break apart, and disperse. Thus, while the unitary self of liberal humanism remains the prevailing notion governing Western understanding, and the West's configuration and discipline of selfhood even in the twentieth century, that universal self and the traditional narratives through which it seeks to consolidate itself have lost some of their cultural privileges.

But despite the dissolutions of the old metaphysical selfhood—what we might call the selfhood of the father—modernist and postmodernist challenges to the notions inherited from the nineteenth century have not always dispersed the cultural hold on the embodied subjectivity of woman. Twentieth-century challenges too often assume masculinist privileges precisely because discursive practices continue to specularize woman, albeit in provocative new ways. Thus while "man" has begun to change figures, "woman" remains the object of, and in, contestatory male discourses—psychoanalytic, political, genealogical, philosophical, literary—and as such remains "muted, elided, or unrepresentable in dominant discourses."[10]

For instance, when Freud rewrote the trajectory of human development, he maintained, even while rewriting and sometimes contradicting himself, the fundamental essentialism of woman.[11] Continuing to naturalize female difference and inferiority through what he claimed to be a scientifically sound explanation, he reinvested the evolutionary theory of Darwin with his own theory of psychological development. Thus the characteristics of female essentialism promoted by the Victorians and their precursors carried over into Freudian theorizing—only now the language describing woman's psychological drama was informed by a radical theoretical framework that broke the Victorian cultural taboo against openly discussing human sexuality. In Freudian theory signs of

sexuality were everywhere visible, or in the case of woman paradoxically invisible. With the development of the female self tied
irrevocably to the absence apparent on the female body, Freud
located female identity in the profound experience of absence, of
lack. This new physiological and "scientific" explanation, although
simultaneously rather mythical and mystical (because untestable),
reaffirmed the "natural reality" of female selfhood as essentialist.
Female subjectivity became associated after Freud with an apparently new but merely renewed set of descriptive terms: "feminine
masochism, feminine passivity, feminine castration, feminine penis
envy."[12] Freudian revision located woman's difference even deeper
in the sexuality latent in the unconscious and in biological de-
terminism, although even Freud manifested some confusion about
the social origins of sexual difference.

Moreover, with Freud woman remains tied to a procrustean,
teleological script of femininity. She is required to pass efficiently
through the early phallic, the oedipal, and later adult stages of
female development. If she is healthy, she accepts the rule of the
phallus as the law, accepts the responsibilities of self-sacrifice and
self-effacement, and assumes her place as mother at the center of
the home, accepting her lack and worshipping first the man and
then the son who has what she has not. She remains the non-self,
the silent other to man's one. Her sexuality is the none that is the
nothing to be seen. Man, who has one, is her authority.

Woman does not exist as an independent subjectivity outside
Freud's specular representations of her as essentialized being. As a
result, argues Jane Gallop as she reads Luce Irigaray, the subject
itself remains normatively phallic, male. "The neutral 'subject' is
actually a desexualized, sublimated guise for the masculine sexed
being," she writes: "Woman can be subject by fitting male standards which are not appropriate to, cannot measure any specificity
of femininity, any difference. Sexual indifference is not lack of
sexuality, but lack of any different sexuality, the old dream of
symmetry, the other, woman, circumscribed into woman as man's
complementary other, his appropriate opposite sex."[13] Paradoxically, it remains the essence of woman to have no essence but
opposition, otherness.

More recent postmodern critiques of the old essential self, while promising to subvert all essentialist notions of selfhood (including, one would expect, woman's embodied selfhood), fall short of the promise. At its worst, poststructuralist nominalism threatens to reduce woman to a fictive status, universalizing her once again, erasing the specificities of her differences. Lacan, for instance, would reduce woman to the gap between her legs, to an absence of access to the phallus as universal signifier. In making woman "a non-identity, non-figure, a simulacrum . . . distance itself," Derrida situates woman outside the essentializing discourse he calls logocentrism.[14] But in placing her outside, in making her a marginal site of resistance in western logocentrism, he also calls her to a position of universalized negativity. Privileging sexuality as a category of genealogical import, Foucault nonetheless erases gender from his screens of meaning and remains indifferent to what Teresa de Lauretis describes as the "differential solicitation of male and female subjects" and "the conflicting investments of men and women in the discourses and practices of sexuality."[15] While postmodern theories often make a place for the "feminine," they tend not to offer space to specific women and their heterogeneous experiences of oppressions and empowerments. Women's experiences in the world as well as the experiences of people of color are thereby elided.

Moreover, in the new romance with discursive subjection, postmodernism, warns Linda Alcoff, threatens to erase "the subject's ability to reflect on the social discourse and challenge its determinations."[16] Already elided, woman now confronts the impossibility of ever finding a space in which to assert her own agency. Thus while the breakdown of the universal subject undoes the authority of the father in one of his guises, it threatens another kind of subjection that would erase real women outside the "text," silence the heterogeneous specificities of their experiences, including the experiences of oppression, in service to the impersonal and homogenizing technologies of rampant textuality. As a result, women and other muted groups are theoretically stripped of the power, however complexly exercised, to affect change. Most critically, they are stripped of their multiplicities of differences in deference to a procrustean sexual difference. They remain subject to and subjected in their bodies.

Autobiographical Remnants

This brief overview cannot, of course, capture the complexities and fuller sophistications of the cultural shift from the old metaphysical self to the more recent understandings of subjectivity[17] nor the complexities of the way in which the bodies and subjectivities of "women" fare within that history of change. That project would require its own extended study. It is meant to be suggestive and to play off the opening discussions of universal and embodied subjectivities. Obviously, it is from the point of view of these more recent theories of the subject that the discussion of nineteenth-century discourses of selfhood derives. A fuller engagement with issues of subjectivity, identity, and the body takes place in the discussions of autobiographical projects that follow. So let me return to some prefatory remarks about autobiographical practices in the twentieth century.

Like the old self, the coherence of traditional autobiography begins to break apart, to disperse. "With each deeper penetration into the workings of the text," notes William C. Spengemann, "the connections between autobiography and what it appears to describe have become increasingly problematical, and the differences between autobiography and other written forms correspondingly indistinct, until there no longer seems to be anything that either is or is not autobiography."[18] The splitting of "I"'s—into narrator, narratee, and what Paul Smith calls the ideological "I"—guarantees the obfuscation of distinctions between factual and fictional "lives."[19] The textualization of the signature ultimately erases "life" outside the text. Since there remains no self, no authority, no truth outside discourse, traditional autobiography loses any special status. As the end of this century approaches, the genre seems threatened with generic extinction. Experiments in alternative autobiographical writing practices, like those of Roland Barthes, for instance, push as far as they can against the former call to a unified, univocal self and a teleological itinerary.

Yet as the certainties and comforts of that self evanesce and the western romance with old notions of selfhood wanes, people seem no less preoccupied with the autobiographical "I," perhaps more preoccupied with it. For James Olney, "the heart of the explanation for the special appeal of autobiography to students of literature in recent times" has been "a fascination with the self and its profound, its endless mysteries and, accompanying that fascination, an anxiety about the self, an anxiety about the dimness and vulnerability of that entity that no one has ever seen or touched or tasted."[20] The genre of choice among literary and cultural critics, autobiography's place in the panoply of forms and fashions, has shifted from the margins of critical inquiry to what Domna Stanton claims is "the very center of modernist concerns."[21]

This fascination derives not only from the elusiveness of the old self and destabilization of its cultural hold on us but also from the desire of autobiographical subjects to splinter monolithic categories through which they are culturally identified, such as the monolithic category of "woman," and to reassemble various pieces of identity, experience, and knowledge into another kind of subjectivity. For these purposes the perhaps underrated flexibility of autobiographical forms, a flexibility we have seen in the discussion of Harriet Jacobs's slave narrative, offers promising opportunities. Surely, traditional autobiographical forms have been complicit with the reification of a certain kind of western subject. Configured as white, middling, and male, the old self overrode white middle-class women, working-class men and women, and men and women of color, who, if they wrote autobiography at all, spoke mutedly, circumspectly, and still could not be sure that their "lives" would be read or readable. After all, the stark truth, despite the current proliferation of readings of Harriet Jacobs's slave narrative, is that this slave narrative was consigned to obscurity for over one hundred years. It went unread, perhaps because it was, precisely, unreadable. Nor could diverse peoples always maneuver their stories inside the lines of the provided subjectivities and the provided narratives culturally available to them. The form may have done more to them than they to it, but not always or not consistently so. For autobiography has continued to provide occasions for the entry into language and self-narrative of culturally marginalized peoples, of peoples who are assigned inauthentic voices by the dominant culture. When newly articulate autobiographical subjects come to write, they not only enter a generic engagement through which they recapitulate the contours of subjectivity promoted in dominant discourses; they also speak as "unauthorized subjects" who are pulled and tugged into complex and contradictory subject positions. Moreover, they fashion and refashion, then fine tune various identities through which they make meaning out of their experiences. Their maneuverings within their unauthorized positions and their engagement in fluid entanglements with subjectivity, identities, and narratives have often resulted in unconscious or conscious interrogations of traditional autobiography and its autonomous, free, coherent self, interrogations that position them to take advantage of this time of generic instability.[22]

There is tremendous elasticity of autobiographical forms, a fact that we discover in any perusal of bookstores and libraries. There seems an endless variety to personal writings, autobiographical novels, personal essays, journals, diaries, collections of letters, travel literature, oral histories, ethnographies, testimonials, and prison narratives. Autobiographical subjects are everywhere. And the cacophony of autobiographical voices invigorates autobiographical narrative. In fact, it is a wonderful time of autobiographical experimentation as well as autobiographical traditionalism. Fractures in the old forms generate new modes of self-narratives. Chafings in the new subjectivities open up new spaces of resilience and resistance. In the shifting relationships of master narratives and alternative practices, positions in borderlands, to invoke Gloria Anzaldúa's phrase, command cultural visibility and currency. Less tied down to conventional figures, "locals" in a time of tumult and instability find exhilarating and necessary, if painful, the pursuit of alternative narratives, of alternative orientations to the subject. And they are prepared to grapple with the problematic nature of self-narrative since that problematic already inheres in the confrontation between hegemonic and nonhegemonic epistemologies and strategies of storytelling. That preparedness, especially as it affects women, is something Germaine Brée acknowledges when she speculates that "at this time of spectacular change in our sense of the macrocosm we inhabit—women, because until now they have had little occasion, therefore little inclination, to 'construct meaning' on a grand scale, are in a better position to see beyond the constraints of our conceptual representations, beyond our dichotomies and abstractions (not the least of which is the male-female dichotomy) and to look to the 'multiplicity of the real.' "[23]

In the following chapters I want to explore the multiplicity of autobiographical strategies some twentieth-century women in the West employ to negotiate the autobiographical "I." I turn first to three modernist writers, Gertrude Stein, Virginia Woolf, and Zora Neale Hurston, to see what trouble they make for traditional autobiography as they engage time, memory, and history to contest the cultural constraints of assigned identities. Then I conclude with two chapters that look at more recent, and extremely diverse, autobiographical practices by Annie Dillard, Cherríe Moraga, Jo Spence, Hélène Cixous, Gloria Anzaldúa, and Donna Haraway. In the first of these two chapters I am interested in texts that take up the body as a source of self-knowledge. In the final chapter I am interested in manifestos that use autobiographical practices to put forward new subjects.

Influenced by modernist, postmodernist, and postcolonial theories and by increasingly sophisticated interrogations of a multitude of differences, these women use autobiography as one prominent ground for cultural critique and resistance. While negotiating various identifications (of gender, race, class, ethnicity, sexuality), they discover points of resistance to the integumentary strains of provided subjectivities. Their contradictory and fluid subject positions lead them to intervene in those cultural fictions, interrogating, cannibalizing, rereading the stories to their own purposes.

Wrenching autobiographical form to their own purposes, these autobiographers write "beyond the ending" of conventional narrative and its closures, to use a phrase from Rachel Blau DuPlessis.[24] As they do so, they resist the discourses that come from "other's people's mouths, in other people's contexts, serving other people's intentions," to invoke the epigraph from Bakhtin. They challenge dominant discourses with combative power, dramatizing sometimes unsettling encounters with subjectivity, identity, and the body. Contesting old notions of self and story, they effectively destabilize generic norms, rendering the genre flexible, heterogeneous, a carnivalesque form for differences, as any perusal of the many autobiographical forms in the century attests. Contesting old closures, the old decidables of meaning and power, they investigate—invest themselves in—alternative technologies of autobiography.[25]

IV

"STEIN" IS AN "ALICE" IS A "GERTRUDE STEIN"

What is the use of being a little boy if you are to be a man what is the use.

Gertrude Stein, *Everybody's Autobiography*

The making of a portrait of anyone is as they are existing and as they are existing has nothing to do with remembering anyone or anything. . . . In a cinema picture no two pictures are exactly alike each one is just that much different from the one before. . . . Each time I said the somebody whose portrait I was writing was something that something was just that much different from what I had just said that somebody was and little by little in this way a whole portrait came into being, a portrait that was not description and that was made by each time, and I did a great many times, say it, that somebody was something, each time there was a difference just a difference enough so that it could go on and be a present something.

Gertrude Stein, "Portraits in Repetition"

The autobiography of Rose . . . is the autobiography of Rose even if her name is not Rose.

Gertrude Stein

When she came to the scene of autobiography, Gertrude Stein found herself triply discomfited. Neither the old autobiographical "I" of the fathers nor the sexually marked and remarkable "I" she brought to the page nor the conventional narrative itinerary through which the normative autobiographical "I" progressed could do the textual work she wanted to do in *The Autobiography of Alice B. Toklas.* The genre itself, driven by chronology, multiple levels of referentiality, and a normative subjectivity seemed incapable of accommodating her modernist experimentations with time, referentiality, the instrumentality of language, and the erotics of lesbian desire. And so she had a challenge of almost impossible proportions facing her in writing autobiography. How could she displace the center of autobiographical narrative away from a unified subject? How could she keep the identity of the sexually marked subject out of the autobiographical text and keep the celebration of lesbian coupling in the text? How could she keep the materiality of the body and language in the autobiographical text? How could she resist the teleological thrust of traditional autobiographical narrative and insinuate a time of repetition? How could she render an explicitly (as opposed to a fictional[1]) autobiographical narrative nonreferential? In other words, how could she break the paternal instrumentality of the genre? In grappling with such questions Stein came up with an experimental form through which she both trespassed upon the grounds of the universal subject and restaked its topological and tropological boundaries by engaging in a duplicitous out-of-body ruse.

The original edition of *The Autobiography of Alice B. Toklas* carries a ring-shaped insignia embossed on the cover. Lettering in the shape of a band reads, "Rose is a rose is a rose is a rose. . . ." "Alice" tells us later in the text that, after discovering the phrase in a Stein manuscript, she "insisted upon putting it as a device on the letter paper, on the table and anywhere that she would permit that I would put it."[2] This device functions as a multiply valent signature on the cover of the autobiography and points to a variety of phenomena that mark the disruptive nature of Stein's autobiographical text. First, the band creates a border between an inside and an outside, thereby calling attention to zones of adjacency and separation, the identity and difference of inner and outer space, as well as the interdependencies of margins and centers, outsides and insides.[3] Second, the band as circle signifies the seamless relation-ship of beginnings and endings, as well as the possibilities of nar-rative repetition just as the sentence "Rose is a rose is a rose is a rose" turns back upon itself to start again at the beginning where it only provisionally ends. Third, the ring-shaped insignia becomes pictorially a wedding band, signifying the erotic union of Alice B. Toklas and Gertrude Stein, as the text itself signals that erotic union. Fourth, as Lisa Ruddick among others has noted, in Stein's work the rose is associated with female genitalia, the color rose with menstrual blood, and the circle with the vaginal opening.[4] Thus a metaphorical trace of the female body marks the cover, the ground of the autobiographical text. Finally, the band functions as a kind of silent authorial signature, for no author's name appears on the cover. Authorship remains a mystery, a phenomenon of undecidability. In all these ways the cover calls into question the nature of the text to follow, the complex relationship of "Alice" and "Gertrude," or as critics have noted, of "Gertrice/Altrude,"[5] and the undecidability of boundaries between the autobiographical subject and the other in autobiography.

So too does the title page and its accompanying Man Ray photo-graph in which Gertrude Stein sits at her desk writing while Toklas, silhouetted in the light, enters/exits a door at the back left. The light surrounding Toklas in the doorway repeats the light directed on Stein's hands and paper, effectively joining the two actions: Stein writing and Toklas entering, or more imaginatively, Stein writing Toklas or Toklas entering the writing Stein. Thus the photograph reveals the authorship that the title page refuses to name. More-over, the title of the photograph, "Alice B. Toklas at the door," once again signals the notion of borders, or doorways between inner and outer spaces. Toklas strides into Stein's writing room in the gesture of interpenetration of object and subject. Like the rose insignia, the photograph and title page confuse the notions of self and other, identity and difference, narrator and narratee, "I" and "you," and they visualize in their semiotics, as the ring does, the lesbian couple, going in or coming out of the writing closet.[6] The pleasures of the text (that is, of writing) and the pleasures of the body (that is, of lesbian coupling) are here foretold.

Although she offers hints of the real authorship of *The Auto-biography* throughout the narrative, Stein sustains this undecidability until the end, when she reveals the joke.[7] "Alice" writes that "about six weeks ago Gertrude Stein said, it does not look to me as if you were ever going to write that autobiography. You know what I am going to do. I am going to write it for you. I am going to write it as simply as Defoe did the autobiography of Robinson Crusoe. And she has and this is it" (252). As critics of the text have noted, in these last few sentences Stein confounds readerly expectations about generic contracts and autobiographical subjects by identifying herself with Defoe and Alice with Robinson Crusoe and, therefore, identifying autobiography with fiction "simply." But the simply belies the complexity with which that identification proceeds.[8] In fact, Gertrude Stein has created a fictive autobiographer, "Alice B. Toklas," not in order to present her own autobiography. She does so, as Leigh Gilmore argues, in order to represent the lesbian couple.[9]

As Julia Watson remarks, "Women's sexuality has usually been presumed as heterosexual except when spoken otherwise,"[10] both in and out of autobiography. If that is one of the laws of genre operative in autobiographical practice, then Gertrude Stein had to make trouble within the conventions of the genre. This troubling project of representing the lesbian couple forces Stein both to engage in the sacrifices[11] necessary for autobiographical narrative and to disrupt the dominance of that unitary subject which requires sacrifice. By doubling autobiographical authority, doubling identity in the text, Stein explores the ambiguous nature of the autobiographical subject.[12] Thus demarcations between autobiography and biography, Gertrude Stein and Alice B. Toklas, fictive and autobiographical subjects, are radically renegotiated as are the connections between subjectivity, identity, and the body.

Narrative Interventions

Writing as "Alice," Stein intervenes purposefully in the autobiographical contract by breaking the monopoly of the old universal subject and its metaphysical "I," that bar crossing the page of traditional (and normatively male and heterosexual) autobiography. "What makes *The Autobiography of Alice B. Toklas* so interesting," suggests James E. Breslin, "is that it admits the conventions of memory, identity, chronological time—in order to fight against and ultimately to transcend their deadening effects."[13] On the most obvious level, the text erases the "I" of memory, identity, and time altogether. Stein plays with what Gilmore calls "the superabundance of *I*"[14] by emptying the "I" of the abundance expected in the autobiographical contract. "Alice" is an "I" emptied of "I-ness," emptied altogether of subjectivity, emptied of the body behind or before the "I." What Stein said of San Francisco ("There is no there there") might just as well be said about "Alice." The "I" of "Alice" is a "fictive fiction," to use Philippe Lejeune's term,[15] not an autobiographical fact, not even an autobiographical "faction."[16] Neither "Alice" nor Stein exist in the text as virtual "I"s.

Rather, we might say that the autobiographical "I" here is an "I" of two-ness since the voice of the text is not singular. In braiding the voices of Stein and Toklas, the narrator continually forces the reader to equivocate in specifying who speaks at any textual moment. Sentences contain traces of at least two voices as the narrating Stein captures the rhetorical structures, rhythmic cadences, and witty perspective of Toklas as well as her own stylistic experimentations and vision. Thus there is a "we-ness" to the textual "I," a "we-ness" constituted through a linguistic mixing, what Françoise Lionnet describes in another context as a practice of *metissage*.[17] And this mixed "we" acts to qualify the promise of coherence and univocity privileged in traditional (nineteenth-century) autobiographical practice.

Through the narrative strategy and rhetorical artiface of the autobiographical speaker who is no "I," Stein alters the perspective through which the autobiographical subject materializes. As a result, the boundaries between inside and outside in autobiography blur. Instead of the autobiographical narrative emanating from the consciousness of the autobiographical subject, that subject is situated as an object of autobiographical discourse. This vexed relationship of outsides to insides fascinated Stein, as "Alice" affirms when she comments that with the writing of Ada and the beginning of the long series of portraits, Stein's style changed: "She says hitherto she had been interested only in the insides of people, their character and what went on inside them, it was during that summer that she first felt a desire to express the rhythm of the visible world.

It was a long tormenting process, she looked, listened and described. She always was, she always is, tormented by the problem of the external and the internal" (119). In assuming the narrative body and voice of the other, Stein develops a means to shift the narrative perspective to an externalized subjectivity. As a result, Stein "excreates"[18] herself in the text as entity, as the noun, "Gertrude Stein."

Presenting her story from the externalized perspective of "Alice," Stein effectively makes herself this noun by figuring herself as a genius of a specific history abstracted out, distilled, the verbal equivalent of the painted figure in Picasso's portrait of her. Briefly describing Picasso's early portrait of Stein in the opening pages of the text, "Alice" writes: "Yes, he said, everybody says that she does not look like it but that does not make any difference, she will, he said" (12). Picasso's portrait represents Stein as stark, powerful, full-framed. Her body is solid; the faceted face reflects the cubist's preoccupation with multiple angles and constantly moving perspectives. Her eyes are piercing, her nose is large, and her clothing is substantial, earthen-colored, like peasant's clothing. In this portrait Gertrude Stein is monumental: She fills the frame, shimmering with presence and power.

And throughout the text, "Alice" presents Stein as the central figure in Paris intellectual and artistic life. Sitting calmly in her chair, pronouncing on the art and life of those around her in an oracular voice, "Alice's" Stein is much like Picasso's. A genius, she is figured as the center of creativity, a calm voice issuing wisdom and originality. Simultaneously and paradoxically, she is constantly in motion, as the surface of the cubist painting is in motion, a figure of the dynamism, mobility, and synchronicity Stein identified with the twentieth century.[19] "Stein is not created as a realistic, psychologically complex character," says Breslin, invoking the term *character* here for what we might call identity, "she is, rather, an abstraction, a deliberate simplification—a mythical figure whose peaceful self-sufficiency allows her to transcend external circumstances."[20] And the repetition of the name over and over again, Gertrude Stein, Gertrude Stein, Gertrude Stein, makes of that name an incantation. Always referring to Stein in this way, "Alice" identifies Stein as a modern icon by placing her at the geographical (note the repetition of "rue de Fleurus") and spiritual center of the text, the city of Paris, and twentieth-century modernism. Or, to put it another way, "Stein" becomes a noun full of thingness just as the rose on the front cover of her autobiography is full of its thingness.

With "Alice" as narrator and "Gertrude Stein" as abstract entity rather than psychological or self-conscious subject, the auto/ biographical text is evacuated of the teleological trajectory so central to nineteenth-century notions of the universal subject. Stein's use of "Alice" as autobiographical narrator aids and abets her desire to escape origins. For "Alice" the story of Gertrude Stein begins when Alice herself arrives in Paris. While she turns back momentarily to summarize Stein's early life, those years are relatively unimportant to the narrative. By narrative implication, Stein's real life begins with the relationship that marks Stein's break from her brother and her bourgeois past. Nor can "Alice" take the reader on a psychological journey into Stein's past in an effort to recover the psychological origins of her development as a writer. Thus there is no story of evolutionary selfhood here, no attempt to find the essential thread of a Gertrude Stein that winds through childhood, adolescence, early adulthood, and into her mature years as a writer.

The teleological trajectory of traditional autobiographical texts requires a certain kind of time in narrative, but this linear time-sense is displaced in "Alice's" narrative by another more abstract time-sense. "Alice" provides the reader with a minimalist sense of chronological time, using the titles of the chapters as signposts of chronology. They are time, but time broken up, time placed and displaced, time past and time forward. Continually "Alice" breaks the forward movement of narrative or linear time with digressive asides, anecdotes, circuitous micronarratives, flashbacks, fastforwards, with notices to her reader that she will return again to a particular moment.[21] And as "Alice" insists that she will begin with a certain time or story, but does so again and again after numerous interruptions, the narrative resists the stability of one origin and its line of descent.[22] Moreover, the disruptions to chronological time introduce an insistent repetition into the text, what Ruddick and Marianne DeKoven call earth-time because it is allied with natural cycles and the mother. Thus linear time is constantly confused and unwound as the narrator creates a sense of the synchronicity of past, present, and future.

The following passage, in which "Alice" compares the composition of Ada to the composition of the autobiography, captures "Alice's" timely playfulness: "I began it and I thought she was making fun of me and I protested, she says I protest now about my autobiography. Finally, I read it all and was terribly pleased with it. And then we ate our supper" (114). When precisely did she do the reading? When precisely did they eat their supper? With this shimmering movement of times past, present, and future, movement analogous to the shimmering quality of lines and space in cubist paintings, Stein is effectively able to reorient the reader's time-sense and generic expectations. The anecdotal breaks in chronology, the confusion of past, present, and future, as well as the externalized portrait, subvert the notion of clearly defined developmental stages of growth, of the subordination of time present and future to time past in autobiographical narrative, and the notion of a coherent, unified core of selfhood.

The Trouble with (Sexual) Identity

According to DeKoven, Stein differentiated "entity" or "human mind" from "human nature" or "identity," explicitly in such essays as "What Are Master-pieces and Why Are There So Few of Them" (1936) and *The Geographical History of America; or, the Relation of Human Nature to the Human Mind* (1936). "Entity" exists in timelessness, "independent of memory, the past, all forms of embeddedness in history and human relations." "Identity" is a contingent phenomenon, "imbued with self-consciousness and relatedness." In assuming the narrative position of "Alice," Stein is able, in her modernist autobiographical practice, to resist various embedded forms—in teleological time, in a personalized and contingent past, in an absorbing narrative self-consciousness, in the realm of human nature or identity. Stripped of the contingencies of a suspect identity, "Gertrude Stein" does not speak autobiographically as a "coherent, separate, uniquely individuated bourgeois-patriarchal self."[23]

This resistance to identity has everything to do with Stein's troubles with sexual identity. Self-styled and self-proclaimed genius of twentieth-century modernism, Stein had throughout her early (and most experimental) years as a writer assumed what Catharine Stimpson describes as the cultural linkage of "masculinity and towering creativity,"[24] a linkage explicit in one of her notebooks where she writes: "Pablo & Matisse have a maleness that belongs to genius. Moi aussi, perhaps."[25] Her early preoccupation with typologies of human beings led her to position herself, at least in her notebooks, as a "masculine type" and in her novels to project her struggle onto a male protagonist, onto Jeff in "Melanctha" and onto the "aggressive" and "loyal" son of *The Making of Americans*.[26] For Stein, maleness was identified with intellect, power, knowledge, creativity, boldness; and femaleness with such stereotypical traits as filth, stupidity, lethargy, wiliness. Construing male and female in this traditional and essentialist way, Stein was caught in the dilemma of the woman as genius. She conceptualized genius and femaleness as mutually exclusive identities. In so doing, she participated in an essentialism that forestalled the understanding of gender as socially constructed and forced herself into contortionist impersonations and identifications against her very body.

Male identification had also to do with her "errant" sexuality. Trying to wrest meaning out of a lesbian sexuality that in the early twentieth century was considered a "pollutant," that made of her a "singular,"[27] Stein at first found in Otto Weininger's theories a meaning to and justification for her lesbianism. For Weininger lesbian sexuality signified in women "an invigorating dose of 'maleness.'"[28] Because she had to confront the psychological and cultural problematic of her lesbian sexuality and because she desired that "dose of maleness," Stein transgressed the culturally constructed boundary differentiating naturalized sexual identities. She cross-identified in order to love women and to love one woman in particular. This identification of her lesbian sexuality with that "dose of maleness" may account for the way she and Alice configured their singular relationship. As many friends and critics have remarked over the years, the two women established an apparently conventional patriarchal marriage: Stein played the role of "husband" to Toklas's performance of the effaced and doting "wife." As Stimpson admits with some regret: "Most problematically, Stein was husband, Toklas wife. Not only did Stein write, and Toklas type and edit, but Stein ate, and Toklas cooked and served."[29] Thus to both write as genius and to love as lesbian, Stein negotiated the cultural position of man, effectively identifying against herself as woman. DeKoven suggests that Stein's "self-hatred was such that she was psychologically compelled to identify herself as a man in order to be a happy, sexually active person and a functioning writer."[30]

But DeKoven suggests that her eventual acceptance by the public in the late twenties and thirties caused some relaxation in her role as misunderstood outcast, as a literary and sexual "singular." And Stimpson suggests that "though Stein was never a public feminist, during the 1920s she began to cut the cord she and Western Culture had tied between masculinity and towering creativity."[31] With the connection loosened, Stein could take her experimental writing into new areas. "The more secure Stein felt in her male professional persona," claims Ruddick, "the freer she felt, within her dense texts, to burrow into an infantile and maternal territory and to challenge habits of thinking connected with male dominance."[32] And, we might add, with "compulsory heterosexuality." For in her increasingly satisfying lesbianism she came to experiment with the artificiality of gender differentiations. Certainly a poem such as "Lifting Belly" points to gender play between Stein and Toklas: "Please be the man. I am the man."[33] Sexual identity here becomes unfixed, fluid rather than instrumental, just as Stein's wordplay unfixes language from a procrustean instrumentality.

The sexual ambiguities inherent in her identity as a "singular" woman of genius inform her relationship as writer to the literary forms of the patriarchy. This was especially true of autobiography because it was a form to which she was drawn and with which she constantly played. In *Everybody's Autobiography* Stein would later write: "There is too much fathering going on just now and there is no doubt about it fathers are depressing." She then asked: "What is the use of being a little boy if you are to be a man what is the use."[34] This "rejection of fathers," notes Shirley Neuman, "repudiates *any* traditional sense of identity; it categorically denies any literary interest or function to either one's psychobiological past or the seed-time of one's soul."[35] Chronological narrative is an old story, an old father's tale. And childhood as the origin of identity is part of that paternal legacy.[36] Gertrude Stein's "life" begins, she implies through the voice of "Alice," not in childhood and not in her paternal legacy. It begins when Alice B. Toklas displaces, both physically and emotionally, Stein's brother Leo, son of the father, and as such the figure of patriarchal lineage, power, and control, and when, as a result, Stein inserts herself into his "paternalistic" role and assumes the position of the singular, as the man/woman of genius. As she pursued her singular genius against the norm, she pursued an autobiographical practice against the norm, resisting, as we have seen, the evolutionary story, the self-conscious narrator, the identification between autobiographical narrator and autobiographical subject, the unitary voice, all the rhetorical and narrative components of a patriarchally inscribed identity. From the writing position of the "man/woman" of genius, she could critique the narrative of paternal origins and the identities those origins secured.

This is not to suggest that Stein unfixes patriarchal gender identities in any simple way in *The Autobiography of Alice B. Toklas*. The course of her undoing is complex and vexed, and it is tied to the sexual politics of the text and to strategies of disembodiment.

The Text's Sexual Politics

"Alice" informs us that Gertrude Stein, registering the significant similarities between Americans and Spaniards, notes "that they are the only two western nations that can realise abstraction. That in americans it expresses itself by disembodiedness, in literature and machinery, in Spain by ritual so abstract that it does not connect itself with anything but ritual" (91). As an "american," Stein sought to constitute herself autobiographically as the abstract noun, "Gertrude Stein," through the very disembodiment that would extract her from a fixedness in identity. With *The Autobiography*, she manages a kind of tour de force, a radical "out-of-body" experiment in which the autobiographical body seems to be erased entirely from the autobiographical subject. Stein sheds her own body and enters the narrative body of "Alice," thus confusing one body and another, the object and the subject of discourse, the relationship of speaker to words.[37] Even the words of the text have been un/mouthed in the sense that the words are "Alice's," even though the text/mouth is Stein's.

But we need to look further at the sexual politics of the text, at the relationship of this out-of-body autobiographical writing practice and the sexual practices of the body, and to ask what Stein does with sexual identity. It is the female-sexed body that Stein writes out of and the female-sexed body that she writes herself into, or through which she speaks the autobiographical subject. How then can she be implicated in both reinscribing and resisting a kind of identity politics? And what does the evasion of both embodiment and subjectivity have to do with that resistance to identity?

To get at this question we need to look at the complex positionality of "Alice." For me it is useful to think of "Alice's" positionality through the concept of "host(ess)ing." Her identification as hostess takes place early in the text when she talks about the axiom bequeathed her by her father: "He . . . told me that a hostess should never apologize for any failure in her household arrangements, if there is a hostess there is in so far as there is a hostess no failure" (5). She tells her readers that she enjoys "the pleasures of needle work and gardening," that she is "fond of painting, furniture, tapestry, houses and flowers and even vegetables and fruit trees" (3–4). As a narrator, she confesses that she "inevitably takes my comparisons from the kitchen because I like food and cooking and know something about it" (41). "Alice" thus figures herself (and Stein figures "Alice") as the quintessential hostess, a role she embraces with ironic wit and relish: "The geniuses came and talked to Gertrude Stein and the wives sat with me" (87).

But "Alice" is not only figured as the hostess in the text. She is the hostess of the text. At the metaphorical level "Alice" functions as narrator-hostess since her text hosts the succession of Stein's guests, the geniuses, near-geniuses, and friends who move through their lives. Through anecdote after anecdote, "Alice" makes a home in her text for the artists and intellectuals of the early twentieth century. More significantly, "Alice" is the hostess of Gertrude Stein, or we might, by introducing yet another meaning of *host,* that meaning which identifies the host as part of the Eucharist, say that she is the sacrificial victim[38] through whom Stein's story is told.

Sacrificing her own story to Gertrude Stein's story, "Alice" reproduces a very conventional narrative, a "woman's story." In the role of devoted wife to Gertrude Stein's husband, "Alice" seems to embrace her identity as a woman as well as the conventional script of woman's essentialized selfhood by dedicating her text to the enhancement of her spouse, making Stein the entity or artistic genius who inhabits the center of all significant historical and textual activity and relegating herself to the margins of the story. She serves as a virtual host who sacrifices her own life for the life of her spouse. This generic convention traces its roots back to the seventeenth century, when women such as Margaret Cavendish, Duchess of Newcastle, and Ann Lady Fanshawe wrote biographies of their famous husbands, biographies through which they attempted to secure the (sometimes suspect) reputation of their husbands for posterity. And it continued as a formulaic mode of female address within an increasingly bourgeois culture. The testimony of the wife insisted on and celebrated the distinction of the husband and secured the status of the husband as a "man of action." So long as she spoke the life of the heroic man, the subordinate woman could speak publicly.

In fact, in *The Autobiography*, female self-effacement is pushed about as far as it can be pushed. "Alice" sacrifices her very subjectivity to her husband since, in fact, Stein ventriloquizes "Alice." Stein as the author of "Alice" assumes the position of the man who speaks for woman, in this way appropriating the wife's very voice, effectually silencing her to the degree that he/she makes her speak.[39] From one point of view this gesture of gobbling up the host is an outrageous act of masculinist appropriation.

But what does speaking as "Alice" enable Stein to do textually? And what does it have to do with identity practices? If woman is the sacrificial victim of patriarchal culture, what does it mean for Stein to speak as one of the victims? If women are the repressed ground upon which patriarchal culture rests, what does it portend for Stein to inhabit that repressed ground?[40]

By speaking through the voice of Alice B. Toklas, Stein pursues an art of camouflage. The relationship of cubist painting and camouflage is remarked by "Alice" as she recalls the cannon in camouflage on the Boulevard Raspail in Paris. And later, she notes the significance of camouflage in World War I as she recalls touring the front after the Armistice: "The idea was the same but as after all it was different nationalities that did it the difference was inevitable. The color schemes were different, the designs were different, the way of placing them was different, it made plain the whole theory of art and its inevitability" (187). Using "Alice" as a piece of camouflage, Stein can make herself the egotistical center of the text and the influential center of twentieth-century modernism. She can, as Timothy Dow Adams argues, publicize herself through a "tall tale" in which "she creates herself as a legendary figure, given to outrageous bragging and superhuman abilities."[41] That is both the art and artifice of her text.

The camouflaged Stein displaces her "monumental egotism" into the self-effacing voice of "Alice." Through this disembodiment, she can simultaneously present herself as genius and protect herself from the reader's expectation that women should avoid egotistical self-display and self-assertion. Imagine the difference in effect if the following passage contained "I's" instead of "she's": "She realises that in english literature in her time she is the only one. She has always known it and now she says it" (77). The laughter would have been missed for the pretension. Stein uses "Alice" to escape her identity as the patriarchally defined female, even as she herself participates in exacting the sacrifice of "Alice"/woman as wife.

The art of camouflage can also be seen as a strategy for normalizing a culturally abnormal sexual relationship. Assigning "Alice" to the wife position and "Gertrude Stein" to the husband position in the text, Stein reinforces the relationship of self-sacrifice to female-ness and genius to maleness. In doing so she situates in her text a traditionally arranged rhetorical couple that represents the traditional coupling of heterosexuality. Invoking a politics of heterosexism, in order to normalize her "aberrant" sexuality, she appears to be honoring a masculinist hierarchy through which male and female identities are constituted.

But while *The Autobiography of Alice B. Toklas* seems to promote a patriarchal gender hierarchy with its essentialized sexual difference and compulsory heterosexuality, it does so at the same time that it challenges the very bases of that identification. Just as there is "no there there" in the "I" of the autobiography, there is no there there in the invocation of the heterosexual couple, the lesbian couple as butch-femme couple. "Stein camps up both gender and heterosexual roles in the wife/husband depiction of Alice and the Genius; she allegorizes their relationship through this depiction and in effect undercuts the referentiality on which this representation of domesticity depends," suggests Gilmore.[42] In fact, Alice's performance of the wife's role is a travesty through which Stein is displacing the heterosexual couple and heterosexual coupling, resituating in its stead, in its textual homestead, the lesbian couple and lesbian coupling. Moreover, it can be seen/heard as an outrageous jest/gesture/ingestion.[43]

Speaking "Alice," Speaking the Body

Catharine Stimpson talks about the two ways in which representations of Gertrude Stein effectively undermined the power of her voice, the sensuality of her body, and the centrality of her place in the avant-garde. On the one hand representations domesticated her by depicting her ensconced within the confines of her home at 27 rue de Fleurus. On the other hand, representations removed her from time by identifying her with figures such as Caesar, creating a "personage" extracted from contemporary time. In both ways the body of Stein was erased as source of pleasure and power. "If the first set of metaphors drains monstrosity of its threat by enclosing it," suggests Stimpson, "the second does so by casting it out and away from daily history, and in part, these metaphors transmogrify Stein into a sacred monster—to be sought after by some, cursed by others."[44]

Paradoxically, in the disembodied strategy of *The Autobiography of Alice B. Toklas* Stein stages a subversive return of the repressed body. The domestic scene and the gendered arrangements of domesticity that have traditionally neutralized female sexuality here become charged with eroticism. Stein effectively deterritorializes the domestic scene, the site of bourgeois arrangements, by emptying it of heterosexuality and filling it with lesbian pleasure. Describing a Zeppelin raid over Paris in the the winter of 1914–15, "Alice" writes:

> I had as was and is my habit gone to bed very early, and Gertrude Stein was down in the studio working, as was her habit. Suddenly I heard her call me gently. What is it, I said. Oh nothing, said she, but perhaps if you don't mind putting on something warm and coming downstairs I think perhaps it would be better. . . . Well I . . . said

when she woke me, is it a revolution and are there soldiers. No, she said, not exactly. Well what is it, said I impatiently. I don't quite know, she answered, but there has been an alarm. Anyway you had better come. I started to turn on the light. No, she said, you had better not. Give me your hand and I will get you down and you can go to sleep down stairs on the couch. I came. It was very dark. I sat down on the couch and then I said, I'm sure I don't know what is the matter with me but my knees are knocking together. Gertrude Stein burst out laughing, wait a minute, I will get you a blanket, she said. No don't leave me, I said. She managed to find something to cover me and then there was a loud boom, then several more. It was a soft noise and then there was a sound of horns blowing in the streets and then we knew it was all over. We lighted the lights and went to bed. (157)

This passage, different in tone than the rest of the text and full of potentially doubled meanings, follows a brief reference to the composition of *Tender Buttons,* the collection of poems and pieces charged with wordplay, feminist revisionism, lesbian eroticism, and gnosticism.[45] It captures the tenderness, care, compatibility, humor, and sexual pleasure of the lesbian couple even as it presents the vulnerability of "Alice" and the authority, knowledge, and protectiveness of "Gertrude Stein."

Thus lesbian eroticism is partially played out through conventional role performances. Yet, while this eroticized exchange may seem to proceed through butch and femme identities that are, according to Judith Butler, "in some sense 'replicas' or 'copies' of heterosexual exchange," the scene simultaneously calls into question "the very notion of an original or natural identity." For Butler, "it is precisely that question as it is embodied in these identities that becomes one source of their erotic significance." In the very unfixedness of heterosexual identities, says Butler, lies a subversive, comedic potential: "Heterosexuality offers normative sexual positions that are intrinsically impossible to embody, and the persistent failure to identify fully and without incoherence with these positions reveals heterosexuality itself not only as a compulsory law, but as an inevitable comedy. Indeed, I would offer this insight into heterosexuality as both a compulsory system and an intrinsic comedy, a constant parody of itself, as an alternative gay/lesbian perspective."[46]

Even as Stein situates "Gertrude Stein" and "Alice" in apparently heterosexualized roles, she undoes any necessary, natural, essential sexual identity through an alternative perspective on sexual identity. Who is speaking? A "man" (the "husband" "Gertrude Stein")? A "woman" (the "wife" "Alice")? A "woman" playing a "man" playing a "woman"? A "female" "man" playing a "woman"? Stein and her text participate in what Butler describes as "the subversive recombination of gender meanings"[47] as "Gertrude Stein" and "Alice" reveal the gender discontinuities of bourgeois heterosexuality.

Moreover, in *The Autobiography,* Stein both camouflages and announces her lesbian sexuality in her strategic decision to enter the body of the lover. Stein enters the mouth of her lover and takes up lodging in the body of "Alice" for the purposes of writing the autobiography. "Alice" in turn enters the mouth of her host writer through whose body she speaks. This commingling of subjects in the text is thus an act of erotic union, signed by the wedding band/vaginal image on the cover. Ultimately, Stein, in commingling her story with "Alice's" story, hosts her lover in return. And so the text becomes what Catharine Stimpson calls a "somagram" of lesbianism.[48]

The very language of Stein's text is implicated in its erotics. The sentences of the text are both Alice's and Stein's as the stylistic commingling mirrors the bodily commingling. Through Stein's invocation of Alice's colloquialisms and cadences, through her braiding of the language of the lovers, she enters into the materiality of language of the loved one. The word issues through the body of the lover as four lips speak together.[49]

The digressive asides, the gossipy anecdotes, are all sources of textual pleasure as they "cut," to use Ruddick's analytical term, across the chronological time-sense of the narrative. At any moment "Alice" moves off her linear trajectory to talk about conversations, meals, romantic relationships, imbroglios, fates of friends. A gossipy anecdotal style is a kind of narrative wordplay. The anecdote gives pleasure in and of itself; it satisfies the voyeuristic desire for "the real dirt" about people.[50] Moreover, the anecdotal style is repetitious because it always calls for a return to the narrative thread, disruption and return, creating a kind of compelling rhythm that Stein herself understood as erotic.

And I do not want to omit the effect of the almost incantatory quality of "Alice's" use of the phrases "Gertrude Stein" and "she says" or "she always says."[51] Over and over "she" weaves the full name of and pronominal references to the lover into her text. While such references constitute Stein as entity, they also function to constitute the multidimensional "pleasure of the text," to invoke Roland Barthes's phrase.[52] They signal the pleasure of Stein as the author of the text; the pleasure of Stein as the lover of "Alice," the pleasure of "Alice" in her lover, and our pleasure in the *jouissance* implicit in repetition and the release of the signifier from its signified into its word-ness and sound.

In her celebration of "Gertrude Stein," "Alice" unashamedly evinces pleasure in the life and achievements of her lover. But of course that is the fiction of pleasure Stein creates. Even as she positions herself in the text as allied with the sun and the domain of the father, Stein herself is taking her own pleasure by speaking as Alice, and by implication as a "woman" (since "Alice" identifies herself early in the text with the "moon").[53] To put it another way, she takes pleasure in absorbing entirely the body of the other/lover, of filling herself up with "Alice" and then of emptying "Alice" out of her. This movement of filling up and emptying out, according to Ruddick, reflects Stein's metaphorical understanding of the creative process as well as the rhythm of sexuality as allied with bodily processes. It links, for this modernist, writing and the body. In this way the metaphor also enables Stein to contest, according to Ruddick, "a Cartesian dualism that historically has devalued and marginalized women" in the sense that it "undermine[s] the polarities of pure/impure and mental/material, polarities that are patriarchal in the sense that they tend to devalue woman along with matter."[54]

If, as Stimpson has argued, Stein was figured by her contemporaries and by her critics as a kind of female monster, if her body was masculinized in order to deny it its palpable sexuality, then Stein paradoxically reclaims her body through this out-of-body experiment. She is playing the joke on a public that would make of her the monster, the sexually unattractive/inactive woman by playing out before them the very pleasures of the autobiographical body. Without actually naming what Watson and others call "the unspeakable," Stein makes the unspeakable of lesbian coupling speak. Through the camouflage of normative gender arrangements of heterosexuality she encodes the "abnormative" alignment of desire. Camouflage is only camouflage when it is known to hide something.

Stein has taken that most common of female autobiographical forms—the self-effacing biography of the public figure by his spouse—and made it the vehicle through which to speak of her most uncommon and transgressive sexuality. While she seems to mime, to invoke Monique Wittig's analysis, "the discourses of heterosexuality" that "prevent [lesbians] from speaking unless we speak in their terms,"[55] she has worked to undo through subversive laughter the naturalness implicit in those discourses. As Gilmore suggests, however much "Alice" might play the role of the wife, there is no wife there because the regulatory practices of compulsory heterosexuality have not successfully produced "Alice" as a wife. Moreover, "Alice's" invocation of the phrase "the wives of geniuses" again and again turns it into a comical expression, demystifying it. And however much "Gertrude Stein" might play the husband, that husband is indeed a woman. This woman too has not been successfully produced as wife. We might say that Stein has both filled and emptied the autobiographical "I" of the heterosexuality that marks it in the paternal order. Simultaneously, Stein disperses the authority of paternal narrative, including autobiography, by subverting the old stabilities of identity and chronology. The cultural radicalism of Stein's modernism and her lesbianism invigorate one another. The text's eroticism and its radical disruptiveness are one and the same.

"Alice" identifies Stein with the sun—that symbol Stein invoked as a sign of maleness—when she says of Stein in Spain, "she could even lie in the sun and look straight up into a summer noon sun, she said it rested her eyes and head" (55). The figure of Stein staring at the sun can be read at least two ways. She stares into the sun in a gesture of identification with the sun. She stares into the sun in a gesture of defiance, challenging the sun to make her turn her gaze away. Substituting "two" for "one" in *The Autobiography of Alice B. Toklas*, Stein looks both ways.

V

THE AUTOBIOGRAPHICAL EYE/I IN VIRGINIA WOOLF'S "SKETCH"

These were two of the adventures of my professional life. The first—killing the Angel in the House—I think I solved. She died. But the second, telling the truth about my own experiences as a body, I do not think I solved.

Virginia Woolf, "Professions for Women"

To relax I read little Dorrit and think of going on with my Au[tobiograph]y. Never have I been so set on my own spinning. Gerald Heard's book spun me to distraction last night. . . . [H]is fanatical starved or as he would say strangulated individuality presides. A scream, a distracted scream issues, instead of the soaring spirit.

Virginia Woolf, *Diary*, Wednesday 25 October 1939

Then dipped into my memoirs: too circuitous & unrelated; too many splutters; as it stands. A real life has no crisis; hence nothing to tighten. It must lack centre. It must amble on. All the same, I can weave a very thin pattern, one of these days, out of that pattern of detail.

Virginia Woolf, *Diary*, 1 November 1940

The surveyor of woman in herself is male: the surveyed female.

John Berger, *Ways of Seeing*

Within a page of opening her autobiographical "A Sketch of the Past," Virginia Woolf critiques traditional autobiographical texts and their privileging of metaphysical selfhood: "They leave out the person to whom things happened," she concludes: "The reason is that it is so difficult to describe any human being. So they say: 'this is what happened'; but they do not say what the person was like to whom it happened. And the events mean very little unless we know first to whom they happened."[1] Thus she counters tradition by attempting to capture the quality of the "I" to whom things happened, to capture the subject's ineffability. She does not structure the narrative around the achievement of career or public recognition, a coherent and chronological template of evolutionary development that had characterized traditional Victorian autobiography. Nor does she try to dig deep inside to discover the hard core, the granite at the center of her being. For Woolf too many disparate forces converge on the individual, too many diffusive forces connect the individual to others.

Like her contemporary Gertrude Stein, Virginia Woolf experimented with autobiographical writing at various points in her life. Her first experiment with memoirs was the early "Reminiscences" (1907), expressly a biographical piece about her sister Vanessa addressed to Vanessa's son, Julian Bell, but effectively a memoir of her own childhood. Between 1920 and 1936 she wrote several autobiographical papers which she delivered to the Memoir Club, a group of friends who, according to Jean Schulkind, "gathered at intervals to read memoirs in which they were committed to complete candour."[2] And toward the end of her life she returned to autobiographical writing as she worked on what she would leave behind as the unfinished "Sketch." By then, as the comments quoted above indicate, Woolf confronted considerable disjunctions between the inherited, and what she considered patriarchal, traditions of life writing and her own modernist interventions in traditions of narrative time, voice, and subjectivity.

Reading biographies, autobiographies, memoirs, and collections of letters voraciously during the writing of the "Sketch,"[3] Woolf persistently defined and redefined in her diary what kind of personal writing worked for her and what did not. She seems to have read memoirs and autobiographies for a certain elusiveness of vision, a preoccupation with "visions and dreams" rather than "actions or . . . dramatic scenes."[4] She certainly found an enemy of personal narrative in any kind of "strangulated individuality," which, as the epigraph indicates, she described as "a distracted scream" that interferes with "the soaring spirit."

At the same time as she read various forms of life writing critically, she also confronted the limitations of strangulating individuality in her writing projects, for she wrote "A Sketch of the Past" while struggling with both the biography of Roger Fry and "Pointz Hall" (which would become the novel *Between the Acts*). Writing the Fry biography was particularly painful to her. Her diary records that she continually worried about the writing, editing, publishing, and reception of the work. She accepted the challenge as a duty, a commitment to his memory and to his friends. But in accepting the obligation she entered into a generic contract that went against the grain of her sensibilities and her imaginative vision. She worried that her account was too dry, tied too much to the details of his life and to chronology and not enough to the quality of his life and his influence on others, to the sights and smell, the feeling of his days and his friendships. The aesthetic difficulty here had to do with the demands of biographical writing. For one, there was the demand of censorship, the careful screening out of material that might offend those still alive. Second and more important, the biographical subject required a clear, unerring focus on the individual. That focus was precisely what Woolf was trying to dislodge because she associated individuality with male privilege and hierarchy.

In her fiction she had been working to disrupt the traditional sequence and sentence of patriarchal narrative, especially in the later novels, "Pointz Hall" among them, where she eschewed a singular protagonist in favor of what Rachel Blau DuPlessis calls a communal or choral protagonist.[5] Diverting the narrative focus away from the single controlling consciousness to a communal protagonist, Woolf found a means to contest the engendered plots of nineteenth-century fiction—romance and *bildungs*—and the assumptions permeating that fiction, "beginning" argues DuPlessis, "with gender polarization and the dichotomy of male and female, public and private spheres, and moving to hero and heroine and the 'hard visible horizon' of the isolated individual."[6] She also found a means to undermine the hierarchization of subjects. Since, as DuPlessis notes, "the promotion of any given character to a position of greatest importance in a narrative indicates dominant values and marks social hierarchies," Woolf "equalized the characters" with the effect that "no one stands higher in the plot than any other: the final conveyor of value is plural."[7]

The intensity of her desire to banish the isolated individual and "his" hard nut of selfhood from both fictional and autobiographical texts has to do with the historical circumstances surrounding the writing of the "Sketch" and the interpretation she gave to that history. With the onset of World War II, a new kind of disturbance characterized life at Mecklenberg Square and Monks House. German planes flew continuous raids over southern England, their deadly intrusions creating terror and a sense of vulnerability. Woolf's final diary is punctuated with references to bombing raids, sirens, damage assessments, and records of deaths. While references to the war are sporadic in the "Sketch," they are nonetheless poignant, as in the following passage: "The battle is at its crisis; every night the Germans fly over England; it comes closer to this house daily. If we are beaten then—however we solve that problem, and one solution is apparently suicide (so it was decided three nights ago in London among us)—book writing becomes doubtful. But I wish to go on, not to settle down in that dismal puddle."[8] As she argued in *Three Guineas,* that strangulated individuality and the patriarchal arrangements that support it lead inevitably to authoritarianism, fascism, and wars of aggression, to those bombs falling around her as she writes, to those bombs that render her own life one of inescapable vulnerability.[9]

Beyond the real pressure of the German assault on England lay another patriarchal assault, that of the "sons" on their "parents." Younger male writers had begun to turn against their predecessors, Woolf among them, rejecting and redefining the kind of modernism identified with Woolf's novelistic experiments, effectively marginalizing her. In this way, her audience was disintegrating. So Woolf was vulnerable on at least two fronts.[10] In her own way, Woolf is saying as emphatically as Stein that "there is too much fathering going on just now and there is no doubt about it fathers are depressing."

Of course, when Woolf wrote her memoir, she could not erase all trace of the narrating "I." She was, after all, telling the story of her own past directly, without the refracting lenses of fiction or polemical prose. But we might say that in her "Sketch" Woolf tried to write "between the acts" of traditional auto/biography and choral fiction. Like Stein, then, Woolf dislodges the old "I" from autobiography, but she takes the destabilization of boundaries between one subject and another in a different direction than Stein does, for she moves not into one other but into multiple others as she pursues a diffusive rather than unitary subjectivity. The challenges she faces are as considerable as those facing Stein, who also sought to break the instrumentality of paternal narratives. How could she use the personal signifier, "I," without becoming authoritarian in relationship to her self, her past and the world, without becoming one of those trees haunting male writing? How could she disperse the "hard visible horizon" of that universal "I," with its dominance, aridity, and patriarchal privileges, and effectively transform the old autobiographical "I" into that communal "we"? Or to put it another way, how could the self-narrating "I" of autobiography achieve a kind of anonymity and thereby escape the narcissism and egotism inherent in autobiography.[11]

And, finally, what did this anonymity have to do with the formerly unspeakable "truth about [her] own experiences as a body"? Might not anonymity become a kind of out-of-body experience through which she could escape the vulnerabilities of the body, the violence of the identity contents assigned to it by the patriarchs, and the inherited narratives with which they bombarded her? It is to the history of the body informing Woolf's "Sketch" that I want to look first.

Inaugural Memories and the History of the Body

To inaugurate her narrative, Woolf opens her unfinished "Sketch" not with historical details of family lineage, not with paternal and maternal origins, but with the "orts and fragments" (to invoke a phrase from *Between the Acts*) of her earliest memories, those prelinguistic moments of sensual pleasure and receptivity before the infant body has been unhinged from mind and imagination. Two moments in particular capture her memory. Sitting on her mother's lap, she is enveloped by the large passion flowers on her mother's dress. Lying in her crib at St. Ives, she feels the wind, listens to the sounds of water, wind, and window covering, sees the light play through space. These privileged moments of preindividualized being she associates with ecstasy—with the semiotic pleasure of pure sensation and experiential wholeness, with instinct and passion. Here is the moment before repression has begun its work.[12] "If life has a base that it stands upon," she claims, "if it is a bowl that one fills and fills and fills—then my bowl without a doubt stands upon this memory" (64).

To the experience of preoedipal bondedness and boundlessness in which her body and her mother's body are the sources of ecstasy, Woolf juxtaposes several horrifyingly vivid memories that signify for the older narrator the transition from the childhood of nondifferentiation to the young womanhood of overdetermined sexual identification. For Woolf, the fluidity of infancy carries over into the experience of childhood. The early world of Virginia, Thoby, Vanessa, and Adrian is fluid, indistinguishable, unmarked by the divisions of rigid sex roles, since she has yet to be engendered. But the memory of standing before a mirror, ashamed of the figure she sees projected in the glass, marks a radical change. In trying to understand the significance of this memory, she concludes: "I must have been ashamed or afraid of my own body" (68). In the mirror she sees reflected a bounded, totalized body, a body captured in the gaze. Hard-edged, impermeable, confined, that body lacks the fluidity, the openness, the permeability identified with her earliest memories, ones that she says provided her with rapture and ecstasy. Here body and background, ground and figure, are dramatically separated from one another.

Woolf follows this memory with her dramatic revelation of childhood sexual abuse:

> There was a slab outside the dining room door for standing dishes upon. Once when I was very small Gerald Duckworth lifted me onto this, and as I sat there he began to explore my body. I can remember the feel of his hand going under my clothes; going firmly and steadily lower and lower. I remember how I hoped that he would stop; how I stiffened and wriggled as his hand approached my private parts. But it did not stop. His hand explored my private parts too. I remember resenting, disliking it—what is the word for so dumb and mixed a feeling? It must have been strong, since I still recall it. This seems to show that a feeling about certain parts of the

body; how they must not be touched; how it is wrong to allow them to be touched; must be instinctive. It proves that Virginia Stephen was not born on the 25th January 1882, but was born many thousands of years ago; and had from the very first to encounter instincts already acquired by thousands of ancestresses in the past. (69)

Then directly after this revelation, she remembers a (perhaps) oneiric vision in which she catches a glimpse of herself in a mirror, only now there is an animal visible behind her. In the latter vision, the specular conjunction of body and animal graphically identifies her body with the animal world, with the low, the irrational, the contaminating and unruly, thus with the grotesque or carnivalesque. Graphically Woolf renders her body as a source of lowliness and animality, of disgust and shame, and reveals the motivations for her inhibitions, her repressions.

Several aspects of this succession of memories command the reader's attention. First, with the revelation of sexual abuse Woolf introduces a liminal scene in which the young girl experiences the loss of her own body to the sexual domination and exploitation of the patriarch, an older brother and putative protector. Her body is literally taken away from her. With the intrusion of Gerald Duckworth's hand, the child experiences the painful recognition that her body is not hers to control, that it is there for others to handle. If that handling is physically invasive, it is also culturally pervasive. For Woolf interjects here her memory of childhood injunctions against bodies being touched.[13] Therefore, it is not only Gerald Duckworth's sexual abuse but bourgeois Victorian taboos surrounding the body that effectively remove the feeling subject from her own body, from that specific source of ecstasy.

Second, the feeling of horror she recalls derives from her knowledge, however conscious or unconscious, of that specular self which encloses her in the prisonhouse of gender, in identity's body. That very body defines and delimits her as female subject, tying her to her destiny as woman. In the mirror she sees what Hélène Cixous has called "the uncanny stranger on display—the ailing or dead figure, which so often turns out to be the nasty companion, the cause and location of inhibitions."[14] But something more happens here. If, as John Berger has argued in considering the specular relationship of women to the mirror, "the surveyor of woman in herself is male: the surveyed female,"[15] then the recollection of uneasiness is a recollection of a shift in the subject's position. As the "I" who looks at that body becomes the observer, and the body the observed, that "I" assumes the place of the male subject. Looking in the mirror as "tomboy" (a childhood identification she has noted), the young Virginia gazes at her body as men will later do. Thus the act of looking in the mirror implicates her in the very practice that she will later so vigorously abjure, the experience of her stepbrother's creation of her as the object of the public gaze, as a woman in the heterosexual economy.

These memories reveal the symbolic and imaginary processes whereby the female subject is consolidated in ways that support the privileges of the male/bourgeois subject, what Julia Kristeva describes as the "coding of his repulsion in relation to the other in order to autonomize himself,"[16] and the consequent coding of the self-revulsion of the female subject. The young Virginia is positioned in a body that she experiences as a source of shame and alienation. The regulatory processes brought to bear on the imagination render the female body other, animal, therefore abject, and exclude that body and its unruliness from the domain of the higher subject. Woolf's oneiric vision glimpses the internalization of this symbolic consolidation. Simultaneously bourgeois culture locates women in their bodies, imposes the total identification of woman with her body. A woman becomes the cultural abject, identified out in her difference, solidified in her very embodiment. Woolf's specular "moments of being," or rather, moments of splitting, reveal how as a woman she is doubly indemnified. She is the cultural abject: she abjects her own body.

The degree of abjection is revealed in the subtle movement of narrative voice in the passage about Gerald's invasive hand. Woolf shifts the narrative voice away from the "I" of the narrating subject by invoking the distancing device of third-person narrative, referring to herself as the object "Virginia Stephen." Moreover, she increasingly distances her responses from their immediate source in the subsequent analysis of motive. First, she suggests the shame might have derived from her fear of being caught looking at herself since to do so would violate her childhood identification with a "tomboy code" (67). But she proceeds to trace it back further to ancestral predispositions over which she has no control. Recalling that "femininity was strong in our family," she suggests that the Stephen women were famous for their beauty, a beauty she finds gives her "pride and pleasure," but she also notes that her "natural love for beauty was checked by some ancestral dread" (68). This dread may reach back only two generations to a "spartan, ascetic, puritanical" grandfather from whom she inherited "some opposite instinct." Or it may go further back to prehistory, to the ancestresses of the race to whom she traces discomfort with invasions of her body. She takes the source of bodily disgust away from her own family experience to the instinctive life of the human species. She cannot, as Sue Roe notes, even describe the sensations in this passage as she could in describing her earliest memories; she seems to have no words for talking about her own sexualized body and no personal narratives for conveying her response.[17]

Other early moments of being recapitulate the sense of the abject body. In a fight with Thoby, her body suddenly goes limp, paralyzed. By the apple tree that the child identifies with Mr. Valpy's suicide her body cannot move. Before a puddle, she cannot move her body nor can she find anything physical to touch. After being accosted by an "idiot boy," she huddles in one end of the bathtub, "motionless." In all these recollections, the young girl's vulnerable body goes "dead."

These specular moments of being separate Woolf's narrative of childhood from her narrative of young adulthood and signify for the older narrator the transition from the childhood of sexual nondifferentiation to the young Victorian womanhood of overdetermined sexual identification. The female body has placed her socially in a procrustean identity. For the older writer, the figure in the mirror represents female selfhood shackled to the female body and engendered through specific social, cultural, and historical conditions. What shocks the young girl does not shock the older woman, who recognizes too clearly the ways in which the fabricated body and the female subject in that body are constituted out of the "invisible presences" of patriarchal ideology: "Consider what immense forces society brings to play upon each of us," writes Woolf, "how that society changes from decade to decade; and also from class to class; well, if we cannot analyze these invisible presences, we know very little of the subject of the memoir" (80). The autobiographer thus proceeds to track, if sketchily, the social construction of sexual difference within the Victorian household.

First, she describes the centrality of the mother in her childhood (a great cathedral space) and the shock of her mother's death. Her deathbed scenes bring together various motifs: the distressing mirror, but now with no body reflected in it; the washing of the dead body; the coldness of the body to the kiss of the child ("When I kissed her, it was like kissing cold iron" [92]); and the distancing of the child from the feelings of grief ("I said to myself as I have often done at moments of crisis since, 'I feel nothing whatever' " [92]); and afterwards the oppressive playing of "parts that we did not feel," the "fumbl[ing] for words that we did not know" (95). It is as if symbolically her mother's death finally takes the body from the young girl in a grand anesthesia.

She tracks the next phase of her grand anesthesia through her subsequent relationship to mothering. In a series of in/habitations of identity, the young Stella replaces the dead mother, Vanessa replaces the dead Stella, and Virginia joins Vanessa in assuming the cultural place of dutiful daughterhood.[18] Against their wills, the daughters/sisters are fashioned into models of nurturant femininity. The connection between the mirror scene and this narrative of displacements is joined in the female body. If the earlier reflection in the mirror confronts her with her own abjection, a sense of bodily dispossession, the subsequent filling-in-the-place-of-the-mother forces her back to total embodiment.[19] In the gaze of the men around her she is possessed entirely by the body of woman. The latter part of the "Sketch" thus focuses on the socio/familial regulation of her very body.

For one, her body determines her assignment to certain household spaces since bourgeois gender ideologies spatialized the separate spheres through the physical division of the house into study and drawing room. Her body locates her in the drawing room. It also locates her in certain clothes, the "habits" about which the older narrator remembers feeling so much discomfort. "Everything to do with dress—to be fitted, to come into a room wearing a new dress," she confesses, "still frightens me: at least makes me shy, self-conscious, uncomfortable" (68). The dress becomes a costume of the body, a costume of the mind, enclosing the young woman literally and figuratively within a particular representation of female identity. "Vain trifles as they seem," Woolf had written in *Orlando,* "clothes have, they say, more important offices than merely to keep us warm. They change our view of the world and the world's view of us. . . . Thus, there is much to support the view that it is clothes that wear us and not we them; we may make them take the mould of arm or breast; but they would mould our hearts, our brains, our tongues to their liking."[20] Woolf recognized how effectively clothes, external signs of sexual difference, influenced hearts, brains, and language. And in "Sketch" she suggests how social life becomes synonymous with female bodily display as she remembers the distress she felt when her brothers introduced her into society. In one more way, they handled her by turning her into an object of the male gaze, by turning her body into a source of male pleasure.

Not only are spatial assignments and clothes components in the regulation of her body; so too are manners, those sets of behaviors associated with space and dress. As "regulations of the body," suggest Peter Stallybrass and Allon White, manners "become the site of a profound interconnection of ideology and subjectivity, a zone of transcoding at once astonishingly trivial and microscopically important. Traversed by regulative forces quite beyond its conscious control, the body is territorialized in accordance with hierarchies and topographical rules which it enacts automatically, which come from elsewhere and which make it a point of intersection and flow within the elaborate symbolic systems of the socius."[21] Ultimately, Woolf's female body becomes a commodified body, designed, produced, and consumed, a process Woolf acknowledges in her imagery of the machine: "And so, while father preserved the framework of 1860, George filled in the framework with all kinds of minutely teethed saws; and the machine into which we were inserted in 1900 therefore held us tight; and brought innumerable teeth into play" (131).[22] Those teeth are so many sets of manners, gearing her up for the finished product, a young lady.

By the final page of the unfinished "Sketch," the narrative fizzles out in the total paralysis of the subject who cannot escape the social topography of separate spheres, the travesty of sex roles, the gender hierarchy of compulsory heterosexuality, and the social regulations of the body, a subject who cannot escape the sense of distance between herself and her experience:

> There they were, on the verge of the drawing room, these great men:
> while, round the tea table, George and Gerald and Jack talked of the
> Post Office, the publishing office, and the Law Courts. And I, sitting
> by the table, was quite unable to make any connection. There were
> so many different worlds: but they were distant from me. I could
> not make them cohere; nor feel myself in touch with them. (136–37)

Woolf's narrative breaks off (with her suicide) at a point in the
history of the sexed subject far distant from the inaugural moments
of infancy when she felt entirely "in touch with" her body and the
body of the mother. It is as if the "Sketch" breaks off amidst the
psychological ravages inflicted on the young "Virginia" through
the psychological, intellectual, and physical wars of aggression that
Victorian men waged on women and their bodies.

The Body Displaced

The body with which Woolf felt so much discomfort, however,
rematerializes in a metaphorical elsewhere. Even as the body in the
mirror continues to haunt the narrative as the "uncanny stranger,"
another material figure displaces the narrator's body. In fact, the
body is fragmented into a writerly metaphor, or rather the materiality of the body is concentrated into a metaphorical orb, a kind of
transparent eyeball. Her resistance to her own body (and her early
memory of being positioned in her mother's lap as a sensate being)
sends her vision toward the transparent eyeball, away from the
solid individuality of embodied subjects.

In an essay entitled "Street Haunting," Woolf describes leaving
the Clarissa-esque narrow room of self to become absorbed in the
street where "the shell-like covering which our souls have excreted
to house themselves, to make for themselves a shape distinct from
others, is broken, and there is left of all these wrinkles and rough-
nesses a central oyster of perceptiveness, an enormous eye."[23] Only
too aware of the constrictions, foreclosures, stillnesses, and nar-
rowing rigidities of the totalized "shape distinct from others," an
individualized subject who takes shape through sexual politics, this
modernist writer bemoans the unitary self's tendency to foreclose
and silence "those embryo lives which attend about us in early

youth until 'I' suppresse[s] them."[24] Woolf understood how one by one these possible trajectories of subjectivity are foreclosed by the fixedness of identity, and are submerged in the wake of the powerful, totalizing "I." But by taking trips, geographical, cultural, psychological, the subject can "penetrate a little way, far enough to give oneself the illusion that one is not tethered to a single mind, but can put on briefly for a few minutes the bodies and minds of others."[25] By traveling out of one's own body, the subject can escape a constraining identity. Thus, an alternative subject to the hard (male) nut is "something so varied and wandering that it is only when we give the rein to its wishes and let it take its way unimpeded that we are indeed ourselves."[26]

Significantly, Woolf reworks this figure of the "central oyster of perceptiveness" in "Sketch" as she identifies her infant self with a transparent eyeball, although the exact image is one of fruit. She has "the feeling, as I describe it sometimes to myself, of lying in a grape and seeing through a film of semi-transparent yellow" (65). This great grape eyeball is sense itself, open to impressions, absorbing color, sound, smell, rhythm: "I am hardly aware of myself, but only of the sensation. I am only the container of the feeling of ecstasy, of the feeling of rapture" (67). "Grape" subjectivity is fluid, open to the multiplicity of sensations that pass between the child and the mother. Always permeable, this preindividualized subjectivity immerses itself in the "cotton wool" of daily life and remains always an invitation to exchange. The time of the great grape eyeball is the moment before the totalizing "I" intrudes, before interpretation and alienation disrupt the seamless exchange between the experiencing subject and the experienced world. It is the time before entry into the symbolic realm maps out for people the difference of subject and other. It is the time before the mirror presents the girl with the image of her body, locus of sexual difference and discomfort, locus of both embodiment and bodily homelessness. Paradoxically, the great grape eyeball is the sensate body disjoined from an earthly, socially commanded embodiment.

This figure of the transparent grape eyeball is critical to Woolf's critique of metaphysical selfhood and its regulation of the body. A material entity, a sensual organ, it takes in, imbibes the external world, acting as conduit for external experience. Yet it is simultaneously a metaphorical locus of spirit, vision, illumination, interpretation, a place of writing. Conjoining both matter and spirit, external reality and internal vision, the transparent eyeball lies on the border between inside and outside, mind and matter, subject and other. Disembodied, the transparent eyeball as locus of ecstasy is not tied to a finite body but functions as an experiencing point of contact between inner and outer. The older woman's metaphor of the transparent eyeball effectively connects her to the grape-infant Virginia who experienced the pure ecstasy of semiotic union, the commingling of self and other, the seamless transition between inside and outside that she identifies with her earliest memories.

In memoriam, Woolf's writing practice mediates the distress of separation, from the preoedipal bond of infancy, from her mother, from her own body. It links her to the rich sensuality of that cathedral space she responds to when as a child she goes to Paddington to pick up Thoby (who has returned home after her mother's death): "I walked along the platform gazing with rapture at this magnificant blaze of colour. . . . It impressed and exalted me. It was so vast and so fiery red. The contrast of that blaze of magnificent light with the shrouded and curtained rooms at Hyde Park Gate was so intense. Also it was partly that my mother's death unveiled and intensified; made me suddenly develop perceptions, as if a burning glass had been laid over what was shaded and dormant" (93). And immediately following this recollection comes her memory of reading a poem from *The Golden Treasury* and being struck by its meaning: "I had a feeling of transparency in words when they cease to be words and become so intensified that one seems to experience them" (93). The sensuality of the child before separation from the mother becomes for the young girl and for the mature artist the erotic materiality of language and the transparency of vision. Writing the subjectivity of the transparent eyeball provides an imaginary means to achieve once again union with the body of the mother.

Anonymity, Subjectivity, and the Critique of Autobiography

Signifying the desire of the subject to traverse permeable ego boundaries, the metaphor, in linking her to that earlier moment of pleasure in the body of the mother and in her own body, promises a diffusive and absorptive rather than appropriative subjectivity. And the metaphor materializes through specific narrative practices and implicit critiques of traditional autobiography in the "Sketch."

Take, for instance, the role of memory in Woolf's narrative. The repertoire of memories specific to the individual are essential to subjectivity. As integuments of subjectivity, memories are so many umbilical cords connecting the narrator to the swirl of others surrounding her. Thus Woolf emphasizes that her story is as much the story of others, the mother, sisters, brothers, who hold her in place, as her own, that to tell hers is to tell theirs since self and other join together in a seamless horizon of intersubjectivity. Of the influence of other people she writes: "Yet it is by such invisible presences that the 'subject of this memoir' is tugged this way and that every day of his life; it is they that keep him in position. . . . If we cannot analyse these invisible presences, we know very little of the subject of the memoir; and again how futile life-writing becomes. I see myself as a fish in a stream; deflected; held in place; but cannot describe the stream" (80). Of her brothers and sisters she writes: "And if I were to describe myself, at fifteen, I should have to describe Nessa and Thoby, both in great detail; for they [were] as much my life as anything" (107). And of her mother she writes eloquently, lyrically, and specifically, as in the following passage in which she describes the similarities (and physical differences)[27] between mother and daughter:

> Then I see her in her white dressing gown on the balcony; and the passion flower with the purple star on its petals. Her voice is still faintly in my ears—decided, quick; and in particular the little drops with which her laugh ended—three diminishing ahs . . . "Ah-ah-ah . . ." I sometimes end a laugh that way myself. And I see her hands, like Adrian's, with the very individual square-tipped fingers, each finger with a waist to it, and the nail broadening out. (My own are the same size all the way, so that I can slip a ring over my thumb.) She had three rings; a diamond ring, an emerald ring, and an opal ring. My eyes used to fix themselves upon the lights in the opal as it moved across the page of the lesson book when she taught us, and I was glad that she left it to me (I gave it to Leonard). (81–82)

Later she writes of her mother, "she was the whole thing" (83), thus linking the influence of her mother to the development of her aesthetic sense of writing as a way of seeing the pattern, "the whole thing." And "the whole thing" is a communal rather than an individual whole.

Through this movement into the stories of those around her, through this exploration of the traces of their lives within hers, Woolf incorporates others into the "floating vessel" of her subjectivity.[28] Pursuing the anonymity of communal subjectivity, she expands the subject beyond the narrow boundaries of an isolated, unitary core of selfhood, beyond the distracted screams of strangulated individuality. She also expands the subject beyond the cultural framing of the female body reflected in the mirror, the necessary and specular other to the strangulated individual. Hard-edged boundaries between self and other are illegitimate borders of self-containment to be resisted in favor of a soaring, or floating transindividualism. In effect, the nomadic, incorporative subject escapes through intersubjectivity the prisonhouse of singular identity, escapes through disembodiment the regulated female body. This anonymity is thus an aesthetic response to the firm boundedness of the body in the mirror as well as a visionary response to the hard nut of the individualized phallic "I." As such it becomes a means through which Woolf critiques the traditional subject of autobiography.

She also critiques the traditional plot of autobiography. Roaming back and forth through time and memory, Woolf, while acknowledging some need for a "thin pattern"—the memoir in fact carries forward the history of the body noted above—eschews the conscious use of memory to construct a linear narrative of evolutionary selfhood, eschews the narrative tendency to put these people and these memories in their right place. Constructed plots, tracing the development of a strangulated individuality invite authorial control and promote an authoritarian stance on the part of the narrator toward both the subject of the memoir and his or her past. When she registers her response to rereading an early draft of the "Sketch" in the diary, Woolf registers her resistance to plotting with its insistence on distorting crises: "Then I dipped into my memoirs," she writes, "too circuitous & unrelated; too many splutters; as it stands. A real life has no crisis; hence nothing to tighten. It must lack centre. It must amble on. All the same, I can weave a very thin pattern, one of these days, out of that pattern of detail."[29]

Far from being prelude to the present and thus a point on a narrative line, time past for Woolf constitutes the presentness of the present. In fact, past and present are coextensive, not disjoined through a hierarchy that subordinates the former to the latter through a controlling design.[30]

Nor is the subject of the "Sketch" in control of the past. Scenes from the past break upon the present moment, deluging the autobiographical subject in memory. Moments of being in the past, these scenes are moments arbitrarily revisited, not scenes entered into purposefully or consciously by the autobiographical subject. Revisited, these moments sometimes become "more real than the present moment" (67). "Always a scene has arranged itself," she notes, "representative, enduring. This confirms me in my instinctive notion; (it will not bear arguing about; it is irrational) the sensation that we are sealed vessels afloat on what it is convenient to call reality; and at some moments, the sealing matter cracks; in floods reality; that is, these scenes—for why do they survive undamaged year after year unless they are made of something comparatively permanent" (122). In the language of this passage about memory Woolf invokes in yet another context the notion of the subject as a floating vessel, drifting in a fluid medium. The significance here is that floating is an activity not entirely under the conscious control of the subject—if the "instinctive notion" is "irrational," so is the position of the floating subject. The drift carries the subject along; the subject is opened to the deluge, to change and movement. Scenes, the real, cannot be kept out, controlled. Thus the narrator is subject to memory, not its controller, not its authority. Neither predictable nor easily maneuvered, memories come and go. And, as Shari Benstock notes in her analysis of "Sketch," memories are not dependable because "they slip beyond the borders of the conscious world" and "are traversed and transgressed by the unconscious."[31]

Moreover, life for Woolf encompasses moments of nonbeing as well as moments of being; but the unsaid, the unconscious, the unknowables exist in an elusive subtext, forever unavailable. The invocation of the remembered implies the silences of the unremembered. Woolf was only too aware that any attempt to capture the history of the subject is doomed. As she concludes after describing her early memories, "the things one does not remember are as important; perhaps they are more important (69). This

acknowledgment of the unremembered in one more way undermines the authority of the memoir's subject to "capture" the
past. "This shows that among the innumerable things left out in my
sketch I have left out the most important—those instincts, affections, passions, attachments—there is no single word for them, for
they changed month by month—which bound me, I suppose, from
the first moment of consciousness to other people" (79–80). In fact,
Woolf rejects the narrative stance of the person who "knows." She
calls into question the truth of the early memories she relies upon to
ground her story: "Perhaps," she says of one of her first memories,
"perhaps" she was on her way to St. Ives. She does not know,
cannot know the full truth of that moment. The narrator also
rejects the tendency to pin down and to know other people and
their lives as she constantly undercuts her attempts to understand
others, for instance, her mother or her father. Others cannot be
consolidated in a singular gaze. That is the interpretative action of a
strangulated individuality, the violence of the patriarch. Any subject needs to be refracted through multiple gazes, as "Virginia" is
refracted through her mother and father, Stella, Vanessa, and
Thoby.

Everywhere the narrator of "Sketch" concedes the impossibility
and the undesirability of the old autobiographical project. Breaking
the power of the central protagonist of autobiography as a figure
present unto itself, controlling, unitary, Woolf disperses herself into
the past, into the stories of others, into a communalized subjectivity, refusing to name the truth, refusing to contain her narrative in a
coherent chronology, resisting the position of authoritative narrator. This anonymous, interdependent subjectivity enables her to
escape into a stream of life, into that fluid time and place of history,
memory, being, nonbeing, where the subject is constituted provisionally through the contextualities of history, family, and individual experience.

Over the Dead Body of the Angel in the House

The metaphor of the great grape eyeball provides a way for the
older writer to elaborate another kind of subjectivity than that of
the universal human subject with its strangulated individuality. In
addition, it allows her to displace that pervasive phallocentric trope

of vision, the one Luce Irigaray describes as "man's eye—understood as substitute for the penis."[32] Finally, the metaphor allows her to transform the alienating homelessness she feels as she confronts the baseness of her body to a visionary homelessness, a disembodied writing, that signals release from the social fabrication of female embodiment and the compulsory heterosexual identity that embodiment anchors. Positioning herself in the transparent eyeball, Woolf can escape the confining boundaries of that singular body that so shamed her and the gender hierarchy that so violently constrained her.

This escape from identity's body is, for Woolf, the necessary trajectory of the artist, the wordsmith. "One's life is not confined to one's body and what one says and does," she writes: "one is living all the time in relation to certain background rods or conceptions. Mine is that there is a pattern hid behind the cotton wool" (73). The meaning of writing for Woolf has to do with the way a disembodied writing practice enables her to make meaning out of what she calls the "sledge-hammer blows" of life so that she no longer feels vulnerable, powerless, and embodied. Through writing she transforms the blow into revelation:

> It is only by putting [the blow] into words that I make it whole; this wholeness means that it has lost its power to hurt me; it gives me, perhaps because by doing so I take away the pain, a great delight to put the severed parts together. Perhaps this is the strongest pleasure known to me. It is the rapture I get when in writing I seem to be discovering what belongs to what; making a scene come right; making a character come together. From this I reach what I might call a philosophy; at any rate it is a constant idea of mine; that behind the cotton wool is hidden a pattern; that we—I mean all human beings—are connected with this; that the whole world is a work of art; that we are parts of the work of art. *Hamlet* or a Beethoven quartet is the truth about this vast mass that we call the world. But there is no Shakespeare, there is no Beethoven; certainly and emphatically there is no God; we are the words; we are the music; we are the thing itself. And I see this when I have a shock. (72)

In a kind of transubstantiation the body becomes the word, the word without identity's body. That I take to be the meaning of her erasure of Shakespeare and Beethoven as "identities."

Woolf's narrative reveals how various technologies of self-representation call the early twentieth-century middle-class body and its female bourgeois subject into being. The narrative simultaneously charts an imaginary route by which the alienated subject tries to escape identity's body in a gesture of sublimation that extrudes a disembodied, higher artistic vision from the grotesque body. This struggle with the ultimate unspeakability of physical passion, this redirection of female eroticism into an alternative artistic vision is also played out, according to Roe, in Woolf's last novelistic experiment, "Pointz Hall."[33] In the autobiographical fragment as well as the novel, the need to escape the female body effectively joins the need to resist the distracted scream of the strangulated individuality of the male "I." Resistance to one kind of carnivalesque image (the animal in the glass) leads to another variation of the carnivalesque image—the boundless eye of the artist who entwines ecstasy and vision, as when she writes of her response to the love of Stella and Jack Hills: "It was bodiless; a light; an ecstasy" (105).

But the contradictions of the anonymous, disembodied "I" are inescapable in Woolf's narrative. As it seeks to escape bounded identifications, the floating eyeball functions as a locus of resistance to stable topographies of class and gender identities. It cannot be kept in its place/space/singular identity. Yet the elevation of the disembodied eyeball also sustains the baseness of the body. And the assignment of baseness to the body anchors the bourgeois subject, the embodiment of woman, and the more traditional practices of autobiography. Part of the "truth" that Woolf tells "about my own experiences as a body" is the unspeakable truth of repression. Woolf's text reveals a nostalgia for the body before the cultural construction of identity (and the very real trauma of sexual abuse that testifies to the politics of gender) intrudes and partitions her off in identity's body. To escape the grotesque body, she imagines herself a disembodied spirit, the transparent eyeball. While the metaphor energizes certain aesthetic practices, such as the pursuit of narrative anonymity through which Woolf contests the cultural consolidation of male identity and strangulated individuality, it also sustains, through its contradictions, the troubled relationship between the autobiographical subject and the female body.

VI

DIASPORAN SUBJECTIVITY AND IDENTITY POLITICS IN ZORA NEALE HURSTON'S *DUST TRACKS ON A ROAD*

—and I am of the word-changing kind—

Hurston, *Dust Tracks*

I did not know then, as I know now, that people are prone to build a statue of the kind of person that it pleases them to be. And few people want to be forced to ask themselves, "What if there is no me like my statue?" The thing to do is to grab the broom of anger and drive off the beast of fear.

Hurston, *Dust Tracks*

Gertrude Stein evades fixing in the autobiographical "I" and its paternal legacy of compulsory heterosexuality by entering the narrative body and ventriloquizing the narrative voice of "Alice B. Toklas." The unitary subject of autobiography, the one, becomes the textual lesbian couple, the two. Virginia Woolf evades fixing in the authoritarian "I"—that I "as hard as a nut"—by escaping identity's body through the great grape eyeball and traversing a transindividual, communal sphere of fluid intersubjectivity. The unitary subject of autobiography disperses into an impersonal refracted many-ness. For both modernists, specific experiences of the body send them to such evasive narrative strategies. For both, the out-of-body strategies of evasion signal complicities with and interventions in the cultural assignment of women to an identity with specific bodily contents. As a result, in both Stein's *Autobiography* and Woolf's "Sketch" an elusive "I" undermines the generic laws of self-reference.

Zora Neale Hurston joins Stein and Woolf as the elusive autobiographical subject intent on evading a specific identity in her *Dust Tracks on a Road*. But the experiential context of elusiveness is significantly different for Hurston. She turned to autobiographical writing less than enthusiastically; as commentators have noted, she wrote her autobiography at the request of her editor at Lippincott. Apparently the editor recognized the salability of this woman's "life." In effect, the publishing house paid Hurston to turn her life into a commodity to be consumed by a predominantly white audience that wanted to know who the famous novelist was. Perhaps it is the commercialization of the project with its distressing racial politics and Hurston's unwillingness to write that contribute to the frequent assessment that the elusiveness of the autobiographical subject in *Dust Tracks* signals not the success of an experimental modernism inflected with racial politics but the failures of the autobiography itself.

For instance, Robert E. Hemenway, Hurston's biographer and editor of the "restored" edition of the autobiography, points to what he sees as the "confusion" and "untrustworthiness" of *Dust Tracks*. He notes several glaring omissions and narrative evasions: Hurston's failure to provide information about her career as a novelist and about her marriages, her refusal to reveal her date of birth, her silence covering some ten years of her life, and her "nonconfrontational strategy" in "creating a document intended to further the progress of American race relations," that is, her failure to "fix" her ideas on racial politics.[1] *Dust Tracks* is not condemned solely for its biographical and political evasiveness, however. For Craig Werner, the text is an artistic and psychological failure because, despite Hurston's "complex stylistic experiments" in other works, "the voice of *Dust Tracks on a Road* gives little sense of her awareness of the deconstructive potential inherent in the intersection of Afro- and Euro-American discourse."[2] To support his contention, he points to the narrator's lack of self-reflection about the relationship of writing to self-constitution.

But other critics have probed further into the unsettling elusiveness of Hurston's autobiographical "I." Emphasizing that Hurston was paid to represent the black world to the white world (as her patron pays her to represent a black person in her jaunts about New York), Barbara Johnson suggests that she turned her own life "into a trickster tale of which even the teller herself might be the dupe" and in this way called into question, however unconsciously, "the possibility of representing the truth of identity."[3] Attentive to Hurston's unwillingness to write her autobiography, Claudine Raynaud elaborates the practices of "signifying" through which Hurston sought to divert both editorial pressures and the pressures of the confessional autobiographical mode that promoted self-revelation.[4] For Nellie McKay, *Dust Tracks* is "a deliberately staged work" in which the famous author, "negotiat[ing] the dangerous shoals of white male and female race and class oppression and white and black male sexism," controlled "what she wanted her readers to know."[5] And Françoise Lionnet argues elegantly for the subversive potential set loose in Hurston's "an-archic autoethnography."[6] These readings of *Dust Tracks* suggest that the elusiveness of Hurston's "Zora" is purposeful, culturally specific, and subversive.

Within the first several lines of *Dust Tracks,* Hurston signals to the reader that she will not participate in any fixing of the autobiographical subject. "So you will have to know something about the time and place where I came from," she claims, "in order that you may interpret the incidents and directions of my life."[7] Then she fills her narrative with allusions to "lies" and "lying" as well as "specifying." Through this linkage of storytelling and lying, Hurston destabilizes the very grounds upon which readers can do the work of interpretation she assigns them. She will not let them fix the autobiographical subject, "Zora Neale Hurston," as a unified subject of autobiography, as a kind of statue. Culturally provisional and individually improvisational, Hurston's autobiographical "I" engages in a jazzed-up performance of diasporan subjectivity. Through her textual performance, the black woman resists her reader's attempt to fix her in the identity of the exceptional black woman by undermining the bases upon which that identity is founded. Thus the autobiography contributes to the mystification of Hurston, who, as Joanne Braxton remarks, remains "one of the most enigmatic and elusive figures in black American literary history."[8]

Unfixing Temporal/Teleological Identity

Apparently conforming to audience expectations that famous people who write their autobiographies will track their rise from obscurity to prominence, Hurston begins her narrative in historical origins. In the ethnographic opening, the narrator recalls a frontier culture, locating her story in the history of the Eatonville folk from whence she has come. She chronicles family history, the courtship of her parents, and the subsequent marriage of alternative cultural voices represented by mother and father. The narrative of childhood follows, a pastoral idyll full of fantasy and magic, language and love, increasingly punctuated by the child's developing sense of inner homelessness and fate. Homelessness emerges as the controlling metaphor with the death of the adolescent girl's mother and her subsequent search for economic security and educational opportunities. Having narrated the story of her formal education, Hurston then erases chronology altogether, introducing what Raynaud calls "a vertical organization, *une topique,* a series of 'common places.' "[9]

At this point Hurston abandons the larger structural principle of chronology altogether; but even in the chronologically organized chapters she unsettles personal chronology. She refuses to specify dates, those facts that anchor the autobiographical subject in historical time and the reader in a secure textual relationship to the autobiographical subject. If specifying dates in autobiographical writing is one of the technologies whereby a text constructs the historical individual—dating makes the "man," so to speak—then refusing to date, refusing to fill the gaps in the chronological record, interferes with conventional technologies of developmental individuality and by implication with the laws of genre.

The specificity of chronology, of secular progress, is not the only structural principle introduced, only to be forestalled, then abandoned altogether. Early in the autobiography, Hurston introduces another structural principle that promises a kind of cartographic plotting to her life (56), the plotting of the spiritual quest, a commonplace in autobiographical confession. She recalls how as a child she saw her life laid out before her in twelve visions. But, as Lionnet notes, Hurston does not proceed to track a spiritual quest in the traditional tripartite structure of death, conversion, rebirth that is so characteristic of black spiritual autobiography. In fact, she projects her life as already read, so to speak, already mapped, reversing the normative autobiographical trajectory whereby the writer looks back upon the past in order to discover the quest pattern. Moreover, despite the dramatic possibilities of visionary mapping, Hurston refuses to reveal the map summarily or to organize the text as a slow, incremental revelation of the visions. Nor does she specify what exactly the visions portended, how exactly they were fulfilled. Eventually the reader can no longer keep track of the relationship of the twelve visions to the narrative. Hurston thereby undoes the normative expectations established through the conventions of spiritual autobiography and pursues instead what Lionnet calls an an-archic structure.[10]

In effect, the secular and spiritual "tracks" in a developmental path turn to "dust" since they do not stick. In this way, as Raynaud recognizes, Hurston's very title is proleptic: "the temporariness of the traces left on the road, the fleetingness of dust announce the silences and the voluntary omissions."[11] And with the evacuation of temporality and teleology from the text, something happens to the autobiographical "I." Raynaud suggests that in the latter chapters of *Dust Tracks* the text is voided of the "I" as Hurston writes essays on such topics as love, religion, and race relations. "On the verge of becoming discourse (*discours*)," she suggests, "history (*histoire*) is emptied of the 'I,' another of Hurston's diversionary tactics to subvert the confessional goal of the autobiography."[12] While I agree with Raynaud that Hurston has no intention of confessing to her reader, I do not agree that the text is voided of the "I." It is not so much voided of the "I" as it is supercharged with a problematized "I." If the "I" is not fixed in a developmental pattern, whether the pattern of secular progress or spiritual quest, how does it fare in other loci of identity?

Unfixing Racial Identity

Hurston turns other trackings of identity to dust through her narrative and discursive strategies. In the unpublished but restored version of the chapter entitled "My People, My People," the narrator much more vigorously (than in the chapter originally published) confronts identity politics in the black community, sometimes in a self-parodying manner. She works her way through a series of identity behaviors, attitudes, characteristics, doing the work of the anthropologist who catalogs just what "the Negro" is. But she thwarts any attempt at formal anthropological fixing of racial identity by critiquing each definition and by multiplying the numbers of "the Negro" throughout the chapter. At the conclusion of the catalog of descriptors she states: "But maybe, after all the Negro doesn't really exist. What we think is a race is detached moods and phases of other people walking around. What we have been talking about might not exist at all" (304). Hurston implies here that behaviors are contextual, not essential.

At other points, she recognizes the sometimes subtle and sometimes blatant connection between "race" behaviors and "class" behaviors. For instance, in the published "My People" chapter, she elaborates the gulf that exists between the "educated Negro" and the "underprivileged" Negro: "The educated Negro may know all about differential calculus and the theory of evolution, but he is fighting entirely out of his class when he tries to quip with the underprivileged" (217). Thus she dispatches any unified scientific explanation of race. She also uses folklore to dispatch any essentializing categorization of peoples supporting the discourses of race. Invoking the folk explanation of God's assignments of colors to the different races, she comments colloquially: "So according to that, we are not a race. We are just a collection of people who overslept our time and got caught in the draft" (306).

Hurston also refuses to posit the materiality of the body as a ground upon which to establish racial identity and difference. Throughout the restored "My People" chapter, Hurston critiques the body as constitutive of the sign "race." "After all," she argues, "the word 'race' is a loose classification of physical characteristics. It tells nothing about the insides of people" (325). This is not to say that the body does not exist, but that it need not ground alignments of difference in the body social. "Priding yourself on your physical makeup," comments the narrator, "something over which you have no control, is just another sign that the human cuss is determined not to be grateful" (327). Or, she asks, "Why waste time keeping conscious of your physical aspects?" (326). Hurston diffuses attention away from the body as the origin of identity. The variety of human bodies destabilizes any boundary marker established to separate one kind of body from another, markers that racialist discourses seek to stake out. Intermingling of "races," an intermingling signaled by the heterogeneity of specific bodies, makes nonsense of "race" as a unified or essentialized or natural category within the body politic. "There's a man white enough to suit Hitler," Hurston writes of James Weldon Johnson, "and he's been passing for colored for years" (295). Depending "too much on skin" to establish identity, she suggests, will only lead to being "mis-put on your road" (295).

Nor can recourse to a unified experiential base ground identity politics. In the published version of "My People," Hurston uses the testimony of personal experience to dispatch the notion of a unified racial identity: "I maintain that I have been a Negro three times—a Negro baby, a Negro girl and a Negro woman. Still, if you have received no clear-cut impression of what the Negro in America is like, then you are in the same place with me" (237). In other words, "you" consider "me" to be a "Negro," but even I cannot specify what the essential identity of "the Negro" is since my own experience has multiplied identities. And most ironically, Hurston situates her (white) reader "in the same place" that she occupies, thus blurring the grounds upon which racial differentiation can proceed.

More problematically for critics such as Darwin T. Turner, Hurston repudiates the communal history of victimization as the unified ground upon which the essential difference of "the Negro" can be established. Contrarily, she places her origin in an empowered black life: "I was born in a Negro town. I do not mean by that the black back-side of an average town. Eatonville, Florida, is, and was at the time of my birth, a pure Negro town . . . the first attempt at organized self-government on the part of Negroes in America" (3). Situating Eatonville outside an oppositional relationship—it is not the black back-side to the white frontside—she gives the black community a history of self-government and economic independence outside oppression, an origin outside abject poverty and the brutalities of slavery or indentured servitude, those experiences that often form the basis of racial solidarity and thus identification in the black community.

This is not to say that Hurston erases the experience of racial oppression from the text. Throughout *Dust Tracks* she incorporates biting analyses of various forms and effects of racial oppression. She acknowledges the vulnerability of the black community and affirms the courage of its members in the face of pervasive violence when she recalls the hushed childhood evening when her family waited in a darkened home while the men went to the aid of a black man they feared was being attacked by whites. In the descriptions of the series of jobs she takes as a household servant, she reveals the tenuous relationships of blacks to white employers, especially of black women to white male employers.[13] In the story of her sojourn as manicurist in the barbershop in Washington, D.C., she sympathetically considers the economic motivations for black complicity in segregationist practices. In the restored chapter entitled "Seeing the World as It Is," she makes explicit connections between colonialism and slavery: "I must confess to being a little dry around the eyes. I hear people shaking with shudders at the thought of Germany collecting taxes in Holland. I have not heard a word against Holland collecting one twelfth of poor people's wages in Asia. Hitler's crime is that he is actually doing a thing like that to his own kind" (342). While much of the commentary is explicit, some is implicit, as is the excessive gratitude of the black artist who knows she depends on the largesse of white patrons for support, a perhaps strategic excess more evident in the unpublished version of the friendship chapter than in the published version.[14]

But Hurston does not position herself as the victimized black subject since she does not locate the origins of her subjectivity in the history of oppression or the violent psychology of race relations in America. In this way, she eludes being assigned any provided subjectivity and foils any attempt on the part of the white reader to fix her as a "representative" of her race. On the contrary, she challenges the reader to see her as a singular individual.

I would note also that through her an-archic subjectivity Hurston eludes fixing in the generic conventions of the African-American autobiographical tradition. According to Stephen Butterfield, the history of victimization motivates the autobiographical subject to speak as a representative of the people rather than an individual, stressing communal identification rather than individuality:

> The 'self' of black autobiography on the whole . . . is not an individual with a private career, but a soldier in a long, historic march toward Canaan. The self is conceived as a member of an oppressed social group, with ties and responsibilities to the other members. It is a conscious political identity, craving sustenance from the past experience of the group, giving back the iron of its endurance fashioned into armor and weapons for the use of the next generation of fighters.[15]

But Butterfield's trope cannot account for Hurston's resistance to identity politics based on the common experience of oppression. Alice A. Deck suggests that "the self in Zora Neale Hurston's *Dust Tracks on a Road* is one example of a black American who never considers enlisting in the regiment, because she defines herself in her text in terms other than warrior or defiant black activist."[16] Hurston's resistance may derive from her understanding that the warrior fights against something, and the activist organizes in protest against something.

Like James Baldwin, who came of writing age in the next decade, Hurston challenges the privileging in the African-American literary tradition of the protest work, either autobiography or novel.[17] Hurston refuses to accept her nomination as the representative of her race, precisely because representatives get fixed by all the people who see them as representative. Moreover, since representative victims are victims of something, they are assigned an "identity with predictable contents," to invoke Biddy Martin's phrase.[18] Thus protest keeps people positioned in oppositional identities. And while victims may invoke pity, even incite action for change, they also sustain operational hierarchies. To invoke pity may simultaneously be to posit one's communal identity as a liability. As Barbara Johnson notes of Hurston's "reversal of implicit white expectations," the narrator of *Dust Tracks* confronts her reader with an autobiographical subject who is "not pitiful but powerful" and who understands being African-American "not as a liability but an advantage."[19]

Hurston's mode of resistance to racial oppression is not to "join the regiment" but to divest racialized identity of any privileged status by undermining the discourses of race, dislodging black and white from their oppositional framework, and looking at people "duck by duck" (235).[20]

Unfixing Gender Identity

Hurston also turns to dust any tracking of gender identity deriving from an essentialized sexual difference. Elizabeth Fox-Genovese suggests that the narrator creates a kind of cross-gendered mythic birth for herself as she describes how she was "delivered" by a (white) man.[21] Then, as she re-creates her childhood, the narrator emphasizes the disjunction between the cultural meaning assigned her sexed body and her independently constructed identity as tomboy. Figuring herself as imaginative and willful, exploratory and independently purposeful, Hurston celebrates the brazen transgressiveness of her desires. Her childhood dream of owning and riding a white stallion aligns her with power, speed, and movement and signifies her desire to cross sexual (and racial) identity barriers.[22]

The narrator also refuses to put her marriages in their "proper" places in the chronology of the text. This refusal to tell the love story is a refusal to confine her story to conventional narrative paradigms, to the conventional "female" plot of love and marriage expected by her bourgeois reader. It is also a refusal to acknowledge formal and therefore ideologically charged structures that reify heterosexual relationships as constitutive of the female subject and gender hierarchy as constitutive of male-female relationships. This is not to say that Hurston does not acknowledge heterosexual relationships. She speaks of a particularly difficult romantic attachment in "Love." But even as she talks of love, she subordinates the desire for heterosexual attachment to the desire for an empowered writing career, for what she calls "rubbing a paragraph with a soft cloth" (264). In fact, the trouble with the relationship is precisely the way in which the involvement in love encourages the man and woman to drift toward a hierarchical marriage in which the man wants his woman to assume the position of wife and the woman begins to slide into her subordinate position. While Hurston puts herself in the place of the lover (an ungendered and equal subject), she does not put herself in the narrative place of the wife (a gendered and unequal identity). Hurston's marginalization of the story of marriage displaces the centrality of the affective domain of domesticity for the female subject.[23]

But even in her transgressive gestures, Hurston is not attempting to situate herself in the place of the male subject. In fact, the privileged relationship in the text is, as it is in Hurston's novel *Their Eyes Were Watching God,* that between women, between the daughter and her mother and by implication between the daughter and her voice.[24] The death of Hurston's mother marks the passing of a childhood world: "Mama died at sundown and changed a world. That is, the world which had been built out of her body and her heart. Even the physical aspects fell apart with a suddenness that was startling" (89). Like Woolf, who identified her mother with "that great cathedral space," the Eatonville daughter loses the very body that centered childhood and home. Alluding to the capacity of the mother to frame the child's world, Hurston writes that it was her "mother's bedroom that fixed the place of the horizon."

The central moment in the first part of Hurston's text is thus her mother's deathbed scene: "Her mouth was slightly open, but her breathing took up so much of her strength that she could not talk. But she looked at me, or so I felt, to speak for her. She depended on me for a voice" (86–87). The friends and neighbors attending the deathbed surround the occasion with folk wisdom in arranging and ordering the scene. For instance, the mirror must be covered to the dying woman. The mother wants the daughter to defy the communal wisdom and to unveil the mirror, but the young girl cannot contend with the adults and their maxims. She cannot "speak for" her mother and assert her power in the face of the forces that would silence the mother's desire.

Of course, much commentary on *Dust Tracks* focuses on the centrality of this death scene and on Hurston's structural invocation of the myth of Demeter/Persephone, the mother/daughter quest for union.[25] In the original myth, the mother searches for the daughter who has been abducted and taken by Hades to the underworld. Every year he agrees to release Persephone for the season of growth and then to receive her back in the season of death. Hurston reverses the pattern. She is the daughter who searches for her mother in the re-search of her mother's community and in the pursuit of a voice adequate to contest with both her black culture and the dominant white culture surrounding her and pressing their "wisdoms" on her.

And much of that wisdom has to do with the disempowerment of the mother and her body, a disempowerment that inextricably conjoins discourses of race and discourses of gender.[26] The stories of (predominantly male) tale-tellers Hurston incorporates in the text situate the black female subject in her body again and again. According to the tale-tellers, the bodies of women are to be beaten, mounted, whipped into shape as men exert power over "their" women. Even more distressing for Hurston is the way in which the body of the black mother is entirely erased from individual histories as people, absorbed by the politics of racial difference, aspire to establish their "whitened" identity by silencing the history of the mother:

> In Jamaica, the various degrees of Negroes put on some outward show to impress you that no matter what your eyes tell you, that they are really white folks—*white* English folks inside. The moment you meet a mulatto there he makes an opportunity to tell you who his father was. You are bound to hear a lot about that Englishman or that Scot. But never a word about the black mama. It is as if she didn't exist. Had never existed at all. You get the impression that Jamaica is a place where roosters lay eggs. That these Englishmen come there and without benefit of females they just scratch out a nest and lay an egg that hatches out a Jamaican. (302)

Even more bitingly focused is her unpublished critique of the Bahaman candidate who, having been supported through law school by a mother who worked as a maid, turns on his mother because of the darkness of her skin, paying her "ten shillings . . . a week to stay away from his house."[27] This passage, which Raynaud finds in the typescript of *Dust Tracks,* is entirely missing from the original and restored version of the published autobiography.[28] In the published version there is a slight trace of this critique, however, when Hurston writes, "I found the Negro, and always the blackest Negro, being made the butt of all jokes,—particularly black women" (225).

As the autobiography attests, Hurston was aware of the politics of chromatism in the black community, that physical calibration of differences in bodies determining the relative status of individuals within the black community, a calibration that mimed the calibration of racialist discourse which situated the black race on the bottom and the white race on the top rung of the evolutionary ladder. And she was keenly attentive to the status of black women as what critics have recently called "the other of the other."[29] As Janie's grandmother in *Their Eyes* comments, "De nigger woman is de mule uh de world so fur as Ah can see."[30]

To disengage the body of the black woman as the "butt" of the joke, to release her from her identity as "de mule uh de world," and to reinsert the body of the black mother in individual and cultural history, Hurston celebrates the physical and verbal strength of black women. Unable as a child to speak for her mother on her deathbed, Hurston speaks for the mother in the autobiographical text as she takes up the mother's voice in the story of her courtship and speaks to her power. Hurston describes how, despite her diminutive stature, her mother defeats rivals for her husband's attention, maintaining authority in her household through the cutting edge of her language. Moreover, Hurston figures her mother as an empowering mentor for her daughter, the mother who defied the grandmother's attempt to stop the lying tongue of the imaginative child—"I vominates a lying tongue" (72)—by "never tr[ying] to break me" (72). Her mother enables her to usurp the male province of storytelling (the scene on Joe Clarke's porch) by bringing the lying home to her imagination. But there are other effective women as well. There is Hurston's Aunt Caroline, who humiliates her husband for his romantic escapades, stripping him of his clothes and booting him out of the house. Later there is Big Sweet, the specifying woman whose words defeat her enemies and protect the young anthropologist from Lucy.[31] And there is Ethel Waters, the black singer whose friendship Hurston celebrates and whose voice fills the friendship. "I am her friend, and her tongue is in my mouth" (245), she writes of Waters. These women are not victims; they are agents, combative, assertive, successful. And language is often the weapon of most resistance. It is the power of woman's word that attracts and in turn reempowers the daughter.

Not only does she recover an empowered mother, she also recovers an empowered mother culture as anthropologist, artist, and philosopher. Lionnet suggests that the inverted myth of Demeter/Persephone adds ethnographic history to the symbolic psychology of the deathbed scene. The trajectory of the early part of Hurston's narrative reenacts the original sojourn in the "mother" country (Africa), followed by the disruption of life that attends the wrenching disconnection from the mother country, the great, sad middle passage, and the diasporan wandering of the motherless child. Thus Hurston's autobiographical text dramatizes the act of remembering the mother and the mother's voice through her own voicing of the history of the folk culture. "The self-portrait Hurston draws in *Dust Tracks,*" Lionnet argues, "is an anamnesis: not self-contemplation but a painstaking effort to be the voice of that occluded past, to fill the void of collective memory."[32] Hurston's "black mama" is not only the personal mother but also the representative mother-culture, that culture suppressed in the dominant white culture (and its languages) where it is considered inferior, a failed imitation, and repressed in the black subject, where it is considered a liability in the move toward a "whitened" identity.

The Mother Tongue and the Material Body

Hurston insists on an empowered mother tongue in several ways. For one, she refuses to evacuate the body from the language of the text. If she does not want to situate an essentialized racial or sexual identity in the body, neither does she want to claim that subjectivity can be constituted without the trace of the material (mother) body. In fact, the female body enters the scene of writing in sometimes unabashed ways. Describing Aunt Caroline's vengeance upon the woman her husband pursues, Hurston writes:

> On another occasion, she caused another lady who couldn't give the community anything but love, baby, to fall off of the high, steep church steps on her head. Aunt Cal'line might have done that just to satisfy her curiosity, since it was said that the lady felt that anything more than a petticoat under her dresses would be an encumbrance. Maybe Aunt Caroline just wanted to verify the rumor. The way the lady tumbled, it left no doubt in the matter. She was really a free soul. Evidently Aunt Caroline was put out about it, because she had to expectorate at that very moment, and it just happened to land where the lady was bare. Aunt Caroline evidently tried to correct her error in spitting on her rival, for she took her foot and tried to grind it in. She never said a word as usual, so the lady must have

misunderstood Aunt Caroline's curiosity. She left town in a hurry—
a speedy hurry—and never was seen in those parts again. (25)

Aunt Caroline, before all the congregation, spits on the rival's
pudendum. When she describes how "company got the preference
in toilet paper" (26), Hurston incorporates bodily needs into a
discussion about propriety and class, lightly poking fun at the
relationships her family establishes between class status and "ass"
status. Describing her feelings when she received the wire accepting
her first novel, Hurston writes: "I never expect to have a greater
thrill than that wire gave me. You know the feeling when you found
your first pubic hair. Greater than that" (212).

For Hurston, the body cannot be elided as a material part of life:
it is rooted, sensuous, natural and humorous, part and parcel of
subjectivity, if not an essentialized marker of identity. Moreover,
the body is celebrated as a source of metaphor and meaning. The
physical world is energetically taken up and embedded in systems
of metaphorical meaning, as, for instance, in the following passage,
which describes Hurston's sense of her place among the other girls
at Morgan: "And here I was, with my face looking like it had been
chopped out of a knot of pine wood with a hatchet on somebody's
off day, sitting up in the middle of all this pretty. To make things
worse, I had only one dress, a change of underwear and one pair of
tan oxfords" (150–51). It is precisely the colorfulness of the body
and its lexicon that gives energy and life to language. Without that
"color" language is denuded.[33]

Nor can the woman be denied her body, for there is another
trajectory of power exerted over the body of the black woman, over
the body of the black generally. Implicit in the cultural surround of
Hurston's narrative is the dominant white culture's association of
the Negro with his/her body and with unlicensed sexuality. That
assignment of a certain identity content to the black female stands
as both a threat and a call to erasure of female sexuality. But the
narrator tries to resist that erasure. Describing her trip to New
Orleans to conduct research on Hoodoo, she recalls how she lay
naked for three days. Her references to body parts are often references to female genitalia. It is as if Hurston wants to remind her
reader, if only sporadically, of the reality of female desire and the
relationship of sexual desire to an empowered subjectivity.

Second, Hurston uses the mother tongue to "educate" through

its "color" the tongue of standard English. Consider, for instance, the following passage that opens chapter 5: "Nothing that God ever made is the same thing to more than one person. That is natural. There is no single face in nature, because every eye that looks upon it, sees it from its own angle. So every man's spice-box seasons his own food" (60). The initial voice is that of the "philosopher" who has grappled with the issue of "relative perspective" and "the real." The statement is a universalized statement; the rhetoric is that of standard English. But the final sentence is aphoristic as Hurston shifts from the voice of the universal subject to the voice of the folk.

The juxtaposition here acts to raise the folk aphorism to the level of sophisticated philosophy, to reveal the depth of wisdom in the "lowly" colorfulness of the folk phrase. In this way Hurston informs the dialect of the folk with the sophistication and abstract capabilities that theorists of race attributed only to "standard" or formal language. For at the time linguists described dialects as deficient languages, failed attempts to mime English and its formal patterns of speech. The effect of such theories influenced the assessment of the culture from which the dialect emerged.[34] The culture itself was considered deficient, primitive, simple. Hurston's juxtaposition counters such theories by calling into question the superiority of European (or philosophic) discourses over folk languages and by revealing the complexity of folk aphorism.

Hurston also reveals the kind of color that has to be evacuated from standard English in order for it to become standard English. We might return to the relationship between the universal subject and the socially abject posited in the opening chapter. As Peter Stallybrass and Allon White state, the universal subject was "constituted through and through by the clamour of particular voices to which it tried to be universally superior. It is on this account that the very blandness and transparency of bourgeois reason is in fact nothing other than the critical negation of a social 'colourfulness,' of a heterogeneous diversity of specific contents, upon which it is, nonetheless, completely dependent."[35] Here and throughout the text, Hurston moves between the neutral language and the colorful language, and by doing so shifts the understanding of what is marginal and what central, what colorful and what universal. To insist on the centrality of the "black mama" tongue is to retrieve the mother culture from its "underprivileged" status, to disentangle it from its liabilities.

Through the dazzling metaphors and verbal facility of her text, the daughter celebrates the body of the "black mama" and the body in the mother tongue. In her refusal to "clean up" or to "whiten" her language by erasing all color and adornment from it, she signals both her resistance to the dominant culture's identity structures and her criticism of the denuded quality of the dominant and neutralized language. Undoing the exclusionary work of standard English that would evacuate color and body from the sentence and the sound, she educates speakers of the neutralized tongue about the cost of the very evacuation of color.

The Diasporan Subject and the Unfixing of Narrative Voice

As an anthropologist, artist, and autobiographer, Hurston retrieves the mother tongue from the occlusions of official histories (with their implicit hierarchies), including histories of languages invoked in racialist discourses. But she goes further to suggest that language, while constitutive of the subject, cannot ground identity politics.

The narrator introduces this insight into her text in the very first chapter when she refers to the early conflict between slaveowners and Native Americans over the identity of escaped slaves. "The sore point of returning escaped Negroes could not be settled satisfactorily to either side," she notes: "Who was an Indian and who was a Negro?" Against the biologist arguments of the slaveowners, the Native Americans posited a linguistic notion of identity: "The whites contended all who had Negro blood. The Indians contended all who spoke their language belonged to the tribe." That is, an escaped slave could shift identity with the shift in language usage. But, of course, the situation created problems in determining where the "slave" belonged. "Since it was an easy matter to teach a slave to speak enough of the language to pass in a short time," Hurston writes, "the questions could never be settled. So the wars went on" (4–5). Like the body, linguistic behaviors cannot establish essential identities. Languages are learned phenomena, and consequently identities can shift with shifts in language usage. Because the boundaries between languages and thus between speakers of languages are breachable, linguistic difference cannot be the primary ground of racial or sexual or national identifications.

Hurston acknowledges the profound implications of this relationship between linguistic identity and context for her own life and work when she describes her early and ineffectual forays into fieldwork. She brought her "carefully accented Barnardese" (175) to the interaction with the people whose stories she hoped to record. But the Barnardese and the identity it established only elicited a profound silence in her informants. She learns that the Barnard identity cannot do the work she needs to do. And so she has to shift words, and thus shift identities, in order to elicit from her subjects the stories she comes to hear. Contextually marked, linguistic usage cannot be disjoined from the relationship of the speaker to the audience or occasion. Since linguistic contexts continually shift, linguistic usage is both improvisational[36] and provisional.

From this point of view, Hurston's entire narrative becomes an improvisational performance of shifts in language. She is, as she says, "of the word-changing kind" (27). Critics acknowledge this phenomenon when they elaborate on the "free indirect discourse" that characterizes Hurston's text.[37] The narrative voice keeps spinning off, slipping toward, taking up temporary residence in, other voices and speaking positions. The narrator slides into the voice of specific individuals like her mother, her aunt Caroline, the white man who attends her birth, Franz Boaz, or into and out of the generalized community of Eatonville whose aphoristic sayings punctuate the rhythm of the text in the same way that they punctuated the rhythm of daily life, into and out of the cadences of the minister and choir at the revival meeting, into and out of blues refrains or the instruction given to her by Barnard students (170–71). She slips in and out of the language of "objective" analysis and of creative metaphor, of the Bible, folk proverbs, the blues, a child's imagination, anthropological science, standard English. The mobility of voice enables her to cross identity lines of race and sex, to cross from one community of linguistic users to another. Take, for instance, the descriptive passage about Polk County (178–85). Here the woman assumes the position not only of anthropologist describing the scene but of the male blues singer whose songs voice the lament of desire deferred.[38]

Barbara Johnson refers to this constant mobility of narrative voice and speaking positions as self-division. I would use another mathematical term, calling it self-multiplication. But I would agree with what Johnson describes as the effect. "The inside/outside boundaries between narrator and character, between standard and individual," she notes, "are both transgressed and preserved, making it impossible to identify and totalize either the subject or the nature of discourse."[39] In the narrator's mouth, language becomes a fluid medium, too malleable to establish fixed identity positions. To invoke the theoretical work of Mae Gwendolyn Henderson,[40] the narrator speaks in multiple tongues. Thus identity politics is troubled by the nature of language itself and by the contextuality that determines what languages cross the tongue of what speaker in what circumstance. In the beginning is the word as creative act or "nommo,"[41] and the word, embraced, is creative to the degree that it improvisationally constitutes the subject but unfixes stable identities, worldly truths, and other words.

Moreover, the more languages the speaker rolls across her tongue, the more expansive and empowering is the subjectivity constituted through such heteroglossia. Describing the poverty of the years following her mother's death, Hurston equates death and "dead dreams" with "this wordless feeling" (116). If death is a wordless feeling, lively experience is the incorporation of ever more words and tongues. "I do not wish to close the frontiers of life upon my own self," the narrator states toward the end of the original version. "I do not wish to deny myself the expansion of seeking into individual capabilities and depths by living in a space whose boundaries are race and nation. Lord, give my poor stammering tongue at least one taste of the whole round world, if you please, Sir" (330–31). Shifting from tongue to tongue adds the knowledges of one tongue to those of another, a phenomenon that the narrator acknowledges when she writes of her early memories that they fit her like a dress and that she needed to put distance between herself and the dress in order to see the past and herself more clearly. The distance thus achieved permits the speaker to critique the constraining identities and oppressive communal wisdoms embedded in any particular tongue and its knowledges. But it also encourages the speaker to see more clearly what is empowering and valuable in a tongue. Shifting fluidly from tongue to tongue thus undermines the cultural privileges of dominant speaking positions (those of class, race, gender, or nationality) and the identities they reify. If you can speak in many tongues, from the tongues of the "lowest" to the "highest," then you begin to intervene in the bases upon which oppressive hierarchies are established and you turn carnival against the forces of corporate identity formation.

Because she is not fixed in a specific tongue, because she is not fixed in a permanent home of identity, Hurston can unsettle the authority that seems to inhere in any specific speaking position. For instance, in the final pages of the chapter entitled "Love," Hurston foils her attempt to bring some kind of meaning to a troubled relationship by dismissing her analysis:

> But pay no attention to what I say about love, for as I said before, it may not mean a thing. It is my own bathtub singing. Just because my mouth opens up like a prayer book, it does not just have to flap like a Bible. And then again, anybody whose mouth is cut cross-ways is given to lying, unconsciously as well as knowingly. So pay my few scattering remarks no mind as to love in general. I know only my part. (265)

Here Hurston refuses to assume the identity of the famous person who can speak authoritatively about personal matters, in this case about love. In fact, she pokes fun at the kind of person who reads about the lives of famous people to find out how to live. Moreover, she frustrates her own totalizing gesture, her own pattern-making, by shifting the burden of interpretation once again to the reader and then, through a turnabout erasure of authority, disappearing on that reader.

In other places she unsettles official knowledges of things, whether the official knowledge comes from blacks or whites, turning words and rhetoric back against the invokers of those words and rhetorical patterns. For instance, in the chapter entitled "Religion," she turns folk language and casual satire to work on the official history of organized Christianity when she writes of Constantine:

> He could not sing like Peter, and he could not preach like Paul. He probably did not even have a good straining voice like my father to win converts and influence people. But he had his good points—one of them being a sword—and a seasoned army. And the way he

brought sinners to repentance was nothing short of miraculous. Whole tribes and nations fell under conviction just as soon as they heard he was on the way. (276)

With her rapier wit, Hurston rewrites history from the point of view of the vanquished, goading her reader to alter standpoints and ultimately to see any history as culturally provisional, written as it is from the point of view of the conqueror.

She does not limit herself to debunking the history and myths of the dominant culture, however; she turns her wit on her own community as well. That may explain the position she espouses on "race men," which her critics have found so problematic. For Hurston, those who espouse and privilege the identity of the race man participate in the same kind of essentializing difference as those whites who use racialist discourse to privilege whites over blacks.[42]

Through her linguistic practice, Hurston declines participation in the univocality and the consequent linguistic exclusions necessary to consolidate a coherent, monadic autobiographical identity of any kind. Thus the narrator's "I" is not, as Raynaud argues, evacuated from the text. It refuses to inhabit a monadic voice, the unified voice of the speaker who knows, who assumes her own authority, who interprets her life for her reader. Originating in no coherent point of departure, traveling along no secure teleological trajectory, this "I" keeps disappearing into heterogeneous voices in a kind of Bakhtinian carnival of heteroglossia. "I am just sort of assembled up together out of friendship and put together by time" (314), she confesses in the restored chapter on friendship. The voice does not settle down because the homesteaded voice would be the fixed voice, defined and confined, the voice emptied of individuality and filled instead with the identity contents that specific communal discourses instantiate.

We might call this wandering, slippery, word-changing "I", the diasporan subject. The homelessness of the diasporan subject becomes a way of being in the world, a condition of radical subjectivity that Hurston identifies not just with the death of her mother[43] and the literal breakup of her home but also with the time during her childhood when she longed to reach the horizon. The diasporan "I" lies simultaneously inside and outside identities, in a personal space of both appreciation and critique. Yet if the diasporan subject, in its homelessness, is always a resident outsider in all the cultures that cross its tongue, it is also intimately tied to community as the other tongue crosses over its tongue endlessly and the other of the tongue speaks. In this way the diasporan subject of Hurston's text moves by incorporation rather than exclusions.

It is this notion of the unfixed subject that Hurston identifies as the "individual." She hails the individual as a way of circumventing the essentializing agenda of identity politics, be it that of professional anthropology, of the dominant culture with its racialist discourse, and of indigenous folk proverbs, three cultures to which she has access as both insider and outsider and three cultures that fix identities along racial, gender, class, and national lines. Yet this is no invocation of the notion of the individual elaborated in chapter 1, the universal bourgeois subject of modernist discourse. For Hurston, individuality is not established in opposition to the community so much as out of the community, out of various communities that cross the tongue of the diasporan subject. Hurston therefore voices individuality as what Henderson calls a "subjective plurality," "an *intrasubjective* engagement with the *intersubjective* aspects of the self, a dialectic neither repressing difference, nor, for that matter, privileging identity, but rather expressing engagement with the social aspects of self ('the other[s] in ourselves')."[44]

Hurston's diasporan "I" is strategic as well as incorporative. In the autobiographical narrative she is an Eatonville daughter, Snidlets, a sacred brown cow, a Morgan girl, a Barnard girl, a silent listener (at the barbershop), an aspiring writer, an anthropologist, a dreamer, a lover, a friend, a southerner (with the traveling show), a destitute teenager, a confident member of the literati, a wanderer, an artist, a collector of tales, a teller of tales, a child, a philosopher, a young girl, a woman, an American, a Negro, an individual, and an inhabitant of the globe. The more she multiplies identities, the more she undermines the fixedness of any identity. It is as if Hurston is saying to her reader, you think I am here, but I'm not. Try to fix me in your interpretations if you can. For my part, I will try to unfix your interpretations, for they would fix me as some kind of statue of the person you would like me to be.

Of course, the problematic context of this creative performance of the diasporan subject complicates our reading of that performance. As a black writer, Hurston found herself in the midst of a white culture that kept her identities as black/woman at the fore, demanded of her that she speak as the black woman, the representative of the black world, the pet of the white world. The editorial interventions Raynaud uncovers reveal the ways in which Hurston's editors as well as the writer herself acted to fashion a black female subject acceptable to a white audience by moderating and sometimes silencing her various voices—the sexual, the political, and the more iconoclastic "Zora." She could not escape the pressure of her reader and her editor entirely. Nonetheless, even within the system of white patronage of black artists in which she was at the time so entangled, she managed to do some culturally troubling work in her autobiographical text. Wreaking havoc with the normative conventions of autobiography through her diasporan subjectivity, she managed to elude the reader who would know who she was.

VII

THE BODIES
OF CONTEMPORARY
AUTOBIOGRAPHICAL PRACTICE

If the body is not a "being," but a variable
boundary, a surface whose permeability is
politically regulated, a signifying practice
within a cultural field of gender hierarchy
and compulsory heterosexuality, then what
language is left for understanding this
corporeal enactment, gender, that constitutes
its "interior" signification on its surface?

Judith Butler, *Gender Trouble*

Woman lives her body as *object* as well as
subject.

Iris Marion Young, "Throwing like a Girl"

What I never quite understood until this
writing is that to be without a sex—to be
bodiless—as I sought to be to escape the
burgeoning sexuality of my adolescence, my
confused early days of active heterosexuality,
and later my panicked lesbianism, means also
to be without a race. I never attributed my
removal from physicality to have anything to
do with race, only sex, only desire for
women. And yet, as I grew up sexually, it
was my race, along with my sex, that was
being denied me at every turn.

Cherríe Moraga, *Loving in the War Years*

The body has been made so problematic for
women that it has often seemed easier to
shrug it off and travel as a disembodied
spirit.

Adrienne Rich, *Of Woman Born*

Harriet Jacobs's struggle for control of her commodified body in an overtly hostile and oppressive body politic, as well as her literal and literary confrontations with homelessness of the body and in the body, dramatically expose the intimate relationship of the auto-biographical body to the body politics of women's self-writing. The subject of autobiography writes the history of the subjected and violated body. Doing so, the nineteenth-century escaped slavewom-an enters into a complex negotiation of rhetorical strategies, subject positions, and narrative paradigms, ultimately troubling the generic edges of the male slave narrative and the narrative tropes of true womanhood. The modernist writers of the early twentieth century also trouble those edges as they tangle with the body and the autobiographical subject. In Gertrude Stein's text the body of the autobiographical subject is nowhere and everywhere at once. In escaping the strangulated individuality of the (male) "I," Virginia Woolf disengages the transparent eyeball from the body of the female artist in a gesture that repudiates an isolating and con-taminating embodiment and works toward an absorptive anonym-ity. In her autobiography of the tongues of Zora, Hurston implicitly connects the recovery of the colorful body of the "black mama" to the constitution of an empowered diasporan subject who both absorbs communal voices into her own working tongue and resists any fixing of her identity in one tongue.

In this chapter I want to consider the ways in which contempo-rary women take up the body through autobiographical practices. But before doing so, I want to ask, as an opening foray, What might skin have to do with autobiographical writing and autobiographi-cal writing with skin? Traditional autobiography most often begins in the midst of "flesh and blood," as the autobiographical "I" opens the narrative with the story of origins, with genealogy. But flesh and blood also moves through other capillary actions since skin is the literal and metaphorical borderland between the materi-ality of the autobiographical "I" and the contextual surround of the world. It functions simultaneously as a personal and political, psychological and ideological boundary of meaning, a contested border of restraint and of transgression through which subjectivity emerges and over which what Nancy Fraser via Michel Foucault calls "the 'capillary' character of modern power" plays.[1] From a certain contemporary perspective, then, subjectivity is the elaborate residue of the border politics of the body. Thus skin has much to do with autobiographical writing, as the body of the text, the body of the narrator, the body of the narratee, the cultural "body," and the body politic all merge in skins and skeins of meaning.

The Body and Its Surround

The clear-boundedness of bodies seem to position autobiographical subjects as demarcated beings separate from others and to locate them in specific spaces and times. Thus the body seems to be the nearest home for the autobiographical subject, the very ground upon which a "notion of a coherent, historically continuous, stable identity" can be founded.[2] But the body only seems to anchor subjects in a finite, discrete, unified surround—a private surround, temptingly stable and impermeable. There is only apparent continuity since, paradoxically, bodies, at once so close as to seem indissoluble from any notion of "me" or "I," can also disrupt the too easy stability of identities,[3] as Hurston's deconstructions of racial identity through recourse to the chromatics of bodies underscores. Bodies sometimes do and sometimes do not secure a correspondence between subjects and their cultural identities.

If " 'being home,' " as Biddy Martin and Chandra Talpade Mohanty suggest, "refers to the place where one lives within familiar, safe, protected boundaries," the autobiographical subject may find the body to be the home of a stranger who is not at home in the body, who is in fact homeless. This sense of " 'not being home,' " Martin and Mohanty continue, "is a matter of realizing that home was an illusion of coherence and safety based on the exclusion of specific histories of oppressions and resistance, the repression of differences even within oneself."[4] This experience of homelessness inside the body derives from the relationship of specific bodies to the cultural meanings assigned bodies in the body politic.

Denise Riley suggests that " 'the body' is not, for all its corporeality an originating point nor yet a terminus; it is a result or an effect." In fact, communal discourses and practices determine how the body is called together as a unified or coherent material reality with specific identity contents. They determine how often and for how long any subject is, to paraphrase Riley, located "in the body" culturally.[5] They determine in good part when the actual and the discursive bodies can fall away from consciousness and when they cannot, when they are invoked and for what purposes. For instance, separate parts of the body are brought together and assigned meaning through the discursive identification of the "female" or "male" body. According to Judith Butler, "numerous features [of the body] gain social meaning and unification through their articulation within the category of sex." But Butler goes on to say that "the 'integrity' and 'unity' of the body, often thought to be positive ideals, serve the purposes of fragmentation, restriction, and domination"[6] since only certain parts of the body are aligned in the consolidation of sexual identification and since those body parts must fulfill specific functions and be positioned in appropriate places to be considered normal.

Paradoxically, a unified body is consolidated on the ground of the fragmented body. Some fragments align into gender identification, some into racial or ethnic identifications. Moreover, while there are unlimited material differences from one body to another, only certain body parts make up the "meaningful" cultural and social differences. And culturally only certain bodies are experienced as different. The body is thus parceled out and policed through discursive systems that establish identities through differences, that normalize certain bodies and render other bodies culturally abnormal, even grotesque. The fragmented materiality of bodies helps sustain the illusion of indisputable continuity between biology and culturally constructed identities such as those of gender and race, the illusion of stable categorizations.

Further, the cultural meaning assigned to the material body permeates the body politic through the metaphorization of the social through the bodily. The body offers itself up in bits and pieces, in its blood, immune system, organs, in its topography and its pathology for use in constructing the social environment and the positions of persons in that environment. This facile movement from the body to the body politic makes the invocation of the body for the purposes of the social a discursive commonplace. Mary Douglas suggests in *Danger and Purity* that "the body is a model that can stand for any bounded system. Its boundaries can represent any boundaries which are threatened or precarious."[7] Drawing on the work of Bakhtin, Peter Stallybrass and Allon White elegantly elaborate in *The Politics and Poetics of Transgression* how "the body cannot be thought separately from the social formation, symbolic topography and the constitution of the subject. The body is neither a purely natural given nor is it merely a textual metaphor, it is a privileged operator for the transcoding of these other areas. Thinking the body is thinking social topography and vice versa."[8] Thus they trace the implications of transcodings between four symbolic domains—"psychic forms, the human body, geographical space and the social order"—as a way of understanding ordering principles of modern western cultures: "Divisions and discriminations in one domain are continually structured, legitimated and dissolved by reference to the vertical symbolic hierarchy which operates in the other three domains."[9] This metaphoric use of the body has consequences for what Fraser calls "the social meanings of our bodies"[10] because any specific body may be overwritten by this social inscription. The body categorized as abnormal becomes associated with those forces threatening the stability of the body politic. It becomes a pollutant, a grotesquerie.

The autobiographical subject confronts all these "bodies" at the scene of writing. And while she finds herself subjected to the social meanings of bodies, she can find ways to resist the kind of body pressed upon her through the body politic. For instance, the autobiographer's specific body is not one culturally charged and categorized body, unified, stable, finite or final. Nor can it be identified along one consuming and unchanging axis. It is the site of heterogeneous axes of signification that become constitutive of the subject of autobiography. Bearing multiple marks of location, bodies position the autobiographical subject at the nexus of culturally specific experiences, of gender, race, sexual orientation, and health among them, and at the nexus of "micropolitical practices" that derive from the cultural meaning of those points of identification.[11] The very complexity of this experientially based history can be used to challenge, disturb, and displace the neat categorizations (and fragmentation/unification) of bodies.

The coherent body and its apparently stable identity are cultural fabrications whose regulation may be only partially effective.[12] And so, if identities are points of departure, they are, to invoke Nancy Miller's phrase, "subject to change,"[13] though not to the inevitability of change. Since change can be brought about through what Martin describes as the "practices of self-representation which illuminate the contradictory, multiple construction of subjectivity at the intersections, but also in the interstices of ideologies of gender, race, and sexuality,"[14] autobiographical practice becomes one means to change. Writing her experiential history of the body, the autobiographical subject engages in a process of critical self-consciousness through which she comes to an awareness of the relationship of her specific body to the cultural "body" and to the body politic. That change in consciousness prompts cultural critique.

I want to trace this politics of the body through three disparate texts written within the last decade. In *An American Childhood* Annie Dillard continues the traditions of bourgeois autobiography as she positions the autobiographical narrator as universal subject. What is interesting about her text is the way in which she participates in the repression of the autobiographical body and the marginalization of the bodies of others as she chronicles and celebrates the unfolding drama of bourgeois self-consciousness. While Dillard keeps the clutter and mess of the grotesque body safely in the imaginative borders of the text, there are others who look directly at the body and its cultural meanings. Through diverse autobiographical practices, Cherríe Moraga, in *Loving in the War Years,* and Jo Spence, in *Putting Myself in the Picture,* use self-writing and self-portraiture as a means to self-knowledge and cultural critique. Through autobiographical writing (and auto/photo-therapy in the case of Spence), they attempt to wrest their bodies from oppressive cultural identifications.

The Body of Annie Dillard's American Childhood

The very title of Dillard's autobiography, *An American Childhood,* signals her identification with the universal subject. The indefinite article followed by the national modifier generalizes the subject of the autobiography. The narrator claims she speaks as an American about a universal cultural experience, a generic American childhood. Rhetorical gestures throughout the narrative solicit the reader's acceptance of the shared nature of experience and assume the reader's identification with the autobiographical subject. The narrator moves facilely in and out of pronouns, shifting from the autobiographical "I" to the communal and inclusive "your," as in "your skin would wiggle," "you walked on sidewalks,"[15] thereby assigning a common history to childhood development. She also universalizes experience by switching to the objective form, as in "an infant watches" (44). She moves glibly in and out of normative generalizations, marked by the introductory phrase "like any child" (11). As they totalize and normalize the child and the childhood, all these gestures establish the narrator as one who knows, as one who is an authority on that common experience.

Dillard's invitation to identification draws the reader into a pageant of dawning self-consciousness. Central to her elaboration of this privatized romantic trope is her deployment of the metaphorics of skin. The word *skin* circulates throughout the text, inviting the reader to consider the specific history of the body that underwrites the romantic journey of Dillard's universal subject.

That journey begins in an idyllic childhood. With loving nostalgia and gentle wit, motivated by a profound sense of the loss of consonance between the subject and the world in adulthood,[16] the older narrator projects childhood as a time when the whole being responds to experience, when body and mind still operate inseparably, when the world and the subject know one another. In this romanticized context, the skin and the subject are one, a phenomenon Dillard captures through an aquatic metaphor. "Like any child," she writes, "I slid into myself perfectly fitted, as a diver meets her reflection in a pool. Her fingertips enter the fingertips on the water, her wrists slide up her arms. The diver wraps herself in her reflection wholly, sealing it at the toes, and wears it as she climbs rising from the pool, and ever after" (11). The suit of skin and the suit of self are identical. Suited up in this way, Dillard's childhood self is assigned an unproblematic identity. There is no suspicion here that the diver might enter a nonidentical reflection/suit, that homelessness in the skin might be an early possibility, for self and skin, and later mind and skin, remain unified. Later, of playing baseball she writes: "I loved living at my own edge, as an explorer on a ship presses to the ocean's rim; mind and skin were one joined force curved out and alert, prow and telescope. I pitched, as I did most things, in a rapture" (97). And, in fact, knowledge derives from skin since the body provides metaphors for understanding and describing the external world: "A baseball weighted your hand just so, and fit it. Its red stitches, its good leather and hardness like skin over bone, seemed to call forth a skill both easy and precise" (100).

As she tracks the inevitable journey of the child toward adolescence, the narrator merges the metaphors of skin with the metaphors of cartography: "An infant watches her hands and feels them move. Gradually she fixes her own boundaries at the complex incurved rim of her skin. Later she touches one palm to another and tries for a game to distinguish each hand's sensation of feeling and being felt. What is a house but a bigger skin, and a neighborhood map but the world's skin ever expanding?" (44). The expansion of consciousness becomes the expansion of borders, and skin serves as the sign of that border between the subject and the outer world: "The interior life expands and fills; it approaches the edge of skin; it thickens with its own vivid story; it even begins to hear rumors, from beyond the horizon skin's rim, of nations and wars. You wake one day and discover your grandmother; you wake another day and notice, like any curious naturalist, the boys" (86). Thus the narrative itinerary of the first half of the text maps a progression of Emersonian explorations: of the near neighborhood and then the larger environment of Pittsburgh, of geology, of biology. There is a sense in which all these explorations become exercises of incorporation. To grow in consciousness is to take everything under the skin, that is, to grow a kind of second skin. Describing her physical engagement with the streets of her expanding neighborhood, Dillard invokes skin as an incorporative medium: "It was your whole body that knew those sidewalks and streets. Your bones ached with them; you tasted their hot dust in your bleeding lip; their gravel worked into your palms and knees and stayed, blue under the new skin that grew over it" (104).

Inevitably, in this romantic scenario the narrative of adolescence stresses the widening gap between the subject and world and the subject and her body. Gradually the material reality around the young girl becomes tedious, a shift the narrator captures through her description of "the boring body" and its adversarial relationship to the imagination of a privatized consciousness:

The actual world is a kind of tedious plane where dwells, and goes to school, the body, the boring body which houses the eyes to read the books and houses the heart the books enflame. The very boring body seems to require an inordinately big, very boring world to keep it up, a world where you have to spend far too much time, have to *do* time like a prisoner, always looking for a chance to slip away, to escape back home to books, or escape back home to any concentration—fanciful, mental, or physical—where you can lose your self at last. Although I was hungry all the time, I could not bear to hold still and eat; it was too dull a thing to do, and had no appeal either to courage or to imagination. The blinding sway of their inner lives makes children immoral. They find things good insofar as they are thrilling, insofar as they render them ever more feverish and breathless, ever more limp and senseless on the bed. (120–21)

There is no place for the body and its demands in the arena of a privatized consciousness. It is seen as disruptive, almost petulant, too demanding, without utility or significance. It is an excess to consciousness, and as excess, expendable. The drift of Dillard's adolescence renders the body unsuitable to the subject.

Unsuitable, too, is the world surrounding the subject. "Private life, book life," she recalls, "took place where words met imagination without passing through world" (120). Thus the latter half of the autobiography traces the narrator's developing sense of alienation from her comfortable bourgeois surroundings. And once again she uses metaphors of the body, now to capture the sense of imaginative frustration with her life. "When rage or boredom reappeared," she recalls, "each seemed never to have left. Each so filled me with so many years' intolerable accumulation it jammed the space behind my eyes, so I couldn't see. There was no room left even on my surface to live. My rib cage was so taut I couldn't breathe. Every cubic centimeter of atmosphere above my shoulders and head was heaped with last straws. Black hatred clogged my very blood. I couldn't peep, I couldn't wiggle or blink; my blood was too mad to flow" (224). Yet here again the body is invoked for its metaphorical possibilities. It is a mad body, a clogged body, a body under the pressure of rage. It is not a body that engenders new knowledge, as did the body of childhood, but a body that operates literally as the irrational and pragmatically as a metaphorical pressure cooker for consciousness.

The rage of Dillard's adolescent "Annie" signals her discontent with the constraining experiences of being a girl in a female body. Of the differentiation between the domains of boys and girls, she writes:

> They had been learning self-control. We had failed to develop any selves worth controlling. We were enforcers of a code we never questioned; we were vigilantes of the trivial. They had been accumulating information about the world outside our private schools and clubs. We had failed to notice that there was such a thing. The life of Pittsburgh, say, or the United States, or assorted foreign continents, concerned us no more than Jupiter did, or its moons. (91)

Suited up in the gendered body with adolescence, the skin no longer functions as a continually breached border of expanding consciousness. The borders of experience close down. In fact, the skin (of the hands) is now covered with the white gloves of bourgeois propriety. The motif of the white gloves that protect the skin of the young girls from touching that of the young boys attests to the cultural constraints attending bourgeois assignments of gender identities. Now the skin has become the skin of sexual difference, a potentially contaminating border not to be breached by contact with an alien world. If the narrator celebrates in elegant prose the breathlessness of a child's body in motion early in the narrative, she captures the stiffness and rage of the gloved body later in the narrative. And she links the gloved hand to the young woman's escape from the body into a universalized imagination, into writing itself, that private domain where words do not pass through world.

Dillard erases the material body, reassembling it imaginatively as the metaphor of skin that sustains self-writing. While the use of skin seems to keep the body before the reader, it works paradoxically to erase the eroticized body and its errant desires, neutralizing the body into the metaphorical language of self-consciousness. As there is little mention of her own sexuality, except a passing description of a fragile and sustained kiss, hers is a noneroticized skin and a repressed body politics. Finally, the skin's only usefulness derives from its service to the scene of writing where its very materiality is dematerialized through metaphorization.

But there are other bodies and another history of the body that circulate through *An American Childhood* and its pageant of romantic individualism: the history of the carnivalesque body. A powerfully rendered scene early in the narrative, which I will call the Jo Ann Sheehy scene, stages the eruption of the carnivalesque. Dillard recalls with a kind of elegiac quality the snowy night when she and her parents watched the Irish girl, Jo Ann Sheehy, skating alone on the street in front of their house. Dillard describes "the world outside" as "dangerously cold." Jo Ann Sheehy skates "recklessly" in "the open street," which was "a fatal place, where I was forbidden to set foot" (31). The scene is oneiric, silent, strangely and magically lit, mysterious, but also "cold" and "black." "Distant over the street," she writes, "the night sky was moonless and foreign, a frail, bottomless black, and the cold stars speckled it without moving" (31). Even as she "watched as if the world were a screen on which played interesting scenes for my pleasure," she recognized that "there was danger in this radiant sight, in the long glimpse of the lone girl skating, for it was night, and killingly cold. The open street was fatal and forbidden. And the apparently invulnerable girl was Jo Ann Sheehy, Tommy Sheehy's sister, part of the Sheehy family, whose dark ways were a danger and a crime" (31).

Their "dark ways" derive from their class status. Jo Ann Sheehy embodies the working-class Irish community at the borders of Dillard's childhood neighborhood. Dillard's narrative suggests that as a child she is intrigued by the Irish children but that she is separated from them most dramatically when her mother disciplines her for calling the family's maid "a nigger," a phrase she has learned from Jo Ann Sheehy's brother. For her mother, the child has spoken forbidden words, words that are a violation of manners, of the right use of language, of a liberal humanism that eschews expressed bigotry. It is precisely this differential use of language that marks the boundaries between classes. Since the Irish are positioned as the crude and unmannerly, when Dillard comes home and repeats Tommy Sheehy's phrase, she effectively speaks as one of the "low." Through that speech she momentarily inhabits the body of the other, and so she comes too close to the "low" for comfort. The borders separating "low" from "middle," the socially abject from the universal subject, are breached, traversed by dangerously fluid identifications.[17] The carnivalesque is not to be played out in polite living rooms.

That snowy evening, the carnivalesque scene taking place outside is essential to the "peace and safety" (31) within. The skating Irish girl, identified with the dark, the mysterious, the forbidden, the bigoted working class, constitutes through her difference and outsider status the snug environment of the family home and middle-class identity. Hers is an errant, erotic body whose pleasure is assigned to outside marginal spaces. For Dillard its power is its imaginative draw to memory, its solicitation to and foreclosure of desire. In this scene, what Stallybrass and White suggest is a "fundamental rule" of identificatory practices occurs: "What is excluded at the overt level of identity-formation is productive of new objects of desire."[18] The low stages a return via the imagination of the middle-class daughter—at a later date and at a safe distance. Dillard establishes her class identity in such scenes and invites our participation in the universal autobiographical subject.

There are other glimpses of the marginal "grotesques" whose exclusion establishes the borders of Dillard's communal identification. The "bums" in the parks she traverses. The working-class people who populate the neighborhood down the hill. The blacks who read books in the Homewood library. The Jewish friend whose parents do not belong to the country club. The homosexuals whose bodies do things that her grandmother Oma cannot imagine. The madwoman in the country club set who "acts out" every once in a while. Dillard notices all of these outsiders. But despite her gentle and even biting irony in pointing to the exclusionary practices of her Pittsburgh world, her narrative and rhetorical strategies move to gently contain those differences, homogenizing human experience in a normative classlessness and racelessness.

The narrator of the text and the narrator's narratee remain fascinated with these bodies, projections of her own sense of outsider status in the comfortable world of Pittsburgh's leading families, of her romantic discontent. And her fascination with the exotic links her to her father and his fascination for New Orleans. The story of his abortive trip down the Ohio River toward New Orleans and jazz, that music of the carnival scene, figures always in the background as the imaginative escape toward carnival from the too stolid, comfortable, and repressed environment of Pittsburgh's leading families and their country club circle and circuit of exchange. Yet the recurrent reference to this journey does not in the end destabilize the narrative so much as it secures the normative romanticism of the universal subject. The challenge to the neutralizing claims of that subject are not voiced by the working-class girl or the Jewish girl or the black maid but rather by Dillard's father, patriarch of the clan, central figure of the privileged class. His desire speaks, but nostalgically and therefore ineffectually. Her father unsuccessfully acts out his romantic discontent and alienation without disturbing the cultural dominance of the bourgeois subject. He cannot get down the river. And his daughter cannot release the carnivalesque body from her own appropriative gaze. It is as if she treats that body narratively as the "madwoman" is treated by her country club set. The madwoman's gestures only reaffirm the boundaries of class by enacting the outsider position. Acting out is allowed because it is ultimately a containable performance of difference.

In her flight from embodiment into a metaphor of skin, Dillard participates in the politics and poetics of exclusion. Imaginatively neutralizing skin, generalizing it as border, drawing it away from the specific body it covers, she erases the specificity of skin with its marks of difference and therefore the cultural meanings assigned people of different skins and physiognomies. This narrative skin, identified with the position of universal subject, reveals its normative whiteness and thus its neutralizing identity practices. What is never said about the skin is the relationship of the white skin to the ease of movement in multiple geographical domains, the neighborhood of the social, of the psychological, and of the literary. Literally and figuratively permitting her to move through ever-expanding neighborhoods, Dillard's white skin, according to Janet Varner Gunn, is "a metaphor for an imperial infantilism that recognizes no boundaries between self and other."[19] What permeates Dillard's metaphor of skin is the comfort of the white skin if not the female skin, the natural and expected fit between skin and neighborhood. No narrative discomfort, no problematics of metaphor complicates this dimension of the text.

Her concluding commentary of memory and meaning invites all her readers to assume the subject position of the universal subject, erasing the specificities of individual skins/stories and the way those stories determine the relationship of individuals to the universal human subject, to the pageantry of that subject and its carnivalesque other. "For it is not you or I that is important," she writes, "neither what sort we might be nor how we came to be each where we are. What is important is anyone's coming awake and discovering a place, finding in full orbit a spinning globe one can lean over, catch, and jump on. What is important is the moment of opening a life and feeling it touch—with an electric hiss and cry—this speckled mineral sphere, our present world" (247–48). It is only those who are fundamentally comfortable in their social position, who can feel so confident that the world wants their touch, that the world will touch back, that there is no violence in that touch. Gesturing toward the reader, whom she appoints as an identical universal subject, Dillard represses the figures of difference that have erupted throughout her text. Specific bodies lose their heterogeneous marks of difference. Dillard is not impervious to the shadowy border areas of class and race that push against the edges of her comfortable skin, to the bodies of the culturally grotesque. And yet in the end she effectively whitewashes identity through her memorial pageant.[20]

Dillard's taking up the position of the universal subject without a body in the writing "I" may be, as Monique Wittig suggests of that strategy, a form of empowerment that enables her to escape gender identity and her position as a "vigilante of the trivial."[21] It is also a form of empowerment complicit in the cultural taming of the colorful.

Warring over and with the Body

Unlike Dillard, who invokes in *An American Childhood* a metaphorical and therefore neutralized skin as the locus of the universal subject's consciousness, Cherríe Moraga in *Loving in the War Years* directs attention to the materiality of skin as the locus of dawning political awareness. Moraga brings the autobiographical body out from under the processes of erasure, assuming her body as narrative point of departure. She discovers that the body functions as a lens through which she comes to see her complex cultural positioning as woman, lesbian, light-skinned Chicana. Her title signals the interrelationship of the body and the body politic, the forced juncture of the personal and the political. "War years" are

the most exigently political years, or perhaps they are the years
when politics has failed. They invoke the battleground upon which
the struggle for cultural meaning is waged—for Moraga, the culturally censored and the self-censoring body of the Chicana. And
"loving" in the "war years" is a kind of revolutionary gesture,
calling as it does "for this kind of risking/without a home to call our
own."[22] "War years" are years of homelessness in and out of the
body.

Throughout the poems and the prose narratives that make up the
text, the narrator insists on being in the body, on the being of
bodies. Bodies surround the text, move in and through it. They are
eaten, for instance, in the memory of her grandmother who gestures
love as edible consumption, or in the poem "An Open Invitation to
a Meal," in which the "I"/lover figures as a "piece of cake" to be
consumed (22). The knees of religious women grind against the
floor of churches (18). The body of the suicide falls through air.
Lips, breasts, thighs, legs, knees, eyes, cunts, backs, skin. Parts
of the body are named, described. Movements of the body are
mapped. Poetry keeps the emotional pulse of the body's experience
beating, alongside, not subordinated to, the prose critique. The
prose analysis keeps positioning the body in its specific discursive
domains of meaning, keeps attending to the mediations enacted on
the body by the body politic. Inscribing embodiedness everywhere,
the narrator challenges the notion of an individuality, an autobiographer distinct from a specific body. Ultimately this new kind
of history of the body motivates an alternative autobiographical
practice through which, as Lourdes Torres notes, Moraga "explores how women are denied a right to their bodies through the
repression of their sexuality, the lifelong threat of sexual violence,
and the denial of reproductive rights."[23]

Thus Moraga writes her body in order to break the circuit of
control over representations of female sexuality in both the dominant Anglo culture and what Mae Gwendolyn Henderson calls the
"ambiguously (non)hegemonic"[24] culture, here Chicano culture.
Yet she does not write the body of a universalized Woman. Moraga's specific body is "female" and "lesbian" and "colored" and
"working class/poor." It is positioned in and out of Chicano culture, in and out of Anglo culture. And compounding the various
specificities of cultural placement, it is a body that can "pass" back

and forth between two cultures, the Anglo and Chicano, the straight and the lesbian. This body founds the narrator's double move: she not only writes the body but critiques the social meaning of that body by elaborating her relationship to the nexus of oppressions inscribed on it: "In this country, lesbianism is a poverty— as is being brown, as is being a woman, as is being just plain poor. The danger lies in ranking the oppressions. *The danger lies in failing to acknowledge the specificity of the oppression*" (52).

The narrator's engagement with her specific body forces her to confront the palpability of color and the politics of chromatism. Anglo culture renders the Chicano body as one of the abject, but the shade of the body determines the relative degree of abjection within both dominant and marginal cultures and the degree of fluidity in both the self-assignment and communal assignment of racial identity. Moraga confronts this chromatism as she considers her positioning in the skin of "*la güera*": "I was '*la güera*'—fair-skinned. Born with the features of my Chicana mother, but the skin of my Anglo father, I had it made. . . . In fact, everything about my upbringing (at least what occurred on a conscious level) attempted to bleach me of what color I did have" (51). Fair skin allows her to escape the abject body of the Chicana figured by her mother and to assume the normatively white body of the dominant culture and its identity structures. This ability to assume the dominant identity sustains the illusion that she can paradoxically escape identity's body, can exist without being called to her body culturally.

But in one of the narratives, she describes how, when her autobiographical protagonist, "Celia," begins living with a black lover, "*color moved in with her*" (36). Discovering that skin color "*meant all the difference in the world*" (36), she finds her skin to be no longer the secure anchorage it had seemed to be, for new knowledge changes inescapably the feel of skin: "*Soon her body began to change with this way of seeing. She felt her skin, like a casing, a beige bag into which the guts of her life were poured. And inside it, she swam through her day. Upstream. Downtown. Underground. Always, the shell of this skin, leading her around*" (36). This psychological homelessness inside her own skin leads to her recognition of cultural homelessness as she comes to understand the ways in which her ability to assume the identity of an Anglo separates her from her family and her community: "I feel at times I am trying to bulldoze my way back into a people who forced me to leave them in the first place, who taught me to take my whiteness and run with it. Run with it. Who want nothing to do with me, the likes of me, the white of me—in them" (95). Her very skin sets her loose from any secure anchorage.

The narrator considers this instability of identification an oppressive rather than a liberating condition: "You call this a choice! To constantly push up against a wall of resistance from your own people or to fall away nameless into the mainstream of this country, running with our common blood?" (97). The surface/color of the skin permits her to change cultural identities, to move noiselessly between two cultures, but "under the skin" she turns against the skin in her, turns against her heritage and thus the source of her subjectivity. She thereby participates in the abjection of her own body. "But at the age of twenty-seven," she writes, "it is frightening to acknowledge that I have internalized a racism and classism, where the object of oppression is not only someone *outside* my skin, but the someone *inside* my skin. In fact, to a large degree, the real battle with such oppression, for all of us, begins under the skin" (54).

Moraga's narrative reveals that because of the color of her skin she could choose to resist identity's body, the cultural consolidation of her body parts into a unified identity as Chicana. But the price of passing was racial disidentification. The operations of sexual disidentification are equally as complex and inextricable from those of racial disidentification. Within Chicano culture the female-in-sex is "*la chingada,*" "the fucked-one." Her very sexuality as expressed in the sexual act becomes grotesque, contaminated, unclean, base (119). Thus, the Chicana is alienated from her bodily home: "If the simple act of sex then—the penetration itself—implies the female's filthiness, non-humaness, it is no wonder Chicanas often divorce ourselves from the conscious recognition of our own sexuality" (119). Denied a pleasurable body, the Chicana is assigned instead another kind of body—the compulsory heterosexual body,[25] even more specifically the repressed heterosexual body.

In the midst of this cultural environment, Moraga recalls how her body moved her in different directions, moved her away from an anchorage in heterosexuality: "I have always known too much. It was too clear to me—too tangible—too alive in the breath of my nose, the pulse in my thighs, the deep exhales that flowed from my chest when I moved into a woman's arms" (116). And so she describes how the dissonance between the cultural injunction to be a heterosexual woman and her own bodily knowledge led her to a state of physical and emotional homelessness, toward yet another kind of grotesquerie: "And if we have lesbian feelings—want not only to be penetrated, but to penetrate—what perverse kind of monstrosities we must indeed be" (119). In yet another powerful technology of (hetero)sexuality, the young girl is driven by the fragmentation of her body toward a reified disembodiment: "I see now that in order not to embody the *chingada,* not the femalized, and therefore perverse, version of the *chingón,* I became pure spirit—bodiless. For what, indeed, must my body look like if I were both the *chingada* and the *chingón*" (120).

The abject female body is not only a personal body, however. It is the community's body, one which threatens to contaminate the body politic, to destroy the very fabric of cultural identity and nationalism. Within Chicano culture the elaborate and compelling myth of Malinche operates to police the female body, and to keep identity fixed in a repressed body whose very erasure consolidates *la familia* and male privilege. Identifying woman's body as the site of cultural betrayal, the myth operates, to invoke Butler, as "the public regulation of fantasy through the surface politics of the body."[26] "This myth of the inherent unreliability of women, our natural propensity for treachery," Moraga insists, "has been carved into the very bone of Mexican/Chicano collective psychology" (101). It effectively alienates the Chicana from her own body and from what Susan Rubin Suleiman refers to as the "wildness of the unconscious,"[27] and weds her to her subordinate position.

If Malinche's myth assigns the Chicana to this specific kind of sexuality, the myth also scripts the effects of her refusal to accept this assignment as it scripts the effects of Moraga's refusing the gender assignments of compulsory heterosexuality:

> The woman who defies her role as subservient to her husband, father, brother, or son by taking control of her own sexual destiny is purported to be a "traitor to her race" by contributing to the "genocide" of her people—whether or not she has children. In short, even if the defiant woman is *not* a lesbian, she is purported to

be one; for, like the lesbian in the Chicano imagination, she is una
Malinchista. Like the Malinche of Mexican history, she is corrupted
by foreign influences which threaten to destroy her people. (113)

The female body opens up to foreign influences, foreign infiltration,
foreign insemination, to foreign meaning and control. It is the
breached boundary that destabilizes inner and outer, that invites
further penetration by the dominant order, the very source of
oppression. It is the opening through which leaks out the (endoga-
mous) life of the people. The body politic thus takes up the female
body in its war with the dominant culture, making the female body
the contestatory middle term between the male/dominant culture of
the Anglos and the male/subdominant culture of the Chicanos. In
the body politic, female sexuality metaphorically and literally saps
the male of his privileges, as it threatens to erase his original
identity.

Insisting on her body as an excluded term in the constitution of
dominant identities, Moraga ultimately places the body of the
Chicana lesbian before the reader in all its materiality, offering a
destabilizing cultural performance. Now the grotesque body speaks
back, "defiantly displaying" in the words of Carroll Smith-Rosenberg, its "own sexuality as a symbol of social resistance."[28] First,
Moraga rewrites the history of Malinche, complicating the act of
treachery by introducing a family tragedy in which the daughter,
Malinche, is rejected by her mother in favor of the son who will
inherit power. The daughter locates the treachery elsewhere than in
Malinche's cooperation with Cortez. She locates it in *la familia*. For
it is a treachery Moraga herself experiences at the hands of her own
mother. Moreover, in rehistoricizing Malinche, Moraga recovers
the body of Malinche and of the Chicana from the legend, and in so
doing she gives her body autobiographically as a gift and as a
source of liberation.[29]

Second, Moraga figures the lesbian as an empowered figure of
desire: "In stepping outside the confines of the institution of heterosexuality, I was indeed *choosing* sex freely. *The lesbian as institu-
tionalized outcast*" (125). As "the most visible manifestation of a
woman taking control of her own sexual identity and destiny"
(112), she is the revolutionary figure whose very relationship to her
body inaugurates cultural critique. And cultural critique, as Linda

Singer suggests, is critical to liberation: "Women who do not know or are incapable of representing what they want are that much less likely to demand or pursue it. The absence of a female-identified discourse adequate to representing women's sexuality in its difference is both a symptom of and instrumental to the continued subjugation of women within the patriarchal order."[30] Third, Moraga makes explicit the connection between the discourse invoked by the body and the acquisition of new knowledge: "It wasn't until I acknowledged and confronted my own lesbianism in the flesh, that my heartfelt identification with and empathy for my mother's oppression—due to being poor, uneducated, and Chicana—was realized. My lesbianism is the avenue through which I have learned the most about silence and oppression, and it continues to be the most tactile reminder to me that we are not free human beings" (52). In scripting a positive, empowered, pleasurable body, Moraga disturbs dominant systems of knowledge that have normalized the female body either as male/the same or as grotesque. Autobiographical writing thus compels the subject toward a new knowledge, a new way of interpreting the practices of the body politic through the material body and its desires.

Fourth, Moraga effectively releases the lesbian body from the pornographic gaze of (male) discourses by writing for an audience she envisions as sympathetic rather than voyeuristic. While she cannot control what kind of readings her autobiographical text will receive, while she cannot filter out all voyeuristic gazes, she can interrupt the specular scenes of lesbian desire with a clearheaded and full-bodied critique of compulsory heterosexuality and its political and institutional implications. And since the body politic of both Chicano and Anglo cultures is founded on the heterosexual construction of men and women, Moraga's empowerment of the lesbian body serves to unsettle normative practices of sexuality that consolidate identity through the fragmentation (the putative unification) of the body.

And finally, instead of parceling out the body, sending various parts toward specific experiences of oppression (skin color toward race, breasts toward gender), Moraga surveys the meanings written all over the body in an attempt to make her meaning out of multiplicity: "Sexuality, race, and sex have usually been presented in contradiction to each other, rather than as part and parcel of a complex web of personal and political identity and oppression" (109). And yet, simultaneously, she resists the colonizing gesture of a false universalization of experience: "As a Chicana lesbian, I write of the connection my own feminism has had with my sexual desire for women. This is my story. I can tell no other one than the one I understand" (139). By keeping the carnivalesque body of the lesbian woman of color always in the fore, by incorporating frag- ments of that body throughout, Moraga insists on the material specificity of the body that speaks and on the specific discourses, practices, and contexts that inscribe the cultural meaning of that body. In effect, Moraga's text/body enacts the return of the political unconscious (in both cultures she straddles) and interrupts a com- placent self-identity founded on the abjection of the lesbian woman of color. Pursuing a sexual discourse adequate to the task of de- scribing and creating knowledge about her specific libidinal econo- my,[31] Moraga politically realigns the lesbian body and dismembers a stifling identity politics, dismembers, that is, identity's body and the disembodiment of the universal subject.

Jo Spence's Propertied Body

Dillard universalizes consciousness, gathers the narrative voice under one monologic authority, and thereby obfuscates the degree to which the terrain of individual consciousness is marked by issues of class and gender. Moraga circulates the specific body of the Chicana and the lesbian in all its colorfulness through her auto- biographical *War Years*. Jo Spence, coming from a working-class background to a middle-class professional identification, uses her autobiographical ph/au/tobiography, *Putting Myself in the Picture*, to take apart the complacencies of a universal subject that is always the classicized subject of representation and to map the trajectories by which the subject can be dismembered and re/membered, repre- sented and re/presented.

One way to read Spence's autobiographical text is to look at it as a history of the photographing subject (both the photographer as subject of autobiography and the subjects of the photographer's images). For the narrative proceeds loosely by chronology as Spence tracks her evolution from working-class photographer's assistant to portrait photographer to student and theorist of photography to photo therapist. In tracking this evolution she introduces the materials of her trade, the specific photographs and exhibit catalogs from various stages of her career. Thus within this teleology there are two times: the time of the reflective narrator and the time of the active photographer. The photographs and the essays and commentary, as Julia Watson suggests, "create a dialogue between her present 'looking' and the texts of memory about the representational power of images to mold perception and behavior."[32]

But a more interesting way of reading/seeing the text is as a history of the photographic body. The kind of photographies Spence catalogs (the plural reinforces the fact that there are many kinds of photography, heterophotographia perhaps) all put the body of the photographic subject in the picture. But that body, as she discovers, is never a transparent body. It is a specific kind of body, and it does specific kinds of ideological work in the frame. From this point of view, then, *Putting Myself in the Picture* can be read as an act of autobiographical recovery since as ph/au/tobiography it tracks Spence's journey from the invisibility and complicity of the poser of photographic subjects behind the camera to the visibilities and subversions of the self-poser before the camera.

Spence chronicles how her career as a photographer began with family portraits, began, that is, in the midst of cultural pageantry that ensures that every photograph of a family effectively reproduces the ideology of the "family" and of compulsory heterosexuality on which bourgeois culture is founded. These photographic practices hold the subject in specific bodily postures since, as she comes to understand, to be posed is to be composed. And to pose is to do the ideological work of one's culture, both to exert power and to reproduce dominant power structures. Family portraits and the family portraitist render invisible the forces of reproduction and thereby act as forces for class production and cultural reproduction. Her artistic journey begins as she turns the camera back on the pageantry itself, explores the invisibilities before the camera, problematizes the very medium that promises to capture moments of the past forever.

Spence's increasing scrutiny of photography leads her toward interventions in the cultural poses of identity's body. In describing

her strategies as a family portraitist, Spence recalls trying to catch
for the photographic subjects "an 'essence,' a sight of themselves,
that *they* knew but nobody else did." [33] But looking for this essence
in bodily gestures and body-image, she recognizes that the sitters
have a low self-image, reflected in their gestures before the camera.
She suggests that they seemed to see the body as grotesque and
desired her to eliminate the grotesquerie, to produce an idealized
body, as they wanted her to produce idealized portraits of their
children and family. Spence sees herself in the mirror of her subjects. As she suggests here and in various textual places, she too had
a low self-image (46), and was uncomfortable in her body. So her
scrutiny of photographic practices becomes more and more the
scrutiny of her own body and body-image.

Becoming involved in the women's movement, Spence turns with
others in various collectives to projects that unfix the old subject of
photography, in part as a way of understanding this discomfort
with the body. Coming to understand that realistic photography
promises to make the subject transparently and thus disarmingly
visible while doing the work of cultural hegemony by rendering
invisible the sources and forces of coercive interpellation, Spence
begins "to use photos to ask questions rather than to try to show
facts" (98). For instance, she includes exhibit photographs of what
she calls invisible labor, the labor of working-class women that
remains unrepresented in many kinds of photography. She does so
to raise the issue of the cultural value assigned to "low" forms of
labor.

Concurrently she moves to question not only the absence of
women's labor in photography generally but also the invisibilities
of class constructions of the subject in photographs themselves.
Early theorizing of photography leads her to understand how "the
invisible class and power relationships into which we are structured
from birth" (92) are erased in photographs yet paradoxically remain as invisible presences. Discovering that "images of women
consistently cut across class differences and disguise them" so that
"class differences . . . are usually hidden in representations of family
life" (72), she learns how complicit traditional photographic meth-
ods are in reproducing the cultural ideology of the middling universal subject by posing the low in imagistic templates of the middling.
The invisible labor of the camera is the cultural interpellation of
middling subjects.

And of sexually marked subjects like herself. In a 1977 exhibit entitled "Disrupting Sexual Stereotypes," Spence displays a series of photographs of one man in various sexualized poses. Modeling him as both man and woman, Spence denaturalizes sexual difference (76) and reveals, as Watson argues, "that 'woman' is constructed through both the spectator's gaze and the subject's participation in becoming 'woman.' "[34] As a result of increasing awareness of her own "socialization as a woman and of the process of 'bourgeoisification' which had taken me away from the working class roots and struggles of my own family" (82), Spence begins to re/vision her own photographic history. In an exhibit entitled "Beyond the Family Album," she gathers photographs of herself and her family and reads them textually, asking questions, introducing memory and history, juxtaposing the camera's gaze that pacified her as a subject to her own script of the past, jarring the apparent meanings out of the frames.

In the process of rethinking her own history as a photographed subject, Spence begins to put herself before the camera as a new subject and as a deconstructed/new body. To discover how she is composed by the camera and certain ideologies of subjectivity, she must learn how to de/compose the photograph and the subject of photography. Through recourse to the carnivalesque body, Spence studies first the relationship of other bodies to representation and then of her own body to representation's body. Moreover, she develops carnivalesque forms, hybrid techniques to unfix the camera's eye: in "Cinderella" she uses captions that call into question the photographic images they accompany as a way of "contradict[ing] and demythologiz[ing] the story" of Cinderella (100); in an exhibit entitled "Remodeling Photo History," she stages photographs of the female body, of her own body, in order to "create a kind of hybrid 'spectacle' " (119) that both mimes and contests the naturalizing processes of various photographic genres, such as ethnography, criminal investigation, advertisement, etc., that use the female body for political purposes. Spence here uses her own body to intervene in the policing technologies of the body politic. Not body-image, but rather staged images of the body undo the invisible labor of conventional photography.

In the last half of *Picture*, the carnivalesque body comes to the fore of theorizing and of autobiographical practice. "I began to reverse the process of the way I had been constructed as a woman," she writes, "by deconstructing myself visually in an attempt to identify the process by which I had been 'put together' " (83). Spence works to undo the social construction of the female subject as heterosexual woman by breaking apart that cultural myth of a unified female subject, of a heterosexual, middle-class "woman's body." Exploring the way in which the bodily surround is not only a material but a fantastic terrain of signs and symbols, the narrator incorporates and critiques photographs of body parts, specifically the breast.

The breast becomes particularly problematic for her when she learns she has cancer. The knowledge of illness and the circulation of her body through the medical community and medical discourse on "the female body" renders Spence a stranger in her own bodily home. In the documentation of her experience with cancer she engages that homelessness by working to extract the breast from its symbolic placement in the body politic, lifting it to the level of metaphor. Since she conceives of herself "as a set of signals or signs, all of which 'meant' something to the viewer," she discovers that she can "control" cultural meanings of the breast by "emphasizing or deemphasizing" (95) it and by constantly resituating the breast in various cultural contexts:

> Given that women are expected to be the object of the male gaze, are expected to beautify themselves in order to become loveable, are still fighting for basic rights over their own bodies, it seemed to me that the breast could be seen as a metaphor for our struggles. The fact that we have to worry about its size and shape as young women, its ability to give food when we become mothers, and its total dispensability when we are past child-bearing age, should be explored through visual representation as well as within healthcare. The two should not be separated out in any way, as our concept of sexuality and our social identity stem from both lived experience and the imaginary self we carry in the mind's eye. Just as the female body is fragmented and colonized by advertisers in the search for new markets for products and is fetishized and offered for male consumption through pornography, so it is similarly fought over by competitors for its medical "care." (155)

Looking directly at the breast becomes part of the process of releasing the body from the gaze of the other, of reclaiming the body, and of reclaiming the subject of that body.

And so I want to consider in more detail two photographs central to the practice of photographic unfixing. The first photograph Spence takes with her to the hospital as a "magic fetish" (157). In a half-frontal shot, Spence looks directly into the camera. Across her left breast is written the interrogative "property of Jo Spence?" This is no glamorized female body: the breasts are large, sagging, taped, and marked for surgery. The photographed subject has refused to pose herself as an idealized or proper female subject whose breasts function as culturally fetishized objects. Moreover, she gazes directly into the camera, returning the gaze of the (male) spectator whose gaze would appropriate the property of the proper name of the subject in the photograph. Spence intervenes in this act of cultural appropriation not only by gazing directly back but by writing "property of Jo Spence" across her left breast, thereby at least appearing to lay claim to her body. But the meanings of "property" proliferate in this image. In philosophical systems, properties of things determine their identity. And so writing "property of Jo Spence" across her breast also signifies Spence's acknowledgment of the way in which the female breast has been culturally determinative of female identity. This fragment of the female body has been constitutive of the whole subject. But property is also a commodity. And linking the breast as "property" to the "proper" name, Jo Spence, also aligns the proper, property, and appropriation, à la Hélène Cixous's "Realm of the *Proper*."[35] Finally, by writing words across her breast Spence points to the process whereby the materiality of the body is inscribed by cultural discourses.[36]

Yet Spence goes further in this inscription of the body. She follows the words with a question mark and thus opens up possibilities for additional meanings of the photographic gesture. The breast seems to be a contested terrain. Is it the property of Jo Spence or not? It may be the property of the medical profession or of the larger culture that takes people's bodies from them. Or maybe the breast is not a "property" of Jo Spence, in the sense of being determinative of her identity. Maybe the breast is dispensable to the aging female body, no longer a determinative property. Maybe the breast is part of what she calls "the 'imaginary bodies' we inhabit as women" (156). Or maybe "Jo Spence" is the contested terrain. Maybe "Jo Spence" is a fiction of the culture's assignment of identity status to the breast. Or maybe the addition of the question mark following the words signals the suspect nature of "self-identity, self-aggrandizement and arrogative dominance,"[37] the very masculine libidinal economy that constructs women through their breasts. Certainly the question mark continues both cultural critique and psychological therapy. It signals her refusal to "collu[de] in [her] continuing infantilization" (158).

In another photograph Spence sets images of her different body parts in circulation around a documentary photograph of herself before a mirror. Upon each body part is written a word, and the sum of the words adds up to the question, How do I begin to take responsibility for my body? The "I" is written across her forehead, the "body" across her buttocks as a way of foregrounding the mind/body split and its impact upon subjectivity and representation. In this photograph the body is broken into bits, fragmented, rendered grotesque, and yet called to the center by the unified subject that is itself split before and in the mirror. Decomposed into its constituent parts, the image opens itself to the low, the ass itself. The abject returns to the subject as the subject tries to assemble a healthy vision of herself. But the photograph holds the fragments and the subject in the mirror in dynamic tension with one another.

In the final pages of *Picture,* Spence turns to a discussion of phototherapy, a process through which she invokes, according to Watson, "the analytical frameworks of psychoanalysis and historical materialism to explore how interrogating gendered subjectivity provides possibilities for political change."[38] Through a process of mutual photography, Spence and her colleague, Rosy Martin, help one another play out before the camera the gendered roles they came to play and the price to the body, for both the heterosexual and the lesbian, of that social construction and its invisibilities. They discover the way in which the female body is suited up in images of the mind that reflect what culture constructs as "natural" gendered subjects; how uncomfortable that body becomes with itself because it always exceeds the fit of the suit; how very unsuitable the suit is.

Most importantly, Spence finds her way to the agency of the subject within what seems a totally determinative cultural environment:

We believe that we all have sets of personalized archetypal images in memory, images which are surrounded by vast chains of connotations and buried memories. In phototherapy we can dredge them up, reconstruct them, even reinvent them, so that they can work in our interests, rather than remaining the mythologies of others who have told us about that "self" which appears to be visible in various photographs. The point where image production in society intersects, through our snapshots, with personal memory is where a disruption can be caused, so that we never see ourselves in quite the same light again. (172)

The photographer can use the camera "for its unfixing, rather than its fixing abilities" (208). She can determine how she wants to put her body in the frame and for what purposes. By asking questions of the photograph she can reveal the invisible labor of the visible image or, as Watson suggests, "'de-censorize' unspeakables for women by making their operations and their normative power manifest."[39] She can even experiment with the (female) gaze itself, posing and demystifying the body of man and the signifying phallus.

Unlike Dillard, whose body metaphors lead her to the privileging of a universal subject, Spence practices a politics of fragmentation, collage, revision: "Out of the broken pieces of the self will come a subjectivity that acknowledges the fragmentation process, but which encompasses and embraces the parts and brings them into dialogue with each other. Out of this, for me, has come new activity, new acceptance, and changes I never considered possible" (198). In this way the body breaks into fragments, into pieces before her, resisting stabilization in the cultural construction of a unified subject which is always a fantasy of class and gender systems. By playing with the body in the picture, Spence discovers that the subject is always in process, that "there is no peeling away of layers to reveal a 'real' self, just a constant reworking process" (97). But Spence does not leave the body in pieces. The empowered subject can bring the body back together again, and again, and again.

VIII

AUTOBIOGRAPHICAL
MANIFESTOS

> Decolonization never takes place unnoticed,
> for it influences individuals and modifies
> them fundamentally. It transforms spectators
> crushed with their inessentiality into
> privileged actors, with the grandiose glare of
> history's floodlights upon them. It brings a
> natural rhythm into existence, introduced by
> new men, and with it a new language and a
> new humanity. Decolonization is the
> veritable creation of new men. But this
> creation owes nothing of its legitimacy to
> any supernatural power; the 'thing' which
> has been colonized becomes man during the
> same process by which it frees itself.
>
> Frantz Fanon, *The Wretched of the Earth*

In the process of putting their bodies in the picture, Cherríe Moraga
and Jo Spence extract the "I" from traditional narrative frames,
those oppressive histories and myths that censor certain bodies and
affect complicit self-censorship. Both women thus engage in overtly
political writing practices. As resisting subjects, they require and
develop resisting forms. Moraga incorporates poetry, prose analysis, journal entries, and sketches as well as multiple languages in a
dialogic engagement with history and fantasy.[1] Spence incorporates
bare chronological data with exhibition catalogs, interviews, articles, and photographs in a textual montage of self-portraiture and
its politics. These hybrid forms join other recent anti-"autobiographical" forms, what Caren Kaplan calls "out-law genres,"[2]
autobiographical but eclectically "errant" and culturally disruptive

154

writing practices. Kaplan includes *testimonio,* prison narratives, collective autoethnography, biomythography, and regulative psychobiography in her discussion of out-law genres. I want to look, in this final chapter, at another one of these out-law genres, what I call the autobiographical manifesto.

By way of introduction to this last autobiographical gesture, let me consider briefly what kinds of autobiographical strategies lead to what kind of political empowerments. One strategic move we might label mimesis. In this move the autobiographer positions herself as the subject of traditional autobiography: that is, she mimes the subjectivity of universal man. Speaking from this location proffers authority, legitimacy, and readability. It also proffers membership in the community of the fully human. For oppressed peoples, such membership can be psychologically and politically expedient and potent. Unselfconsciously embraced, however, mimesis invites recuperation as well as the promise of power, the maintenance of subjection to the self-definitions that bind.

Yet there is another side to this mirroring, the nitrate of mimicry, for something may be exposed here: an unauthorized speaker positions herself in the locale of the universal subject, thereby introducing a menacing suspicion of inexact correlation between representations. "As incomplete mirrors, as the waste of the system that produced the identity of the white male," suggests Linda Kintz, "[an unauthorized speaker] can only reflect back to the male subject a partial representation of himself, a reflection that is askew, flawed, not specular."[3] As a result, autobiographical mimicry may subtly contest the "natural," "commonsensical," "universal" categorizations of difference. In addition to its treacherous invitation to recuperation, then, mimesis may promise escape from an exclusionary configuration of subjectivity.

A second strategy for a contestatory autobiographical practice looks to the politics of fragmentation as the means to counter the centrifugal power of the old unitary self of western rationalism. Promoting the endless possibilities of self-fragmentation, the politics of fragmentation reveals the cultural constructedness of any coherent, stable, and universal subject. It may also reveal how problematic it is to maintain a decisive, unified point of departure for identity as the ground of a liberatory autobiographical practice since the exclusions of unified points are legion. But shattering the old notion of the unitary individual in favor of the split and multiply fragmented subject may not always serve emancipatory objectives; rather, it may serve further oppressive agendas, as Judith Butler cautions: "If oppression is to be defined in terms of a loss of autonomy by the oppressed, as well as a fragmentation or alienation within the psyche of the oppressed, then a theory which insists upon the inevitable fragmentation of the subject appears to reproduce and valorize the very oppression that must be overcome."[4] Any autobiographical practice that promotes endless fragmentation and a reified multiplicity might be counterproductive since the autobiographical subject would have to split itself beyond usefulness to be truly nonexclusionary. And it is difficult to coalesce a call to political action founded upon some kind of communal identity around a constantly deferred point of departure.[5]

Other strategies for oppositional autobiographical practice are grounded in conceptions of "experiential" politics. Difficulties negotiating the terrain of "the real" lead in fact to opposing orientations to experience. For some there is an experience outside representation to which the autobiographical text refers. And there is an ontological basis to identity in this experience. So a potentially emancipatory practice would be one that seeks to uncover the "true" self and the "truth" about that self's experience, the sources of oppression and strength, the essential difference in body, psyche, and modes of knowing and being in the world. For others such a positivist approach to experience neglects the relationship of experience to discourse, the artifactual nature of representation, the operations and apparati of cultural determinations. From this perspective, there is no subject outside language as textuality displaces any transparent experience. And since language operates to fix subjects, the subject of resistance can only engage in a drama of negativity, to allude to Julia Kristeva's theoretical frame, a drama of the what-I-am-not.[6] Now the resisting autobiographer lingers in the space of negativity where she refuses attempts to universalize any "us," "we," or "I." But once again she may be caught in an endless self-qualification that takes her further away from any community of interest and political action.

However problematic its strategies, autobiographical writing has played and continues to play a role in emancipatory politics. Autobiographical practices become occasions for restaging subjectivity, and autobiographical strategies become occasions for the staging of resistance. Thus within what Judith Butler calls "this conflicted cultural field"[7] the autobiographer can lay out an agenda for a changed relationship to subjectivity, identity, and the body. We see this agenda in recent texts by women who pursue self-consciously political autobiographical acts, who issue calls for new subjects, in texts I call autobiographical manifestos. Purposeful, bold, contentious, the autobiographical manifesto contests the old inscriptions, the old histories, the old politics, the *ancien régime*, by working to dislodge the hold of the universal subject through an expressly political collocation of a new "I." In service to a new "social reality," what Donna Haraway describes as "our most important political construction, a world-changing fiction,"[8] the manifesto offers an arena in which the revolutionary subject can insist on identity in service to an emancipatory politics, even if, as Robert K. Martin argues, that identity is "assumed."[9]

The Subject of Manifesto

Dictionary definitions suggest that a manifesto is a proof, a piece of evidence, a public declaration or proclamation, usually issued by or with the sanction of a sovereign prince or state, or by an individual or body of individuals whose proceedings are of public importance, for the purpose of announcing past actions and explaining the reasons or motives for actions announced as forthcoming. Within this definitional context seven constituent aspects of manifesto affect our discussion.

To appropriate/to contest sovereignty

As noted in the introduction, the universal subject consolidates sovereignty through exclusionary practices. These practices figure "others" as "not-an-individualized-'I,' " persons whose humanity is opaque, and whose membership in the human community is negated by relegation to what Nancy Hartsock describes as "a chaotic, disorganized, and anonymous collectivity."[10] Autobiographical manifestos issue from persons assigned to this anonymous collectivity who vigorously reject the sovereignty of this specular *ancien régime* and the dominance of the universal subject.

Through the manifesto, the autobiographical subject confronts the ghost of the identity assigned her by the old sovereign subject, what Paul Smith terms the ideological "I," a fixed object position representing culturally intelligible and authorized performances of identity. These fixed identifications (of "woman," "black," "lesbian," etc.) function as cultural templates for repetition. Repetition, however, breeds contempt; that is to say, repetition brings with it alterations precisely because, as Smith suggests, "imaginary identifications . . . are continually vulnerable to the registration of ever renewed and contradictory interpellations."[11] The autobiographical manifesto confronts this process directly: the tensions set in motion by contradictory identity assignments incite, to use revolutionary rhetoric, self-conscious encounters with the politics of identification and catalyze subjectivity around specific and oppositional contours of "I-ness." Resisting "the taken-for-granted ability of one small segment of the population to speak for all,"[12] the autobiographer purposefully locates herself as a subject, leaving behind the object status to which cultural identities have confined her.

To bring to light, to make manifest (literally struck with the hand)

Since awareness of the pressures to repeat certain cultural identifications is the ground of resistance to repetition, the difficult road to a liberatory autobiographical practice lies through the terrain of cultural critique. And so, when Cherríe Moraga comments in *Loving in the War Years* that "the Third World lesbian brings colored female sexuality with all its raggedy edges and oozing wounds—for better or for worse—into the light of day," she captures colloquially the political agenda of the autobiographical manifesto: to force issues "into the light of day."[13] Intent on bringing culturally marginalized experiences out from under the shadow of an undifferentiated otherness, the autobiographical manifesto anchors its narrative itinerary in the specificities and locales of time and space, the discursive surround, the material ground, the provenance of histories.

To bring things "into the light of day," to make manifest a perspective on identity and experience, affects an epistemological breakage of repetition. The legitimacy of a new or alternative knowledge located in the experience of the margins is affirmed.[14]

The autobiographical manifesto thus attempts to develop what Hartsock describes as "an account of the world as seen from the margins, an account which can expose the falseness of the view from the top and can transform the margins as well as the center. . . . an account of the world which treats our perspectives not as subjugated or disruptive knowledges, but as primary and constitutive of a different world." The individual story becomes the occasion for what Hartsock calls "standpoint epistemologies," analyses of specific confluences of social, psychological, economic, and political forces of oppression.[15] The trajectories, strategies, and tools of these analyses take various forms, some of which I will explore below as part of the enabling myths and motivating metaphors of resistance.

To announce publicly

Autobiographical writing is always a gesture toward publicity, displaying before an impersonal public an individual's interpretation of experience. The very impetus for contemporary autobiographical manifestos, however, lies in the recognition of a vexed relationship between what too easily becomes the binary opposition of the political and the personal. The early rallying cry of the white, middle-class feminist movement was "The personal is political." And through the last two decades the politics of personal relationships, the economics of reproduction, and the politics of psychosexual development have been central to feminist analyses in many fields. In challenging the hegemony of white middle-class feminism, however, theorists of multiple differences have differentiated the personal stakes and psychological impacts of systems of colonization, focusing on the personal experiences of multiple oppressions, of class, caste, race, gender, sexuality, nationality. In this more heterogeneous context, "the private" requires reconceptualization, as Aida Hurtado suggests when she emphasizes that "the political consciousness of women of Color stems from an awareness that the public is *personally* political. . . . There is no such thing as a private sphere for people of Color except that which they manage to create and protect in an otherwise hostile environment."[16] And so a cautionary gesture is necessary here. Different autobiographers come at the private/public duality from different experiences of oppression, from different locales in discourse. As a result the mapping of private/public politics may proceed to lay out different borderlines.

Hurtado argues that we need to attend to the relative positionality of specific women vis-à-vis the "middle-class white man," the prototype for the universal subject who stands centrally in the public space and whose standpoint determines the places of power, the margins of meaning, the geographies of knowledge. As a result the cartography of private space takes its contours from multiple spaces of adjacency. For instance, the white middle-class woman exists alongside "public man," sharing his private spaces. But the woman of color exists separately from that man, generally at a distance from his private space. Different alignments toward the dominant private space condition different cultural constructions of "woman," different cultural practices for women.[17]

The autobiographical manifesto asserts unqualifiedly, even exuberantly, both the politicization of the private and the personalization of the public, effectively troubling the binary complacencies of the *ancien régime* of selfhood with its easy dichotomization of private and public.[18] But the trajectory of its mappings must be considered in the specific cultural locations of the woman who issues the manifesto's call to action.

To perform publicly

While it might seem strange to repeat the former aspect of the autobiographical manifesto with a change of one word, it is important to note separately the performative aspect of the autobiographical manifesto. Expressly a public performance, the manifesto revels in the energetic display of a new kind of subject. The manifesto engages directly the cultural construction of identities and their sanctioned and legitimated performances, engaging the ideological systems pressing specific identities on specific persons. It takes a public stand on behalf of purposeful deflections, intervening in oppressive identity performances, troubling culturally authorized fictions.[19] Historicizing identity, the autobiographical manifesto implicitly, if not explicitly, insists on the temporalities and spatialities of identity and, in doing so, brings the everyday practices of identity directly into the floodlights of conscious display.

To speak as one of a group, to speak for a group

In the manifesto group identification, rather than radical individuality, is the rhetorical ground of appeal. During her public performance the manifesto speaker positions herself expressly as a member of a group or community, an auto/ethnographer, so to speak.[20] The "I" anchored in collectivity is the "I" of what Rita Felski à la Jurgen Habermas labels a counter-public sphere.[21] Counter-public spheres are multiple, invoking identification around various experiences of oppression and exclusions from the central or centrifugal bourgeois public sphere and its ideology of the universal subject. While Felski's particular interest focuses on the dynamics of the feminist counter-public sphere, which she says "does not claim a representative universality but rather offers a critique of cultural values from the standpoint of women as a marginalized group within society," for the purposes of this discussion we need to emphasize the existence of multiple counter-public spheres that operate along analogous lines and generate their specific critiques of universalizing spheres of influence.[22]

Critique in this instance is motivated by the autobiographical subject's desire to contest dominant discourses surrounding the subject, discourses through which the subject is objectified in strategic difference making and rendered abnormative. Moreover, the subject in this instance of the autobiographical manifesto speaks as a member of a nonhegemonic group or counter-public sphere, and that group too has what Mikhail Bakhtin suggests is its own "social dialect," its language/s. For Bakhtin it is through the conflictual, supplementary, consonant action of heteroglossia that consciousness emerges. Psyche, sociality, language converge to link consciousness to critique. But critique does not proceed univocally. Critique is accompanied by what Mae Gwendolyn Henderson describes as "testimony." According to Henderson, testimony derives from the subject's "*dialectic of identity*," that is, from her acknowledgment of a communality of "history, language, and culture" with others of the group.[23]

In the manifesto communitarian auto/ethnography functions as a kind of "nationalism." Bernice Johnson Reagon captures the nationalism inherent in communitarian politics when she suggests that a liberatory space "should be a nurturing space where you sift out what people are saying about you and decide who you really are. And you take the time to try to construct within yourself and within your community who you would be if you were running society . . . [this is] nurturing, but it is also nationalism. At a certain stage, nationalism is crucial to a people if you are ever going to impact as a group in your own interest."[24] Nationalism determines the specific moves through which the manifesto negotiates the landscapes of identity and difference. Postulating a testimonial nationalism, the manifesto quarrels with *"competitive* discourses"[25] and through its narrative itinerary stages a breakage in repetitions. As it does so it struggles to resist the totalizing agenda of the universal subject and proclaims the viability of a nonuniversal position.[26]

To speak to the future

The generic contracts of western literary practices promise something, but what exactly they promise is subject to various theoretical interpretations. Traditionally, western autobiography involves a contractual obligation in which the autobiographer engages in a narrative itinerary of self-disclosure, retrospective summation, self-justification. Thus critics of autobiography, including such contemporary theorists as Philippe Lejeune, emphasize the retrospective aspect of autobiography. Postmodern theorists have shifted the trope to the autobiographical text as the site of a deadly specularity. Paul de Man, for instance, argues that "autobiography veils a defacement of the mind of which it is itself the cause."[27] As a result, "the autobiographical project" becomes, according to Paul Smith, "a privileged kind of impossibility, always given over to uncertainty, undecidability, and, finally, to death."[28] But other theorists resist what they consider the dead end of death in autobiography. For instance, Kathleen Woodward talks of the writing of autobiography as taking place not under the sign of death, defacement, or desire but under the sign of anxiety, "a state of expecting a danger and preparing oneself for it, although the danger may be unknown to oneself, that is, not consciously known." Attempting to suggest a difference between male and female narratives, Woodward suggests that where men may write under the sign of desire and its "emphasis . . . on past loss," women write under the sign of anxiety for future loss.[29]

The autobiographical manifesto offers another sign. Here the "I" does not write under the sign of desire or the sign of anxiety. Rather the "I" writes under the sign of hope and what Hélène Cixous calls "the very possibility of change," emphasizing the generative and prospective thrust of autobiography.[30] Calling the subject into the future, the manifesto attempts to actively position the subject in a potentially liberated future distanced from the constraining and oppressive identifications inherent in the everyday practices of the *ancien régime*. Thus while the manifesto looks back in what Teresa de Lauretis terms "the critical negativity" of theoretical critique, it also gestures forward in "the affirmative positivity of its politics" to new spaces for subjectivity.[31]

Since new interpretations and hopeful futures are "crucially bound up with power," the manifesto always foregrounds the relationship of subjectivity to power.[32] It insists on new interpretations as a means of wresting power, resisting universalized repetitions that essentialize and naturalize. In service to that political cause, the autobiographer issues the call for a new, revolutionary subject, offers an agenda for "I" transformations. Ultimately, then, the manifesto proffers a utopian vision, "a 'waking dream' of the possible," writes Françoise Lionnet, "which might inspire us to see beyond the constraints of the here and now to the idealized vision of a perfect future."[33]

Hélène Cixous's Medusa

I have tried to elaborate some descriptive markers as a way of stimulating certain ways of reading the subject of the autobiographical manifesto. Like theory generally, they are meant not to rigidify and specify all the workings of the autobiographical manifesto but to suggest some lines of inquiry and some originating points for considering variations and problematics. I turn now to a consideration of three autobiographical manifestos.

With its vibrant, provocative, always troubling but never dull prose, Hélène Cixous's "The Laugh of the Medusa" offers a flamboyant and gutsy performance of gender, enacts what Friedrich

Nietzsche describes in *The Will to Power* as "the magic of the extreme, the seduction that everything extreme exercises."[34] Cixous's provocative "Laugh" is certainly a manifesto. The language that establishes its tenor is the language of revolution—future oriented, explosive, subversive. Its expressed gesture is toward both the breaking up of the old and the positing of the new: "As there are no grounds for establishing a discourse, but rather an arid millennial ground to break," she proclaims, "what I say has at least two sides and two aims: to break up, to destroy; and to foresee the unforeseeable, to project" (245). The prose abounds in the terminology and metaphors of revolutionary warfare. There are "sovereigns" to fight, an "empire" to "seize" by a "militant" (253) who goes on "scouting mission[s]" (248). A freedom fighter, Cixous's woman recognizes that "there's no room for her if she's not a he. If she's a her-she, it's in order to smash everything, to shatter the framework of institutions, to blow up the law, to break up the 'truth' with laughter" (258).

For Cixous the revolutionary is a woman fighting for "Woman." Here she promotes a communitarian identity politics based on a foundationalist notion of woman. If the goal of her manifesto is to foster effective revolution, the means to victory may indeed be a "strategic" essentialism, a strategic universalization of Woman (although not biological woman) operating at a specific historical juncture with a "common or shared epistemological standpoint."[35] Cixous herself seems aware of the difference between strategic and ontological essentialism when she declares: "I do not deny that the effects of the past are still with us. But I refuse to strengthen them by repeating them, to confer upon them an irremovability the equivalent of destiny, to confuse the biological and the cultural" (245).

For Cixous the enemies are two: man the oppressor and woman without a body. The former is the entirety of patriarchal culture with its fantasy of the normative human/male. Thus she metaphorizes the male body as a state dick-tatorship (259). The latter enemy is "a woman without a body, dumb, blind," who can never be "a good fighter" because she functions only as a "servant of the militant male, his shadow" (250). Man is the sovereign to be deposed, woman without a body, the specular peasantry holding up the state dick-tatorship. To fight the war of liberation, Cixous's freedom fighter must capture the female body, the lost territory of subjectivity, releasing it from its status as lack, its relegated negativity.

In order to carry out a revolutionary plot, the speaking "I" must become an agent provocateur, infiltrating herself doubly, inside her body and inside history. The two agendas, the one individual and the other collective, are affected through the revolutionary medium of language since writing will "give her back her goods, her pleasures, her organs, her immense bodily territories which have been kept under seal" (250). It will also facilitate her "shattering entry into history, which has always been based *on her suppression*" (250). For Cixous only the writing "I" has the potential to become the revolutionary "I" since writing enables woman to come into agency and to escape the confinement of objectification.[36] The battleground for the freedom fighter is thus the battleground of state representationalism, of language itself. Since language is the revolutionary's arsenal, to be "a good fighter" (250) is to wield "the antilogos weapon" (250), "scoring [her] feats in written and oral language" (251). Hers is a revolutionary mouth, an oral insurgency: "If woman has always functioned 'within' the discourse of man, a signifier that has always referred back to the opposite signifier which annihilates its specific energy and diminishes or stifles its very different sounds, it is time for her to dislocate this 'within,' to explode it, turn it around, and seize it; to make it hers, containing it, taking it in her own mouth, biting that tongue with her very own teeth to invent for herself a language to get inside of" (257). Language must become the revolutionary palace, the symbolic (in the double sense of the term) bastille to be seized: "Writing is precisely *the very possibility of change,* the space that can serve as a springboard for subversive thought, the precursory movement of a transformation of social and cultural structures" (249). And this text, this instance of writing, this "laugh" is such a space of revolutionary seizure and transformation.

To explode the stabilities of phallic history and assassinate authoritarian historians, the revolutionary writing subject must deploy a "feminine practice of writing," a writing whose materiality derives from the recovery of the female body. The relationship between revolutionary practices and the female body coalesces in the manifesto around the two figures of Dora and the Medusa.

Cixous positions Dora as a heroic precursor of the new revolutionary woman, a figure of the formerly repressed woman of "the poetic body" (257), a woman who resisted the inscriptions of Freud's hystericization of her. In this way Dora is identified with Freud's later reference to female sexuality as "the Dark Continent." The manifesto's speaker then links the revolutionary agenda of her emancipatory psychosexual politics to the Black Nationalist movement pressing its anticolonial, anti-imperialist agenda during the late 1960s and 1970s. Like "the colonized peoples of yesterday, the workers, the nations, the species off whose backs the history of men has made its gold" (258), woman is positioned under the sign of oppression/repression. *"The Dark Continent is neither dark nor unexplorable,"* the speaker declares: "It is still unexplored only because we've been made to believe that it was too dark to be explorable. And because they want to make us believe that what interests us is the white continent, with its monuments to Lack" (255). In fact, the speaker goes so far as to identify women with black nationalists: "We the precocious, we the repressed of culture . . . we are black and we are beautiful" (248). Thus the revolutionary potential of woman is magnified by her positioning as surrogate black African: "You can incarcerate them, slow them down, get away with the old Apartheid routine, but for a time only" (247). Blurring the apparently stable boundaries between the personal/conjugal "subjective economy" (259) and the political economy, she links the psychosexual drama of the repressed to the political/economic exploitation of the oppressed: the personal is political, the political personal.[37]

If Dora is the foremother of the New Woman, then Medusa is her mythical mentor. While mythically Medusa figures as a deadly threat to male power and destiny, in the utopian space of new women she functions differently: "You only have to look at the Medusa straight on to see her. And she's not deadly. She's beautiful and she's laughing" (255). Literally laughter breaks up the assembled and calm planes of the face; and as the movement of laughter breaks up the consolidated features of the face, laughter aligns the human with the animal, with the grotesque body. The effect of laughter on the body elides the gap between species and gestures toward the instability of boundaries separating one species from another, unhinging secure placements in hierarchies of meaning. It also breaks up the elegant, cool, controlled planes of statuesque representationalism, forcing the irrational through the lucid planes of reason and control. The sound itself breaks through the language of phallocentrism, a call from beyond, from the body, from elsewhere. Ultimately laughter breaks up the consolidations of a universalized, rational, unifying truth, destabilizing foundational notions of truth by traducing the boundaries of binary opposites: control and abandon, reason and the irrational, body and mind.

As the vatic representative of the oppressed, the seer of the dark continent, the narrator both calls for and practices a revolutionary writing practice that "laughs." Of a feminine practice, she writes: "It is impossible to *define* a feminine practice of writing, and this is an impossibility that will remain, for this practice can never be theorized, enclosed, coded—which doesn't mean that it doesn't exist. . . . It will be conceived of only by subjects who are breakers of automatism, by peripheral figures that no authority can ever subjugate" (253). While definitions confine and delimit, writing can explode old practices, disrupt old patterns. Throughout, the narrator's analysis of the conditions of women's silence and her alienation from her body proceed by turns indirectly and directly. As Linda Singer suggests in her analysis of the comparative politics of the texts of Michel Foucault and Cixous, "to establish her differences from hegemonic forms of authority, Cixous dispenses with or conspicuously transgresses much of the textual etiquette and many of the conventions of academic discourse. Her texts are constructed eclectically. . . . By transgressing disciplinary and paradigmatic boundaries, Cixous positions her work within a different economy of legitimation. Dispensing with conventional footnotes and attributions, she constructs her authority as separate and apart from validation through the chain of fathers."[38] She also destabilizes the notion of narrative progression, moving forward through allusion and language rather than through idea, analysis, and development.

Moreover, in the flamboyant performance of this revolutionary "woman," certain stylistic strategies are deployed exuberantly. Iconoclastic statements common to the manifesto abound: "Let the priests tremble, we're going to show them our sexts!" (255). Excesses of language signal a revolutionary playfulness and cavalier rebellion against the automaticism of common coinage. Thus new

words are formed—*erotogeneity* (246), *frigidified* (247), *sexts*.
Forceful imperatives explode on the page: "Write your self, inscribe
the breath of the whole woman" (250). Pronominal boundaries are
breached as the narrator intermingles the interlocutor and the self,
fluidly moving through the "I," "you," "she," and "who" as a way
of disrupting the certain differentiations separating object and subject, the "I" and the "you." Moreover, the narrator often shifts her
interlocutor—to the "you" of the other woman, to the "You" of
the oppressor. Within a particular passage the narrator shifts perspectives, pronominal locations, and defies the boundaries between
the "I" and the other so that the relative positioning of narrator and
interlocutor seems undecidable. She dismantles the old pronominal
relationships as part of her revolutionary agenda to explode the old
engendering of language.[39] "Blaz[ing] *her* trail in the symbolic," the
narrator destabilizes the old certainties separating pronouns and
the old symbolic configurations of gender, creating what she herself
calls "the chaosmos of the 'personal' " (258). She is herself "flying/
stealing" in "the gesture that jams sociality" (258).

In jamming sociality with the language of the body, the narrator
inaugurates the utopian regime of the New Woman, that newly
coined sovereign. Cixous thus heralds the new age, one in which the
New Woman's "libido will produce far more radical effects of
political and social change than some might like to think" (252).
The new subject is constituted of a "vatic" bisexuality that "doesn't
annul differences but stirs them up, pursues them, increases their
number" (254). In each of us reside "both sexes," which are "variously manifest and insistent according to each person, male or
female," and in each is present the "nonexclusion either of the
difference or of one sex," with the result that the new subject
contains the "multiplication of the effects of the inscription of
desire, over all parts of my body and the other body" (254). This
newly constituted subject will join with others, men and women,
"to render obsolete the former relationship and all its consequences, to consider the launching of a brand-new subject, alive,
with defamilialization" (261). Radical change will occur in love as
Cixous ends her revolutionary manifesto with an almost scriptural
call to love: "In the beginning are our differences. The new love
dares for the other. . . . She comes in, comes-in-between herself me
and you, between the other me where one is always infinitely more

than one and more than me, without the fear of ever reaching a limit" (263–64). With no limits, "she finds not her sum but her differences. I am for you what you want me to be at the moment you look at me in a way you've never seen me before: at every instant" (264). With the Law "blown up," violence, volcanic eruption, destruction subside into the aftermath of a pronominal revolution of new love. The nationalistic revolution with epistemological, psychosexual, ontological, and teleological implications finds its utopian conclusion by ushering in a new history.

Serpentine Subjects and Pastoral Manifesto

The rhetoric of Gloria Anzaldúa's autobiographical manifesto is not a rhetoric of revolutionary explosiveness and exuberant or excessive performance. Anzaldúa's manifesto progresses through the rhetorical focus on the geographical subject signaled in the title *Borderlands/La Frontera: The New Mestiza*. For Anzaldúa the topography of the borderland is simultaneously the suturing space of multiple oppressions and the potentially liberatory space through which to migrate toward a new subject position. The geographical trope is at once psychological, physical, metaphysical, and spiritual, since it functions as a space where cultures conflict, contest, and reconstitute one another. Like Cixous, Anzaldúa actively constitutes and projects a revolutionary subject through metaphor—here the *mestiza* who "has gone from being the sacrificial goat to becoming the officiating priestess at the crossroads."[40]

Because Anzaldúa's text so persistently invokes geography, I want to consider its pastoral qualities and their relationship to the subject of manifesto. I do not mean to imply here that Anzaldúa writes in the pastoral tradition, for that would be to define her manifesto through and contain it within the very history she challenges. I do want to consider what silenced history subtends western notions of the pastoral in order to explore the ways in which Anzaldúa's manifesto resists official histories.

The word *pastoral* invokes a long-lived western tradition, originating with the classical authors Theocritus and Virgil. It is a tradition self-conscious of itself, since later pastoral exercises often echo implicitly or explicitly Virgil and other classic pastoral texts.

The speaker in pastoral evidences knowledge of and thus authorizes his participation in that tradition. Access to the pastoral speaking position is determined by cultural possessions—of specific educational, class, gender, and racial identities. The pastoral speaker tends to be a sophisticated speaker of the aristocratic or middling classes. Even if that speaker speaks as a shepherd, that is, as one of what is called in the theory the "low," the use of literary language and formal rhetoric as well as the thick web of allusion identify the speaker as the sophisticated artist who assumes a place in the genealogy of high culture.[41] Obviously then only certain people can claim a pastoral speaking position. Most often, though not exclusively, the pastoral subject has been male, primarily a privileged male artist. Lowly people, people of color, women, peasants, may have been subjects in pastoral, objects of a pastoral lament, but they have not had the same access to pastoral's primary speaking position.

The term *pastoral* invokes the topography of bucolic spaces, broad landscapes, rural environments, environments that locate pastoral subjects close to nature. In this landscape a simpler, more direct, and less mediated and artificial relationship to experience plays out. Because of its antithesis to the urban environment, pastoral space seems to harken imaginatively if not specifically to an earlier time (in various pastoral visions the golden age, the arcadian scene, the innocent state of childhood), a kind of timeless moment. Pursuing a pastoral relationship to the land and experience, the pastoral speaker thus travels (literally or imaginatively) away from an urban center or metropolis to the rural or local scene. In this space the speaker finds a home-away-from-home, sometimes in the literal sense but most often in a metaphorical sense. The pastoral space (even if only the space of consciousness)[42] promises fullness, and in that fullness lies the possibility of reinvigoration, reorientation, respite from corruption, perhaps a new innocence, perhaps access to "truer" values and selves.

But the simplicity is part of the illusion of pastoral spaces, of that inviting home. In the pastoral mode some power beyond the rural space seems to press ineluctably upon the scene, if kept at uncertain bay. Call the nonpastoral space the metropolis, call it progress, call it urbanization, call it an imperial "civilization." That is, there is a sense of fragility about the pastoral way of life as the grip of the metropolis becomes stronger and stronger, insinuating itself into a simpler way of life that cannot forestall an inevitable transition to another way of life.[43] Or call it time, for there is an implied relationship between this space and time.[44] While pastoral spaces seem to be ahistoricized spaces, the time of history actually functions as a subterranean subtext of pastoral.[45] If the surface of pastoral promotes timeless spatiality, the subtext introduces historical specificity, the very history that undermines the pastoral vision, the very history from which the subject of pastoral would escape.

In that desire to escape the corruptions of the metropolitan center, the pastoral speaker often journeys to colonized territories, there to identify with indigenous peoples, those who seem to have maintained that close relationship to nature and to the essential core of being. And so there is a long history that conjoins pastoral visions and colonization. Virgil's *Eclogues* emerged at the cultural moment when Rome had consolidated its imperial power. The opening up of "new worlds" in the Renaissance renewed interest in pastoral narrative.[46] And throughout the centuries of exploration pastoral descriptions punctuated travel narratives of explorers and colonizers. The pastoral mode has often been complicit in imperial and colonial projects[47] because even when they identify with the "low" or indigenous peoples against the "high culture" of the distant metropolis, subjects of pastoral journeys take a residue of representational violence with them into the countryside. After all, the lowly are projections of the universal subject's desire for innocence, integrity, and uncomplicated meaning. They are not assigned a subjectivity of their own.

With the emergence of national resistance movements and various postcolonial writing practices in the First World, critiques of the politics of pastoral emerge as the indigenous "shepherds" learn to speak and write, not just be spoken as and for. In America, slave narratives functioned as powerful antipastoral challenges to the myth of the southern way of life. Those narratives insisted on making vivid the price of pastoral visions, the exploitation of slaves whose labor underwrote the idyll of country life. Moreover, the narrative of Harriet Jacobs, for instance, emphasized the price exacted on the body of the slave woman to make the pastoral environment thrive. Anzaldúa's autobiographical practice participates in this antipastoral tradition, but with the difference that she writes a new revolutionary subject into being.

Anzaldúa fights the collective amnesia that the colonial situation engenders in borderlands people by engaging in a project of anamnesis: a recollection or remembrance of a past efficiently erased by the forces of oppression and acculturation. But here the amamnesis is not so much personal, albeit the personal punctuates the analysis, as it is collective. The narrator looks through the opacities of colonization for the remnants of the traditions of multiple cultures. For the narrator's purposes, the mythic possibilities of the occluded cultural past are the provocative source of reinterpretation, the new nationalism of the *mestiza* that will encourage a breakage in the repetition of what Françoise Lionnet describes as "historically and Eurocentrically determined racial metaphors of the self."[48]

But the official histories are multiple, not monolithic. There are histories written upon the land, histories that situate the *mestiza* as a certain kind of subject. And so Anzaldúa works to debunk not only colonial history but the history of the colonized as well. It is not enough that she rediscover the land as it was in precolonial days; she must explore the oppressions even within that precolonial landscape, for oftentimes Arcadian ideals, even if energized for revolutionary struggles, are patriarchally organized. Ketu Katrak has cautioned that "in nationalist movements 'traditions' tend to get glorified in order to counteract colonialist, racist attitudes that desecrate native culture. The dangers of reifying 'traditions,' of ahistoricizing them as the transcendent emblems of a culture, are felt most negatively by women, particularly after independence when the rationale of justifying tradition against the enemy is no longer needed" (168). So as a woman, Anzaldúa must untangle the patriarchal web of precolonial history. And in order to counteract the trouble with gender in Aztecan culture, she posits another kind of Golden Age.

To pursue a new nationalism of transformative "hybridization," Anzaldúa's narrator elaborates an "empowering and enabling countermyth."[49] Pressing backward and ever backward through the history of the Mexican and Aztec people, she finds a source of inspiration and countermythology in the "complete" figure of the pre-Azteca-Mexica great goddess. Recovering a precolonial history, the narrator finds that the Goddess *Coatlicue,* "Lady of the Serpent Skirt, contained and balanced the dualities of male and female, light and dark, life and death" (32). Explicitly linked to the Medusa of Greek mythology and of Cixous's manifesto, Coatlicue is "a symbol of the fusion of opposites: the eagle and the serpent, heaven and the underworld, life and death, mobility and immobility, beauty and horror" (47). This serpent state refuses a dualistic ontology, captures imaginatively that "something more than mere duality," that "third perspective."

Inspired by the discovery of Coatlicue, the narrator proceeds to rewrite the history of the Azteca-Mexica nation. She refuses the common story of La Chingada's (Malinche's) culpability, setting forth instead another interpretation of Cortes's victory over the Aztecs: "the ruling elite had subverted the solidarity between men and women and between noble and commoner" (34). Once the Coatlicue "state," in both senses of the word, had been undermined and superseded by a hierarchical/dualistic state, defeat by colonizing armies followed inevitably. This cultural reorganization accounted for colonization, not a discrete moment of a woman's treachery. Adding greater complexity to the cultural history of her peoples, integrating an analysis of the oppressions of gender to those of class and race, the narrator multiplies the sources of colonization. Doing so, she begins to transform the experience of oppression into the call for a new consciousness, and the recovery of an alternative cultural myth empowers her to both critique the sovereign regime and to countervalorize an alternative nationalism. And so Anzaldúa does not linger in this Golden Age of Coatlicue. She carries the history forward and reconstitutes the Coatlicue state as the consciousness of a new kind of subject.

For the narrator, Coatlicue effectively becomes "in my psyche, the mental picture and symbol of the instinctual in its collective impersonal, prehuman. She, the symbol of the dark sexual drive, the chthonic (underworld), the feminine, the serpentine movement of sexuality, of creativity, the basis of all energy and life" (35). Consequently, the recovery of the Coatlicue state is the recovery of body and soul, spirit and matter, that "other mode of consciousness" which "facilitates images from the soul and the unconscious through dreams and the imagination" (37). The insinuating serpent is the figure for the animistic recovery of a larger consciousness, one fuller than the rational self of the universal subject. Such a state uproots the source of violence in the West, the specularization of things and people, and the consequent erasure of spirit from the physical realm (37). Thus the strategic significance of the "serpent skirt" individually and collectively derives from the intervention it encourages in the repeat performances of the "terrorized" self, a self that blames, hates, and divides into the "accusatory, persecutory, judgmental" on the one hand and "the object of contempt" on the other (45), a repressed self from which the body is banished.

Movement toward the new consciousness, the new nationalistic state, is a geographical move that becomes the "crossing," or *travesia,* into a "new territory" (48). Crossing to this "state" the old identities crack, shed and give way to a newly constitutive knowledge that exposes the "falseness of the view from the top":

> Every time she makes "sense" of something, she has to "cross over," kicking a hole out of the old boundaries of the self and slipping under or over, dragging the old skin along, stumbling over it. It hampers her movement in the new territory, dragging the ghost of the past with her. It is a dry birth, a breech birth, a screaming birth, one that fights her every inch of the way. It is only when she is on the other side and the shell cracks open and the lid from her eyes lifts that she sees things in a different perspective. It is only then that she makes the connections, formulates the insights. It is only then that her consciousness expands a tiny notch, another rattle appears on the rattlesnake tail and the added growth slightly alters the sounds she makes. Suddenly the repressed energy rises, makes decisions, connects with conscious energy and a new life begins. (49)

A new autobiographical practice dislodges the old practice of "autonomy," which the narrator describes as "a boulder on my path that I keep crashing into" (50). The old notion of the sovereign self of western autobiographical practice fades from consciousness as she surrenders her conscious "I" to the "power" of her "inner self, the entity that is the sum total of all my reincarnations, the godwoman in me" (50). Surrendering to her mythical and cultural inheritance, she recovers a new sense of subjectivity, a subjectivity multiplied in more than "one" person:

And someone in me takes matters into our own hands, and eventually, takes dominion over serpents—over my own body, my sexual activity, my soul, my mind, my weaknesses and strengths. Mine. Ours. Not the heterosexual white man's or the colored man's or the state's or the culture's or the religion's or the parents'—just ours, mine. And suddenly I feel everything rushing to a center, a nucleus. All the lost pieces of myself come flying from the deserts and the mountains and the valleys, magnetized toward that center. *Completa*. Something pulsates in my body, a luminous thin thing that grows thicker every day. Its presence never leaves me. I am never alone. That which abides: my vigilance, my thousand sleepless serpent eyes blinking in the night, forever open. And I am not afraid. (51)

The new consciousness leads to a state of openness, not self-closure; it is not individual but transindividual, not unitary but multiple. Thus the narrator of *Borderlands/La Frontera* configures the Coatlicue-state in its psychological and political dimensions as a space through which to negotiate ambivalence and heteroglossia.

The new state is achieved through the representational politics of language. In counter-pastoral as in pastoral spaces, the role of the artist is central, as creator of an alternative world. Like Cixous, the revolutionary subject of *Borderlands/La Frontera* must constitute her new subjectivity from her languages. While Anzaldúa specifies three predominant cultural identities constitutive of her borderlands experience—Anglo, Mexican, Indian—she also multiplies the matrices of identifications, the serpent eyes, when she explores the multiplicity of languages spoken throughout her experiential domain. The tongue is the tongue of a linguistic borderland, a wet surface where multiple languages meet and mix, slip and slide. Thus at the beginning of her manifesto, Anzaldúa issues a challenge to the Anglo reader and to the sovereignty of English as the language of self-representation in the United States:

The switching of "codes" in this book from English to Castillian Spanish to the North Mexican dialect to Tex-Mex to a sprinking of Nahuatl to a mixture of all of these, reflects my language, a new language—the language of the Borderlands. There, at the juncture of cultures, languages cross-pollinate and are revitalized; they die and are born. Presently this infant language, this bastard language,

> Chicano Spanish, is not approved by any society. But we Chicanos
> no longer feel that we need to beg entrance, that we need always to
> make the first overture—to translate to Anglos, Mexicans and Lati-
> nos, apology blurting out of our mouths with every step. Today we
> ask to be met halfway. This book is our invitation to you—from the
> new *mestizas*. (Preface)

In not apologizing for the agglomerative linguistic potpourri that is
the language of her autobiographical project, in resisting the pressure to translate the Spanish passages for the Anglo reader, the
manifesto's narrator refuses to reconcile her self-portraiture with
the dominant forms of subjectivity in the West or with the call to
univocity. Many languages intermingle with one another, in a state
of nonhierarchical multiplicity, creating a hybrid language that
captures the multiplicity within the speaking subject and resists the
seductive call to recuperation into the power of the one and the
same tongue. The narrator of *Borderlands/La Frontera* embraces
her multiple voices, multiple identities, multiple positionalities:
Mexican, Anglo, Indian. "I will no longer be made to feel ashamed
of existing. I will have my voice: Indian, Spanish, white. I will have
my serpent's tongue—my woman's voice, my sexual voice, my
poet's voice. I will overcome the tradition of silence" (59). Fighting
the "linguistic terrorism" of the cultural position of Chicanas, she
proclaims the nationalistic allegiance to her specific tongue/s.

The new mestiza works to transcend a dualism that inevitably
hierarchizes everything and thereby determines what histories are
recorded, what voices are heard, what epistemological projects
succeed, what ontological status people bear. She does so through
the autobiographical practice of *metissage,* to use a phrase from
Lionnet's theoretical vocabulary. In the spaces of *metissage,* suggests Lionnet, "multiplicity and diversity are affirmed. . . . For it is
only by imagining nonhierarchical modes of relation among cultures that we can address the crucial issues of indeterminacy and
solidarity. . . . *Metissage* is such a concept and a practice: it is the
site of undecidability and indeterminacy, where solidarity becomes
the fundamental principle of political action against hegemonic
languages."[50]

In fact, she seems determined to speak in tongues and to do so in
the two senses of the phrase Henderson elaborates. She participates

in both glossolalia and heteroglossia. Henderson reminds us that glossolalia usually connotes "the particular, private, closed, and privileged communication between the congregant and the divinity," while heteroglossia refers to "the ability to speak in the multiple languages of public discourse."[51] Through her unique blend of multiple languages Anzaldúa finds a means to represent an ineffable serpent spirit. As tribal storytelling, her self-representational practice induces a "shamanic state" in which her "awakened dreams" (70) enable her to play with crossings of borderlands, with crossings between "my Self" and "the world's soul" in a great "dialogue." Through the great materiality of language she "writes the myths in me, the myths I am, the myths I want to become" and thus feels the power of transformation, the utopian power of recreation, reconstitution, resistance: "My soul makes itself through the creative act. It is constantly remaking and giving birth to itself through my body. It is this learning to live with *la Coatlicue* that transforms living in the Borderlands from a nightmare into a numinous experience. It is always a path/state to something else" (73). But her practice is not only personal but political as she captures the relationship of public discourses to consciousness. This is the discursive borderland where subjectivity emerges out of what Henderson calls the dialogue with difference and the dialectic of identity going on inside her. And the material changes of the written language on the page visualize for the reader the sinuosities of both dialogue and dialectic. This linguistic sinuosity is serpentine work.

The new subject is also the bodied rather than disembodied subject. And that is why the language of the text is replete with physical description and bodily metaphor. If the body is the source of an identity that leads to oppression, the sexed body, the racialized body, then the body must be taken back and honored on the way to speech and writing. "Only through the body, through the pulling of the flesh," the narrator writes, "can the human soul be transformed. And for images, words, stories to have this transformative power, they must arise from the human body—flesh and bone—and from the Earth's body—stone, sky, liquid, soil. This work, these images, piercing tongue or ear lobes with cactus needles, are my offerings, are my Aztecan blood sacrifices" (75). Through the text the body is deployed in endless metaphors of movement, meaning, and metamorphosis, the most provocative of which is the metaphor of the serpent, privileged here against a western mythology that denigrated the serpent.

The serpent as female im/personation and as agent provocateur insinuates itself throughout the narrator's text in a "quickening serpent movement" (81). Like Cixous's, the rhetorical style and structural arrangement of Anzaldúa's manifesto reflect her new *mestiza* consciousness in a performance of the very discursive slippages and tongues she elaborates. Here too we find a pronomial fluidity as the "I" becomes a "she" and the "she" an "I" and both a "we." The narrator breaks the formal boundaries that characterize the *ancien régime,* that old structure of domination through hierarchization. Multiply voiced in its languages, the text does not work toward a totalized vision but celebrates the multiplicity of eyes, voices, and speaking positions that engage in dialogue with one another. Poems, critical essays, prose evocations, fragments from other poets and writers, fragments of street languages, all combine to capture the vitality of cultural politics, the interdependencies of identities, the collage of the new subject. Finally, they coalesce in a defiant call to communal action: "Stubborn, persevering, impenetrable as stone, yet possessing a malleability that renders us unbreakable, we, the *mestizas* and *mestizos,* will remain" (64).

Anzaldúa's invocation of borderlands and her call to the politics of a new subject refuses the traditional pastoral dualism of country and city spaces. Anzaldúa promotes borderlands, ones inscribed on her body and on her tongue as well as on the land. For borderlands are spaces in which history is intensified rather than escaped and where it can never be fixed. Her geography becomes fluid rather than fixed in its oppositional politics. Multiplying identities and histories creates a homelessness—a homelessness that undermines any secure anchorage in one history, even the history that becomes a national romance. The figure of the borderlands also foregrounds the constructed nature of boundaries, including the boundaries of the subject. And so unlike traditional pastoral speakers, Anzaldúa does not linger in the space of pastoral nostalgia. There is a sense of something that has been lost, but her autobiographical narrative takes us further than a whispering loss. As a counter-pastoral manifesto, *Borderlands/La Frontera* interrupts the cycle of nostalgia—both the nostalgia of nativist history, which Edward V. Said has critiqued,[52] and the nostalgia of personal homelessness. In fact, Anzaldúa creates an empowered subject out of language, the language through which she braids the various histories that cannot be escaped.

Beyond the Subject to the Cyborg

Donna Haraway's "A Manifesto for Cyborgs: Science, Technology, and Socialist Feminism in the 1980s" is not an autobiographical manifesto in the ways that Cixous's and Anzaldúa's texts are, but her essay provides a third point from which to consider the possibilities of revolutionary subjectivity.[53] In her "ironic," or, as she suggests, "blasphemous," manifesto, Haraway argues "for the cyborg as a fiction mapping our social and bodily reality and as an imaginative resource suggesting some very fruitful couplings" (191). To celebrate the cyborg is to employ a "postmodern strategy" (194) through which to resist any unitary and therefore imperial subject secured by identitarian politics. Haraway would dislodge all sovereigns, not only the *ancien sovereign* of western discursive practices but the *nouveau sovereigns* of Marxism and feminism with their "dream of a common language" because any dream of a common language, any dream "of a perfectly faithful naming of experience is a totalizing and imperialist one" (215).

Working to undo the old teleology of the western humanist tradition, including its psychoanalytical and Marxist agendas, Haraway deploys the cyborg metaphor in order to subvert the old story of origins, original wholeness, developmental individuation, paternal inheritance, engenderment: "The cyborg is a creature in a postgender world; it has no truck with bisexuality, pre-Oedipal symbiosis, unalienated labor, or other seductions to organic wholeness through a final appropriation of all the powers of the parts into a higher unity" (192). All these narratological templates for identity politics look backward to a natural point of origin, and for Haraway points of origin need to be exposed for the fictions they ultimately are. Points of origin are politically suspect precisely because they map a totalizing uniformity on diverse peoples and experiences through a specified locus of identification. And identity politics are exclusionary, fractured, partial (197). The problem with any "we" is that its deployment colludes in the colonizing naturalization of categories such as "woman." The contemporary project must be to make the category of woman and the category of man evaporate altogether.

The cyborg is a metaphor for its time. Recognizing the importance of historicizing epistemology, of accounting for the metaphorical specificities of particular moments in time, Haraway's manifesto is "rooted in claims about fundamental changes in the nature of class, race, and gender in an emerging system of world order analogous in its novelty and scope to that created by industrial capitalism; we are living through a movement from an organic, industrial society to a polymorphous, information system" (203). The scientific-technical world, governed by the "domination of informatics," renders obsolete the old epistemological certainties of a dualistic world, a world naturalized by the semiotics of dichotomies ("between mind and body, animal and human, organism and machine, public and private, nature and culture, men and women, primitive and civilized" [205]). In the current postmodern surround of a postcolonial global world, the old naturalized categories rearrange themselves into denaturalized categories of meaning. Now the operative organizational mode is that of "coding" at all levels—of the atom, the cell, the information circuit, the multinational economy. And so we must recognize that women live and operate in an "integrated circuit."[54] While the integrated circuit may be constraining and colonizing in new ways and render former oppressions nostalgically preferable, it can also provide "a source of power" through which "fresh sources of analysis and political action" can illuminate a "subtle understanding of emerging pleasures, experiences, and power with serious potential for changing the rules of the game" (215).

Thus the cyborg is "a kind of disassembled and reassembled, postmodern collective and personal self" (205). As an assemblage of "networks" in a surround of "structural rearrangements related to the social relations of science and technology" (214), cyborgs inhabit multiple spaces, presenting multiple identities that expose "the permeability of boundaries in the personal body and in the body politics" (212). In the "utopian tradition of imagining a world without gender, which is perhaps a world without genesis" (192), Haraway embraces the ironic possibilities presented by the cyborg.

While, as she suggests, "the main trouble with cyborgs . . . is that they are the illegitimate offspring of militarism and patriarchal capitalism, not to mention state socialism," they nonetheless provide liberatory possibilities because "illegitimate offspring are often exceedingly unfaithful to their origins. Their fathers, after all, are inessential" (193). Imagining cyborg politics requires imagining unnatural borders. Thus, like Anzaldúa, Haraway explores a "border war," but the topography of her revolutionary skirmish is not originally geographical. Rather her border dispute, her border rearrangement takes place in the space "between organism and machine" (191). Multiple borderlands are breached by the cyborg: between human and animal, living organism and machine, the physical and nonphysical realms (195). Through the breaches, Haraway suggests, "perhaps, ironically, we can learn from our fusions with animals and machines how not to be Man, the embodiment of Western logos" (215).

Thus Haraway's manifesto calls for cyborg performances of "permanently partial identities and contradictory standpoints" upon which to build epistemologies. "Monstrous" and "illegitimate" collocations of animal, human, and machine, cyborgs promise a new kind of politics contestatory of identity politics. This new politics she calls "affinity" politics (196). Denaturalizing the old certainties of identity, the cyborg functions as a de/naturalized locus of affinity, and the politics of affinity promise an escape from the exclusionary impact of identitarian standpoints: "The theoretical and practical struggle against unity-through-domination or unity-through-incorporation ironically not only undermines the justifications for patriarchy, colonialism, humanism, positivism, essentialism, scientism, and other unlamented -isms, but all claims for an organic or natural standpoint" (198).

Finally, cyborgs—such affinity groups as "women of color" who represent "a potent subjectivity synthesized from fusions of outsider identities"—must seize the very technology of preference in the late twentieth century, that is, writing: "Cyborg politics is the struggle for language and the struggle against perfect communication, against the one code that translates all meaning perfectly, the central dogma of phallogocentrism. That is why cyborg politics insist on noise and advocates pollution, rejoicing in the illegitimate fusions of animal and machine" (218) Critically, the cyborg does not chase a dream of a common language but rather deploys "a powerful infidel heteroglossia," through which "she" "recod[es] communication and intelligence to subvert command and control" (217), through which she posits and deconstructs one boundary after another, through which she constantly crosses borders. Concluding with a call to a new revolutionary subject, Haraway places her utopian confidence in affinity with the cyborg: "Although both are bound in the spiral dance, I would rather be a cyborg than a goddess" (223). And she keeps insisting on the energy of a revolutionary "irony," which, she says, "is about contradictions that do not resolve into larger wholes, even dialectically, about the tension of holding incompatible things together because both or all are necessary and true" (190). The incompatibilities of the "I" bring us a long way from the old stabilities of the "I" with which this study began.

The autobiographical manifesto is a revolutionary gesture poised against amnesia and its compulsory repetitions. It is not quite anamnesis (or reminiscence) so much as a purposeful constitution of a future history, the projection of anamnesis into the future. Moreover, the manifesto offers a point of departure for the current generation (of women, of people from the borderlands, of cyborgs) to resist a former generation imposing its multifarious technologies of identity. Through compelling myths and metaphors, these three manifestos map alternative futures for the "I" in the late twentieth century. They point to blurred boundaries, crossed borderlands of multiplicity, differences and divergences, political possibilities and pitfalls, strategies for intervention. They offer fascinating performances of the revolutionary subject, performances which, as Frantz Fanon noted, effectively "transform spectators crushed with their inessentiality into privileged actors, with the grandiose glare of history's floodlights upon them." Whether we follow them or not, whether we pursue some other kind of alternative subjectivity, such performances hold out hope by insisting on the possibility of self-conscious and imaginative breaks in cultural repetitions of the universal subject.

CODA

Pronominal "I"s are historical rather than ontological phenomena. Thus, while the "I" on the page seems such a slight and finite space of assertion, it really becomes a dense point of enunciation. What I've attempted to do in this study is to bring three phenomena to bear on this graphic point and its autobiographical practice: the history of the subject, the history of the body, and the history of narrative laws. Ultimately, these are not three distinguishable strands of attention but one. The imbrications of subjectivity, identity, and the body align variously in the discrete designs of the autobiographical texts I have taken up here. Sometimes identity is the bane of subjectivity's existence, sometimes its ubiquitous point of departure, sometimes its target of narrative opportunity. Sometimes the body tracks the "I"; sometimes it distracts the "I." Sometimes the subject bores through narrative forms; sometimes she bears alternative forms.

Dialogically engaging the laws of genre, autobiographical subjects often take up the old autobiographical forms, piece by piece. They turn them over, around, inside out, to tell another kind of story. In doing so they try to dematerialize the very cultural apparati that would materialize them as specific kinds of subjects. And so these autobiographical occasions are rife with complex negotiations of and resistances to the very laws of genre that would provide cultural blueprints for the alignment of subjectivity, identity, and the body.

In the nineteenth century Harriet Jacobs confounds the ideological assumptions underlying the discourses of true womanhood, including the tropes of sentimental and domestic fiction. The modernist writers of the first half of the twentieth century purposefully develop narrative strategies designed to break the authority of inherited narratives. Gertrude Stein both mimes and undermines the traditional autobiographical mode of the spousal celebration of the "husband," writing an unofficial story of lesbian coupling. Virginia Woolf breaks the grip of strangulated individuality upon autobiographical utterances by speaking anonymously. Zora Neale Hurston confuses reader expectations by abandoning the accoutrements of chronology, the narrative spine of developmental selfhood. By the time they put the period to the autobiographical act, they call into question many of the certitudes of traditional autobiography: chronological time, individuality, developmental selfhood, myths of origins, the fixedness of identity, bodily wholeness, the transparencies of referentiality, the will to knowledge, the unified self. They use revisionary "I"s to break the instrumentality of the genre. On the way they reconceptualize that dense point of enunciation. Stein turns the "I" from the "one" to the "two"; Woolf turns it from the "one" to the none/many of anonymity. Hurston turns the "one" to a kind of vanishing point.

With contemporary writers, autobiographical acts become occasions for searing cultural critique as autobiographical subjects vigorously interrogate cultural subjectivities. Jo Spence mimes a common mode of autobiographical narrative, the story of a profession, not in order to celebrate her professional identity but rather to critique the way the profession constitutes her as a specific kind of subject, and more generally to critique the way in which she (and we) are constructed by the very photography that we naively assume reflects rather than constructs reality. Cherríe Moraga uses autobiographical occasions to do what Woolf claims she was unable to do, that is, "to tell the truth about [her] own experiences as a body" and thus to tell the truth about the complex cultural meanings assigned her body and its desires. For both, autobiographical writing becomes a means to greater self-awareness and politicized consciousness.

Contemporary autobiographical manifestos issue bold calls for new subjects altogether: Hélène Cixous's New Woman, Gloria Anzaldúa's new *mestiza*, Donna Haraway's cyborg. Such subjects require new discourses of identity and new orientations to the body. Cixous propels us through revolutionary language to the provisional subjectivity of a "woman" flying/stealing in her own body/language rather than solidifying in the representations of the phallic economy. Anzaldúa takes us to a new border subject incorporating literally and figuratively multiple cultural identities and bodies. Through what Françoise Lionnet calls *metissage*,[1] she weaves a heteroglossia of languages through a multiplicity of histories and countermythologies. Specifically located, border subjects are neither centered nor marginalized subjects. Thus, they refuse to acknowledge the old positions of dominance and subordination by remapping boundaries and relationships of power. Haraway's manifesto for the cyborg "is an argument for pleasure in the confusion of boundaries and for responsibility in their construction."[2] Turning attention away from essential differences that ensure oppression and trauma at the dense point of the "I," Haraway asks us to think through a new technological register about the evacuation of the fundamental sense of humanness from the subject. Here too we are in the area of borderlands, fuzzy borderlands between human and animal, human-animal and machine, physical and nonphysical. In this new register the very meanings of subjectivity, identity, and the body must be radically rethought. Just how would a cyborg speak autobiographically?

If I have emphasized the signatures of resistance to the old autobiographical "I" in these readings, I have also attended to the ways in which the autobiographical subject may collude in the imperious practices of the "I." That imperiousness is compelling and sometimes disabling for autobiographical subjects, a fact Monique Wittig acknowledges when she calls for the evacuation of that space of enunciation altogether.[3] Her radical solution has been to avoid the "I" and to experiment with the indefinite French pronoun *on* and the collective plural *elles* as the focalizing points of locution outside the history of engendered subjects. Haraway approaches the problem from another angle.

Their radical departures from the old "I" serve as cautionary gestures. As we have seen, autobiographical subjects may participate in the perpetuation of the old "I" even as they chafe against its confining identifications. This is dramatically apparent in Elizabeth Cady Stanton's liberal embrace of the powers of the republican subject and her blindness to the exclusionary grounds of its (and her) privileges. It is also apparent in Annie Dillard's unselfconscious celebration of a universal speaking position, a point of view that erases the specificities of bodies, the differential relationships of subjects to provided subjectivities, and the inequalities of access to privilege.

The complicities in Woolf's resistance are perhaps more subtle. The disembodied eyeball, detached as it is from a body immobilized by actual and cultural violence, functions as a visionary metaphor for another kind of subject, one not consigned to an embodied identity. But it nonetheless keeps the subject separated from her body and thus maintains the cultural injunctions that divide the bourgeois woman from herself. Woolf does not reclaim the body or write a new history of the body. Further, the disembodied eyeball creates the illusion that the subject can escape situatedness in specific social and material circumstances. This illusion of freedom may be part and parcel of the very bourgeois subjectivity Woolf would eschew. Being out of your body is a way of being embodied.

The assumptions underlying the manifesto's call to identification with a new and subversive subject also require careful scrutiny. Cixous's call for a New Woman, for instance, promotes a communitarian identity politics based on a foundationalist notion of "woman." While she is aware of the difference between strategic and ontological essentialism, she nonetheless invokes a universalized "we" implicitly throughout her manifesto. Yet as recent theorists have argued, community is a problematic utopian ideal.[4] Posited on an assumed identification of one subject with another, an idealized community erases differences and contradictory experiences. Thus, as Rita Felski notes, "the ideal of a free discursive space that equalizes all participants is an enabling fiction which engenders a sense of collective identity but is achieved only by obscuring actual material inequalities and political antagonisms among its participants."[5]

Even more problematic is Cixous's recourse to the rhetoric of the black nationalist movement and the figure of Africa as the "dark continent." Deriving from Freud's essay on female sexuality, the metaphor is central to her deconstruction of phallic specularizations of woman. But her position as a white woman speaking as and for "woman" becomes suspect as soon as she introduces that trope. Since she cannot erase her position as a speaker from the "white" continent, her deployment of the metaphor insinuates a racial subtext into the manifesto. This subtext reveals the way in which Cixous establishes a hierarchy of oppressions that privileges the oppression of gender asymmetry. As Moraga warns, "the danger lies in ranking the oppressions."[6] For Moraga the necessary response requires juggling multiple identities at the graphic point of the "I" without dropping any of them. If differences are multiplied as well as identities, the tendency to universalize some kind of subject becomes harder to sustain. As she insists, she writes only "my story" (139) out of the history of her body.

Another danger in resistance is the danger of misinterpretation. Resistance may not be read, or it may be misread as collusion as a result of specific historical conditions. Hurston's narrative strategy is to evade being fixed in any subjectivity culturally available to the public that would consume her story. But the history of critiques of Hurston's text suggests that the strategy of evasion becomes for some readers a strategy of collusion. If the subject persists in evading fixing, she may create the illusion that she has no strong identifications and thus that she is merely a pawn of others. In the context of American racial politics, the failure to be a specific kind of subject may cause problems for both communities of readers but for different reasons. Here a set of political issues affecting the interpretation of resistance and complicity intrude. Who is the reader? And what are the uses to which the reader puts the reading of an autobiographical text?

These comments are meant to suggest the complexities and the contradictions of resistance and of the fine line, if any, that can be drawn between resistance and complicity.

But I want to close not on issues of complicity, but rather on the subversive excesses of autobiographical acts, those excesses through which autobiographical subjects confuse the narrative surfaces of identity and difference, of bodies and subjects. There have been many excessive subjects in these pages. Jacob's unchained subject. Stein's "Alice," or "Alice's" Stein. Woolf's "grape eyeball." Hurston's disappearing subject. Spence's propertied breast. Anzaldúa's *mestiza*. Haraway's cyborg. And there have been the narrative excesses of hybrid forms. Stein's auto/biography. Moraga's pastiche of prose and poetry. Spence's phototherapy. And the manifestos. If we look more broadly, we would find an array of contemporary autobiographical occasions—the comics of Lynda Barry, the quilts of Faith Ringgold, the performance art of Laurie Anderson, the photographs of Eileen Cowin, the comedy routines of Monica Palacios, the provocative videos of Madonna, the post-modern manifestos of Barbara Kruger and Jenny Holzer. On the eve of the twenty-first century, we find autobiographical subjects all around us, and they are stretching textual forms, multiple media, and diverse occasions to fit their excessive negotiations of subjectivity, identity, and the body.

NOTES

1. The Universal Subject, Female Embodiment, and the Consolidation of Autobiography

1. As Woolf's narrator says, this "Mary" could be called Mary Beton, Mary Seton, Mary Carmichael, or "me."

2. Virginia Woolf, *A Room of One's Own* (New York: Harcourt, Brace & World, 1929), pp. 103–104. Further citations will appear in the text.

3. See Isak Dinesen, "The Blank Page," in *Last Tales* (New York: Random House, 1957), p. 104. See also Susan Gubar, " 'The Blank Page' and Female Creativity" in *Writing and Sexual Difference,* ed. Elizabeth Abel (Chicago: Univ. of Chicago Press, 1982), pp. 73–94.

4. Valerie Walkerdine, "Video Replay: Families, Films and Fantasy," in *Formations of Fantasy,* ed. Victor Burgin, James Donald, and Cora Kaplan (London: Methuen, 1986), p. 194, emphasis mine.

5. The phrase comes from bell hooks, *Yearning: Race, Gender, and Cultural Politics* (Boston: South End Press, 1990), p. 38.

6. See Jacques Derrida, "The Law of Genre," trans. Avital Ronell, *Glyph* 7 (1980): 203–204. See also Caren Kaplan, "Resisting Autobiography: Out-Law Genres and Transnational Feminist Subjects," in *De/Colonizing the Subject: The Politics of Gender in Women's Autobiography,* ed. Sidonie Smith and Julia Watson (Minneapolis: Univ. of Minnesota Press, 1992), pp. 115–38.

7. See bell hooks, *Talking Back: Thinking Feminist, Thinking Black* (Boston: South End Press, 1988).

8. Terry Eagleton, *Literary Theory: An Introduction* (Minneapolis: Univ. of Minnesota Press, 1983), p. 131.

9. For the purposes of my argument here the terms *universal, essential,* and *metaphysical* are synonymous. They point to the conception of the human being as a phenomenon separable and beyond the ideologically/culturally constructed. Though I could move between terms, I have chosen to use the term *universal.* I must also move between the terms *self* and *subject. Self* signals an understanding of the human being as metaphysical, essential, and universal. Obviously, *subject* has current theoretical currency. It implies the culturally constructed nature of any notion of "selfhood."

10. Candace D. Lang, in *Irony/Humor: Critical Paradigms* (Baltimore: Johns Hopkins Univ. Press, 1988), suggests that the notion of individuality that emerged during the Renaissance was "favored by both socioeconomic and technological developments: the decline of the feudal system and concomitant increase in capitalist endeavor" (Lang 1988: 14). Lang argues

further that the technology of the printing press, "which would enhance the notion of authorship by saving the text from the relative anonymity of oral tradition," helped foster the emergent notion of individuality. By the nineteenth century, Lang continues, "the notion of the author reached maturity under the aegis of capitalism, with the institution of the copyright, by which the writer acquired sole authority over and responsibility for his works. Historically, that development coincided with the rise of romanticism, which glorified the unique and ineffable self" (14). See also Sidonie Smith, *A Poetics of Women's Autobiography: Marginality and the Fictions of Self-Representation* (Bloomington: Indiana Univ. Press, 1987), esp. chap. 2.

11. J. Hillis Miller, " 'Herself against Herself': The Clarification of Clara Middleton," in *The Representation of Women in Fiction: Selected Papers from the English Institute, 1981,* ed. Carolyn G. Heilbrun and Margaret R. Higgonet (Baltimore: Johns Hopkins Univ. Press, 1983), p. 102. Miller's description of the fixed self itself assumes certain male privileges of power, language, and desire. For instance, his statement assumes that women and men experienced the same access to empowerment through language and its figures of speech.

12. Ibid., p. 101.

13. Seyla Benhabib and Drucilla Cornell, "Introduction: Beyond Politics and Gender," in *Feminism as Critique: On the Politics of Gender,* ed. Seyla Benhabib and Drucilla Cornell (Minneapolis: Univ. of Minnesota Press, 1987), p. 12.

14. Francis Barker, *The Tremulous Private Body: Essays on Subjection* (London and New York: Methuen, 1984), p. 53.

15. Ibid., p. 63.

16. Ibid., pp. 64, 59.

17. See M. M. Bakhtin, *Rabelais and His World,* trans. H. Iswolsky (Cambridge: MIT Press, 1968). See also Peter Stallybrass and Allon White, *The Politics and Poetics of Transgression* (Ithaca: Cornell Univ. Press, 1986), esp. the Introduction.

18. One of Bakhtin's most provocative ideas situates knowledge in a dialogic rather than a monologic relationship of individual to world. See, of course, M. M. Bakhtin, *The Dialogic Imagination,* ed. Michael Holquist, trans. Caryl Emerson and Michael Holquist (Austin: Univ. of Texas Press, 1981). See also Allon White, "The Struggle over Bakhtin: Fraternal Reply to Robert White," *Cultural Critique* (Winter 1987–88): 231.

19. Stanley Corngold, *The Fate of the Self: German Writers and French Theory* (New York: Columbia Univ. Press, 1986), p. 3. Corngold quotes from Jean-Marie Benoist, *The Structural Revolution* (London: Weidenfeld and Nicolson, 1978), p. 184.

20. Iris Marion Young, "Impartiality and the Civil Public: Some Implications of Feminist Critiques of Moral and Political Theory," in *Feminism As Critique,* p. 62.

21. Jane Flax, "Postmodernism and Gender Relations in Feminist Theory," *Signs* 12 (Summer 1987): 624.

22. "Only by expelling desire, affectivity and the body from reason can impartiality achieve its unity" (Young, p. 62). See also pp. 60–67.

23. Lang, p. 62.

24. Young, p. 61.

25. White, p. 231.

26. Eagleton, pp. 131–32.

27. Mary Poovey, *The Proper Lady and the Woman Writer* (Chicago: Univ. of Chicago Press, 1984), p. 27.

28. I now have to shift between the terms *self* and *universal subject.*

29. Stallybrass and White, p. 199.

30. See Julia Kristeva, *Powers of Horror: An Essay in Abjection,* trans. Leon S. Roudiez (New York: Columbia Univ. Press, 1982), esp. chap. 1; and Iris Marion Young, "Abjection and Oppression: Dynamics of Unconscious Racism, Sexism, and Homophobia," in *Crises in Continental Philosophy,* ed. Arleen B. Dallery and Charles E. Scott (Albany: State Univ. of New York Press, 1990), pp. 201–14.

31. See also Stallybrass and White, p. 25. Discourses of the "low" and the "neutral" circulate through various domains of meaning, domains that Stallybrass and White draw into slanted alignments with one another, place, body, group-identity, and subjectivity.

32. Judith Butler, "Variations on Sex and Gender: Beauvoir, Wittig and Foucault," in *Feminism as Critique,* p. 131.

33. Judith Butler, *Gender Trouble: Feminism and the Subversion of Identity* (New York: Routledge, 1990), p. 133. Butler draws her terms from Young's essay, "Abjection and Oppression." See also Butler's analysis of Kristeva's notion of abjection in *Powers of Horror: An Essay in Abjection,* trans. L. S. Roudiez (New York: Columbia Univ. Press, 1982). Butler provides the following summary of Kristeva's notion of the abject: "The 'abject' designates that which has been expelled from the body, discharged as excrement, literally rendered 'Other.' This appears as an explusion of alien elements, but the alien is effectively established through this expulsion. The construction of the 'not-me' as the abject establishes the boundaries of the body which are also the first contours of the subject. . . . The boundary of the body as well as the distinction between internal and external is established through the ejection and transvaluation of something originally part of identity into a defiling otherness" (133).

34. Butler, "Variations on Sex and Gender," p. 133.

35. I mean here the discursive "woman," not specific historical women. Although I have used quotation marks here to indicate the bourgeois ideological construction, "woman," I will not continue to do so.

36. Teresa de Lauretis, *Technologies of Gender: Essays on Theory, Film, and Fiction* (Bloomington: Indiana Univ. Press, 1987), chap. 1.

37. Butler, "Variations on Sex and Gender," p. 133. Butler is here glossing Simone de Beauvoir's analysis of gender difference.

38. Diana Fuss, *Essentially Speaking: Feminism, Nature and Difference* (New York: Routledge, 1989), p. 72.

39. Roberta Rubenstein, *Boundaries of the Self: Gender, Culture, Fiction* (Urbana: Univ. of Illinois Press, 1987), p. 5.

40. Susan Bordo, "The Politics of Subjectivity in the Battle over Reproductive Rights," paper delivered at SUNY-Binghamton, April 1991.

41. Benhabib and Cornell, "Introductions: Beyond Politics and Gender," in *Feminism as Critique,* p. 12.

42. Henry James, *The Portrait of a Lady* (New York: W. W. Norton, 1975), p. 64.

43. See Bordo, "The Politics of Subjectivity." I should note here that the scientific/medical understanding of pregnancy has evolved since Aristotle's day. But as Bordo suggests, there has been a continued propensity to assign active status to the sperm and passive status to the egg.

44. Ian Maclean, *The Renaissance Notion of Woman: A Study in the Fortunes of Scholasticism and Medical Science in European Intellectual Life* (Cambridge: Cambridge Univ. Press, 1980), p. 27.

45. Denise Riley, *"Am I That Name?" Feminism and the Category of "Women" in History* (Minneapolis: Univ. of Minnesota Press, 1988), p. 18.

46. Riley, p. 36.

47. For a stimulating, if flawed, early feminist analysis of woman's relationship to nature, to the private sphere, and to a more personal and particularistic psychological orientation to the world, see Sheri B. Ortner, "Is Female to Male as Nature Is to Culture?" in *Women, Culture, and Society,* ed. Michelle Zimbalist Rosaldo and Louise Lamphere (Stanford: Stanford Univ. Press, 1974), pp. 67–87. For a more recent discussion of the ways in which "liberal conceptions of reason and rationality have rendered the women's point of view either irrational or particularist . . . or concretistic and trivial," see Benhabib and Cornell, p. 11. The authors are summarizing feminist challenges to "liberal" conceptions mounted in *Feminism as Critique,* by Iris Marion Young, "Impartiality and the Civil Public," pp. 56–76, and by Seyla Benhabib, "The Generalized and the Concrete Other: The Kohlberg-Gilligan Controversy and Feminist Theory," pp. 77–95.

48. Hannah More, *The Works of Hannah More,* vol. 1 (New York: Harper and Brothers, 1854), p. 367. See also Linda H. Peterson, *Victorian Autobiography: The Tradition of Self-Interpretation* (New Haven and London: Yale Univ. Press, 1986), p. 127.

49. Horace Mann, *A Few Thoughts on the Powers and Duties of Woman: Two Lectures* (Syracuse: Hall, Mills, 1853), p. 23.

50. George Eliot, *Essays of George Eliot,* ed. Thomas Pinney (London: Routledge, 1963), p. 334; quoted in Lynn Sukenick, "On Women and Fiction," in *The Authority of Experience: Essays in Feminist Criticism,* ed. Arlyn Diamond (Amherst: Univ. of Massachusetts Press, 1977), p. 33.

51. Sukenick, p. 37–38. Sukenick explores in some detail nineteenth-century notions of male and female epistemological differences.

52. For an extended discussion of the ideology of the proper lady in the eighteenth and nineteenth centuries, see Poovey, *The Proper Lady and the Woman Writer*, esp. chap. 1.

53. Riley, p. 41.

54. Poovey, p. 19.

55. For an exploration of Enlightenment notions of the feminine and the identification of the feminine with disruptive cultural forces, see Ruth Salvaggio, *Enlightened Absence: Neoclassical Configurations of the Feminine* (Urbana: Univ. of Illinois Press, 1988).

56. Stephen Heath, "Difference," *Screen* 19 (Winter 1978–79): 111.

57. Alice Jardine, *Gynesis: Configurations of Woman and Modernity* (Ithaca: Cornell Univ. Press, 1985), p. 118.

58. If selves, as Miller argues, "are merely mediated, described, or interpreted by language," then the life of any particular self can be "represented," chronicled from its origins through its teleological course, p. 101.

59. Jane Gallop, *The Daughter's Seduction: Feminism and Psychoanalysis* (Ithaca: Cornell Univ. Press, 1982), p. 81.

60. See Miller for a discussion of the relationship of nineteenth-century realism to the ideology of selfhood which operated from "the presupposition that each man or woman has a fixed character with definite hieroglyphic outlines which may be figured truly, for example in his or her physiognomy or in the figures of speech with which he or she may be described in language" (102). Miller argues further that "the double assumption on which that aspect of realism which involves the mimesis in language of states of mind rests is the following: that there is a prelinguistic self or character and that this in its modes may be expressed, mirrored, or copied without distortion in language" (107).

61. Lang, pp. 72–73.

62. Jean-Jacques Rousseau, *Les Confessions*, vol. 1 of *Oeuvres complètes* (Paris: Pléiade, 1959), p. 5.

63. See Felicity A. Nussbaum, *The Autobiographical Subject: Gender and Ideology in Eighteenth Century England* (Baltimore: Johns Hopkins Univ. Press, 1989).

64. For a discussion of "the triumph of the paradigm of progress" and its impact upon history writing, see Martin Bernal, "Ancient Greece and Modern Racism: Western Self-Images," talk presented at the State University of New York at Binghamton, October 4, 1990.

65. According to Stallybrass and White, the very practice of "produc-[ing] an independent middle subject; this heterogeneity which re-emerges from the very attempt to achieve a formal, balanced and empty neutrality; this vertiginous and disorienting calling of voices from above and below; all this *clutter* and *mess* of the bourgeois Imaginary inevitably forestalled its radical democratic project" (199).

66. See Nussbaum, *Autobiographical Subject*, esp. chap. 2. I am in-

debted to her provocative discussion of both generic theory and ideologies of the subject as they affected autobiographical writing (in England) in the eighteenth century.

67. Stallybrass and White, p. 199.

68. Susan Stanford Friedman, "Women's Autobiographical Selves: Theory and Practice," in *The Private Self: Theory and Practice of Women's Autobiographical Writing,* ed. Shari Benstock (Chapel Hill: Univ. of North Carolina Press, 1988), p. 41.

69. See P. N. Medvedev/Bakhtin, *The Formal Method in Literary Scholarship: A Critical Introduction to Sociological Poetics,* trans. Albert J. Wehrle (Baltimore: Goucher College Series, 1978), p. 14. "The ideological environment," writes Bakhtin, "forms a solid ring around man [*sic*]. And man's consciousness lives and develops in this environment. . . . In fact, the individual consciousness can only become a consciousness by being realized in the forms of the ideological environment proper to it: in language, in conventionalized gesture, in artistic image, in myth, and so on."

70. Toril Moi, *Sexual/Textual Politics: Feminist Literary Theory* (London: Methuen, 1985), p. 65.

71. Gallop, p. 81.

72. Lee Quinby in a paper delivered at the colloquium on "Feminism and Postmodernism," State University of New York—Binghamton, March 1989. See also de Lauretis, *Feminist Studies,* pp. 8–15.

73. Paul Smith, *Discerning the Subject* (Minneapolis: Univ. of Minnesota Press, 1988), p. 118.

74. Paul Smith, pp. xxxiv–xxxv.

75. See Mary Ann Caws, "Ladies Shot and Painted: Female Embodiment in Surrealist Art," in Susan Rubin Suleiman, ed., *The Female Body in Western Culture: Contemporary Perspectives* (Cambridge: Harvard Univ. Press, 1986), pp. 284–85.

2. Elizabeth Cady Stanton, Harriet Jacobs, and Resistances to "True Womanhood"

1. See Regenia Gagnier, *Subjectivities* (New York: Oxford University Press, 1991).

2. For a provocative discussion of the contours of scandal and the body of woman, see Felicity A. Nussbaum, *The Autobiographical Subject: Gender and Ideology in Eighteenth-Century England* (Baltimore: Johns Hopkins Univ. Press, 1989), chap. 8.

3. bell hooks, *Yearning: Race, Gender, and Cultural Politics* (Boston: South End Press, 1990), p. 38.

4. Elizabeth Cady Stanton, *Eighty Years and More (1815–1897): Reminiscences of Elizabeth Cady Stanton* (New York: European Publishing Co., 1898), p. v. All further citations will appear in the text.

5. The phrase is borrowed from Felicity A. Nussbaum's provocative

study, "Eighteenth-Century Women's Autobiographical Commonplaces," in *The Private Self: Theory and Practice of Women's Autobiographical Writing,* ed. Shari Benstock (Chapel Hill: Univ. of North Carolina Press, 1988), pp. 147–71.

6. Estelle Jelinek, "The Paradox and Success of Elizabeth Cady Stanton" in *Women's Autobiography: Essays in Criticism,* ed. Estelle Jelinek (Bloomington: Indiana Univ. Press, 1980), pp. 87–90.

7. Carolyn G. Heilbrun, "Women's Autobiographical Writings: New Forms," *Prose Studies* 8 (September 1985): 17. Heilbrun is reviewing a study by Jill Conway, "Paper on Autobiographies of Women of the Progressive Era," delivered at the workshop on "New Approaches to Women's Biography and Autobiography," Smith College Project on Women and Social Change, June 12–17, 1983.

8. Estelle Jelinek also notes this resistance in "The Paradox and Success of Elizabeth Cady Stanton," p. 72.

9. Nancy K. Miller, "Writing (from) the Feminine: George Sand and the Novel of Female Pastoral," in *Representations of Women in Fiction: Selected Papers from the English Institute, 1981,* ed. Carolyn G. Heilbrun and Margaret R. Higonnet (Baltimore: Johns Hopkins Univ. Press, 1983), p. 125. See also Rachel Blau DuPlessis, *Writing Beyond the Ending: Narrative Strategies of Twentieth-Century Women Writers* (Bloomington: Indiana Univ. Press, 1985), p. 14.

10. Here she invokes the debate among nineteenth-century feminists who fell out along the lines of "influence" or equal rights and suffrage.

11. For a brief discussion of the doubled strands of nineteenth-century feminist ideologies, see Carolyn Steedman, *Childhood, Culture and Class in Britain: Margaret McMillan 1860–1931* (New Brunswick: Rutgers Univ. Press, 1990), p. 121.

12. I am indebted here to an essay by Carroll Smith-Rosenberg, "Misprisioning *Pamela:* Representations of Gender and Class in Nineteenth-Century America," *Michigan Quarterly Review* 26 (Winter 1987): 9–28.

13. See Gayatri Chakravorty Spivak, "Three Women's Texts and a Critique of Imperialism," *Critical Inquiry* 12 (Autumn 1985): 243–61.

14. For discussions of the negation of "the other of the other," see Barbara Johnson, *A World of Difference* (Baltimore: Johns Hopkins Univ. Press, 1987), pp. 166–71; and Michele Wallace, "Variations on Negation and the Heresy of Black Feminist Creativity," in *Reading Black, Reading Feminist: A Critical Anthology,* ed. Henry Louis Gates, Jr. (New York: Meridian, 1990), pp. 52–67. For a critique of various feminist theories that exclude the other woman, see Elizabeth V. Spelman, *Inessential Woman: Problems of Exclusion in Feminist Thought* (Boston: Beacon Press, 1988).

15. Henry Louis Gates, Jr., "Editor's Introduction: Writing 'Race' and the Difference It Makes," in *"Race," Writing, and Difference,* ed. Henry Louis Gates, Jr. (Chicago: Univ. of Chicago Press, 1986), p. 3. Further citations will appear in the text. Elaborating the theories of Hippolyte-

Adolphe Taine, Gates refers to Taine's description of "race" as a "community of blood and intellect which to this day binds its offshoots together" (Hippolyte-Adolphe Taine, "Introduction to *The History of English Literature*," in *Criticism: The Major Texts,* ed. Walter Jackson Bate [New York: Harcourt Brace Jovanovich, 1970], pp. 503–505).

16. For an analysis of black and white bodies in the art and medicine of the nineteenth century, see Sander Gilman, "Black Bodies, White Bodies: Toward an Iconography of Female Sexuality in Late Nineteenth-Century Art, Medicine, and Literature," in Gates, *"Race"* (223–61). See also William L. Andrews, *To Tell a Free Story: The First Century of Afro-American Autobiography, 1760–1865* (Urbana: Univ. of Illinois Press, 1986), p. 3.

17. "Without writing," summarizes Gates, "no *repeatable* sign of the workings of reason, of mind, could exist. Without memory or mind, no history could exist. Without history, no humanity, as defined consistently from Vico to Hegel, could exist" (Gates, p. 11).

18. "Making the book speak," suggests Gates, "constituted a motivated and political engagement with and condemnation of Europe's fundamental sign of domination, the commodity of writing, the text and technology of reason" (p. 12).

19. Frederick Douglass, *My Bondage and My Freedom, Part I—Life as a Slave, Part II—Life as a Freeman* (New York: Miller, Orton & Mulligan, 1855), p. vii.

20. For statistics on the sales of slave narratives, see Charles H. Nichols, Jr., *Many Thousand Gone: The Ex-Slaves' Account of Their Bondage and Freedom* (Leiden, Netherlands: E. J. Brill, 1963), pp. xiv–xv. For further discussions of slave narratives, see Stephen Butterfield, *Black Autobiography in America* (Amherst: Univ. of Massachusetts Press, 1974); Charles Davis and Henry Louis Gates, Jr., *The Slave's Narrative* (New York: Oxford Univ. Press, 1985); Frances Smith Foster, *Witnessing Slavery: The Development of the Ante-Bellum Slave Narratives* (Westport, Conn.: Greenwood Press, 1979); John Sekora and Darwin T. Turner, eds., *The Art of Slave Narrative* (Macomb: Northern Illinois Univ. Press, 1982); Marion Wilson Starling, *The Slave Narrative: Its Place in History* (Boston: G. K. Hall, 1981); Sidonie Smith, *Where I'm Bound: Patterns of Slavery and Freedom in Black American Autobiography* (Westport, Conn.: Greenwood Press, 1974); and Robert B. Stepto, *From Behind the Veil: A Study of Afro-American Narrative* (Urbana: Univ. of Illinois Press, 1979).

21. Douglass, p. vii.

22. Boston *Chronotype,* quoted in Andrews, p. 5.

23. Andrews, pp. 6–7.

24. For a discussion of voice and face, see Gates, pp. 11–12.

25. Mae Gwendolyn Henderson, "Speaking in Tongues: Dialogics, Dialectics, and the Black Woman Writer's Literary Tradition," in Gates, *Reading Black,* p. 120.

26. She achieves legal freedom in the North not through self-agency but through the intervention of her employer, a point to which I will return later.

27. See Abdul R. JanMohamed, "Negating the Negation as a Form of Affirmation in Minority Discourse: The Construction of Richard Wright as Subject," *Cultural Critique* 7 (1987): 247. See also Dana D. Nelson, *The Word in Black and White: Reading "Race" in American Literature 1638–1867* (New York: Oxford Univ. Press, 1992), pp. 133–37.

28. Harriet Jacobs, *Incidents in the Life of a Slave Girl, Written by Herself,* ed. Lydia Maria Child, new ed. Jean Fagan Yellin (Cambridge: Harvard Univ. Press, 1987), p. 19. All further citations will appear in the text. Elizabeth Fox-Genovese explores Jacobs's struggle of wills in "To Write My Self: The Autobiographies of Afro-American Women," in *Feminist Issues in Literary Scholarship,* ed. Shari Benstock (Bloomington: Indiana Univ. Press, 1987), p. 171.

29. Nelson, pp. 136–37.

30. Fox-Genovese, p. 172.

31. Barbara Welter, *Dimity Convictions: The American Woman in the Nineteenth Century* (Columbus: Ohio State Univ. Press, 1976), p. 21. For further discussions of true womanhood, see Julia Cherry Spruill, *Women's Life and Work in the Southern Colonies* (1938; reprint New York: W.W. Norton, 1972); Anne Firor Scott, *The Southern Lady: From Pedestal to Politics, 1830–1930* (Chicago: Univ. of Chicago Press, 1970); Catherine Clinton, *The Plantation Mistress: Woman's World in the Old South* (New York: Pantheon, 1982); Barbara J. Berg, *The Remembered Gate: Origins of American Feminism: The Woman and the City, 1800–1860* (New York: Oxford Univ. Press, 1978).

32. Hazel V. Carby, *Reconstructing Womanhood: The Emergence of the Afro-American Woman Novelist* (New York: Oxford Univ. Press, 1987), pp. 24, 25.

33. "Strength and ability to bear fatigue, argued to be so distasteful a presence in a white woman, were positive features to be emphasized in the promotion and selling of a black female field hand at a slave auction" (ibid., p. 25).

34. What Carby claims for black women after the Civil War applies even more certainly to female slaves before emancipation: "Black women were relegated to a place outside the ideological construction of 'womanhood.' That term included only white women; therefore the rape of black women was of no consequence outside the black community," in "On the Threshold of Woman's Era: Lynching, Empire, and Sexuality in Black Feminist Theory," in Gates, "*Race,*" pp. 308–309. Carby is elaborating the theories of black feminist Ida B. Wells, who explored the politics of lynching at the end of the nineteenth century. See, for instance, Wells, *On Lynching* (New York, 1969), for a collection of her essays. Carby also explores the politics of the black female body in *Reconstructing Womanhood,* pp. 26-32.

35. "In the nineteenth century," writes Gilman, "the black female was widely perceived as possessing not only a 'primitive' sexual appetite but also the external signs of this temperament—'primitive' genitalia" (232). Fascination with this phenomenon of physical and physiognomic abnor-

mality reveals itself in the century's preoccupation with the "Hottentot Venus" whose visual characteristics—large buttocks, flat nose, strange labia—function as signs of her phylogenetic place. The critical significance of establishing the difference of black female anatomy lay, according to Gilman, in the following rationalization: "If their sexual parts could be shown to be inherently different, this would be a sufficient sign that the blacks were a separate (and, needless to say, lower) race, as different from the European as the proverbial orangutan" (235). In the catalog of defining physical characteristics of the female Hottentot, the century read the signs of regression to an earlier state of human evolution. Moreover, in identifying some of those same characteristics as markers of prostitutes (the most sexualized of white women) and in describing the sexual practices of primitive tribes as forms of prostitution, medical anthropologists linked black sexuality and prostitution as two sources of social corruption and disease (syphillis in particular). Sexuality as the dark force in "civilized man" was thus identified with, projected onto, the prostitute and the black female (240-57).

36. bell hooks, *Yearning*, p. 57.

37. Nelson, p. 134.

38. Andrews, pp. 249, 253.

39. Valerie Smith, " 'Loopholes of Retreat': Architecture and Ideology in Harriet Jacobs's *Incidents in the Life of a Slave Girl*," in Gates, *Reading Black*, pp. 220–22.

40. Yellin explores Jacobs's use of the conventions of sentimental fiction in her introduction to *Incidents*, pp. xxix–xxx.

41. Ibid., p. xxvi. Slave marriages were not legally valid. Moreover, the subjection of the female body to the will of the white master, functioning as an effective means of "unmanning" the black male, in one more way destabilized the family and, as Fox-Genovese suggests, left black women with "no satisfactory social definition of themselves as women" (Fox-Genovese, p. 169).

42. See Andrews's extended discussion of the thematics of secrecy in the narrative (254–59).

43. V. Smith, pp. 212–26.

44. The history of the text's fate at the hands of white abolitionists, critics, and literary historians, however, adds yet another story to her story. The text is legitimized by Lydia Maria Child's attestation that it is the authentic story of the author. Recognizing that "it will naturally excite surprise that a woman reared in Slavery should be able to write so well" (3), Child both explains the author's circumstances and assures the reader that she has acted as editor only. This attestation notwithstanding, the text was regarded as fiction by subsequent generations until Jean Fagan Yellin recently verified the authenticity of the places, people, and experiences narrated by "Linda Brent." Ironically, the text as a "technology of reason" spoke against itself. See Yellin's introduction to the text.

45. Alice A. Deck, "Whose Book Is This? Authorial versus Editorial

Control of Harriet Brent Jacobs' *Incidents in the Life of a Slave Girl: Written by Herself*," *Women's Studies International Forum* 10 (1987): 33–40.

46. Child to Jacobs, August 13, 1860, quoted in *The Collected Correspondence of Lydia Maria Child 1817–1880,* ed. Milton Meltzer and Patricia G. Holland (Amherst: Univ. of Massachusetts Press, 1982), p. 357.

47. Deck explores the formulaic patterns imposed by white abolitionists on the experiences and narratives of ex-slaves, pp. 34-36. See also Jean Fagan Yellin, *The Intricate Knot: Black Figures in American Literature* (New York: New York Univ. Press, 1972), and Robert Stepto, *From Behind the Veil.*

48. Gilles Deleuze and Felix Guattari, "What Is a Minor Literature?" in *Kafka: Towards a Minor Literature,* trans. Dana Polan (Minneapolis: Univ. of Minnesota Press, 1986), p. 17. For an elaboration of the deterritorialized nature of women's autobiographical writing, see Caren Kaplan, "Deterritorializations: The Rewriting of Home and Exile in Western Feminist Discourse," *Cultural Critique* 6 (Spring 1987): 187–98.

49. Mary Helen Washington, "Introduction, Meditations on History: The Slave Woman's Voice," *Invented Lives: Narratives of Black Women, 1860–1960,* ed. Mary Helen Washington (New York: Doubleday Anchor Press, 1987), p. 12. See Washington's comments on Jacobs's empowered and assertive voice (11–12).

50. Nelson, p. 141.

51. Carby, *Reconstructing,* p. 49.

52. Nelson, p. 135.

53. For a discussion of Jacobs's implicit and explicit critiques of sympathetic sisterhood, see Nelson, pp. 137–45.

54. Carby, *Reconstructing,* pp. 53–54.

55. See Andrews, p. 251; and Annette Niemtzow, "The Problematic of Self in Autobiography: The Example of the Slave Narrative," in Sekora and Turner, p. 106. Andrew takes issue with Niemtzow's analysis.

56. Yellin, p. xxx; Carby, *Reconstructing,* p. 60.

57. Smith, p. 225.

58. Carby, *Reconstructing,* p. 61.

59. Yellin, p. xxxi.

60. For a discussion of misprision and nineteenth-century readings of the seduction novel, see Smith-Rosenberg, "Misprisioning *Pamela.*"

61. Yellin argues that "instead of dramatizing the idea that the private sphere is women's appropriate area of concern. . . . *Incidents* embodies a social analysis asserting that the denial of domestic and familial values by chattel slavery is a social issue that its female readers should address in the public arena" (xxxii). For a discussion of nineteenth-century versions of "domestic feminism," see Nina Baym, *Woman's Fiction: A Guide to Novels by and about Women in America, 1820–1870* (Ithaca: Cornell Univ. Press, 1978).

62. Nelson, p. 142.

63. Andrews, pp. 247–48.

64. hooks, p. 45.

65. See Andrews, pp. 253–58; Foster, pp. 66–70; Nellie Y. McKay, "Race, Gender, and Cultural Context in Zora Neale Hurston's *Dust Tracks on a Road*," in *Life/Lines: Theorizing Women's Autobiography*, ed. Bella Brodzki and Celeste Schenck (Ithaca: Cornell Univ. Press, 1988), p. 177; V. Smith, p. 217; and Washington, pp. 3–15.

66. V. Smith, pp. 218, 216.

67. Sherley Anne Williams, "Some Implications of Womanist Theory," in Gates, *Reading Black*, p. 72.

68. Fox-Genovese, p. 170.

69. Andrews, p. 280.

70. Craig Werner, "On the Ends of Afro-American 'Modernist' Autobiography," *Black American Literature Forum* 24 (Summer 1990): 204.

71. Werner, p. 209.

72. Henderson, p. 119.

3. Turning the Century on the Subject

1. Candace D. Lang, *Irony/Humor: Critical Paradigms* (Baltimore: Johns Hopkins Univ. Press, 1988), p. 14.

2. "By the turn of the century," write Sandra M. Gilbert and Susan Gubar, " 'the Sea of Faith' had withdrawn when God the *Father* disappeared, and Darwin had shown that man is not a lord of the universe but a 'monkey shav'd.' In addition, during the first two decades of the twentieth century, the Captains of Industry were being threatened by rebellious troops of laborers, Freud was claiming that sons secretly resented and feared fathers, and eventually a generation of sons was destroyed in battle," *No Man's Land*, vol. 1, *The War of the Words* (New Haven: Yale Univ. Press, 1987), pp. 21–22.

3. Lang, p. 14.

4. John Dewey, *The Public and Its Problems: An Essay in Political Inquiry* (Chicago: Gateway Books, 1946), pp. 96–97; also quoted in Germaine Brée, "Autogynography," *The Southern Review* 22 (April 1986): 225.

5. James Olney, "Autobiography and the Cultural Moment: A Thematic, Historical, and Bibliographical Introduction," in *Autobiography: Essays Theoretical and Critical*, ed. James Olney (Princeton: Princeton Univ. Press, 1980), p. 20.

6. See Alice A. Jardine, *Gynesis: Configurations of Woman and Modernity* (Ithaca: Cornell Univ. Press, 1985), esp. chap. 5.

7. Edward W. Said, *Beginnings: Intention and Method* (New York: Basic Books, 1975), p. 293. Quoted in Stanley Corngold, *The Fate of the Self: German Writers and French Theory* (New York: Columbia Univ. Press, 1986), p. 9.

8. Virginia Woolf, *A Room of One's Own* (New York: Harcourt, Brace & World, 1929), p. 4.

9. Said, p. 293.

10. Teresa de Lauretis, "Feminist Studies/Critical Studies: Issues, Terms, and Contexts," in *Feminist Studies/Critical Studies,* ed. Teresa de Lauretis (Bloomington: Indiana Univ. Press, 1986), p. 9.

11. I oversimplify here. Freud's theories about female sexuality are far more complex and ambiguous than I imply. See, for instance, Sarah Kofman, *The Enigma of Woman: Woman in Freud's Writings,* trans. Catherine Porter (Ithaca: Cornell Univ. Press, 1985); Luce Irigaray, *Speculum of the Other Woman,* trans. Gillian C. Gill (Ithaca: Cornell Univ. Press, 1985); Irigaray, *This Sex Which Is Not One,* trans. Catherine Porter with Carolyn Burke (Ithaca: Cornell Univ. Press, 1985); Jane Gallop, *The Daughter's Seduction: Feminism and Psychoanalysis* (Ithaca: Cornell Univ. Press, 1982); Juliet Mitchell, *Psychoanalysis and Feminism* (London: Pantheon, 1974); Mary Jacobus, *Reading Woman: Essays in Feminist Criticism* (New York: Columbia Univ. Press, 1986).

12. Susan Rubin Suleiman, "Writing and Motherhood," in *The (M)other Tongue: Essays in Feminist Psychoanalytic Interpretation,* ed. Shirley Nelson Garner, Claire Kahane, Madelon Sprengnether (Ithaca: Cornell Univ. Press, 1985), p. 354.

13. Gallop, p. 58. She is here elaborating a passage from Irigaray's *Speculum,* p. 165.

14. Jacques Derrida, *Spurs,* trans. Barbara Harlow (Chicago: Univ. of Chicago Press, 1978), p. 49.

15. De Lauretis, *Technologies of Gender: Essays on Theory, Film, and Fiction* (Bloomington: Indiana Univ. Press, 1987), p. 3.

16. Linda Alcoff, "Cultural Feminism versus Post-Structuralism: The Identity Crisis in Feminist Theory," *Signs* 13 (Spring 1988): 417. See also Christine de Stefano, "Dilemmas of Difference: Feminism, Modernity, and Postmodernism," in *Feminism/Postmodernism,* ed. Linda J. Nicholson (New York: Routledge, 1989), pp. 63–82; Rita Felski, *Beyond Feminist Aesthetics: Feminist Literature and Social Change* (Cambridge: Harvard Univ. Press, 1989), pp. 66–71; Jane Flax, "Postmodernism and Gender Relations in Feminist Theory," *Signs* 12 (Summer 1987): 621–43; Nancy Fraser and Linda J. Nicholson, "Social Criticism without Philosophy: An Encounter between Feminism and Postmodernism," in Nicholson, pp. 19–38; Meaghan Morris, *The Pirate's Fiancée: Feminism, Reading, and Postmodernism* (London: Verso, 1988).

17. For an extended analysis of this shift, see Paul Jay, *Being in the Text: Self-Representation from Wordsworth to Roland Barthes* (Ithaca: Cornell Univ. Press, 1984).

18. William C. Spengemann, *The Forms of Autobiography: Episodes in the History of a Literary Genre* (New Haven: Yale Univ. Press, 1980), p. 188.

19. Paul Smith, *Discerning the Subject* (Minneapolis: Univ. of Minnesota Press, 1988), pp. 105–106.

20. Olney, p. 23.

21. Domna C. Stanton, "Autogynography: Is the Subject Different?" in *The Female Autograph,* ed. Domna C. Stanton (New York: New York Literary Forum, 1984), p. 11.

22. The phrase "unauthorized position" comes from Gallop, p. 51.

23. Brée, p. 227.

24. Rachel Blau DuPlessis, *Writing beyond the Ending: Narrative Strategies of Twentieth-Century Women Writers* (Bloomington: Indiana Univ. Press, 1985), p. 21.

25. I am here paraphrasing de Lauretis's title and theoretical phrase, "the technologies of gender." This phrase has also been used by Leigh Gilmore in a paper entitled "Autobiographics as Agency: Technologies of Women's Autobiography," delivered at the Conference on Autobiography, University of Maine—Portland, September/October 1989.

4. Stein Is an "Alice" Is a "Gertrude Stein"

1. See, for instance, Lisa Ruddick's discussion of the autobiographical axes of "Melanctha," *Three Lives* (New York: Random House, 1936) and *The Making of Americans: Being a History of a Family's Progress* (Paris: Contact Editions, 1925), in *Reading Gertrude Stein: Body, Text, Gnosis* (Ithaca: Cornell Univ. Press, 1990), chaps. 1 and 2.

2. Gertrude Stein, *The Autobiography of Alice B. Toklas* (New York: Random House, 1960), p. 138. All further citations will appear in text.

3. S. C. Neuman also explores the inside/outside nature of the ring in *Gertrude Stein: Autobiography and the Problem of Narration* (Victoria, B.C.: English Literary Studies Monograph Series, 1979), p. 15.

4. Ruddick, pp. 148–49.

5. See, for instance, Leigh Gilmore, "A Signature of Lesbian Autobiography: 'Gertrice/Altrude,' " *Prose Studies* 14 (September 1991): 57–58. Also see Catharine Stimpson, "Gertrice/Altrude: Stein, Toklas, and the Paradox of the Happy Marriage," in *Mothering the Mind: Twelve Studies of Writers and Their Silent Partners,* ed. Ruth Perry and Martine Watson Brownley (New York: Holmes and Meier, 1984), pp. 126–30.

6. Gilmore also comments on the semiotics of the photograph in "Signature," p. 66.

7. Timothy Dow Adams tracks how Stein offers various hints throughout the text that the putative authorship is duplicitous, in *Telling Lies in Modern American Autobiography* (Chapel Hill: Univ. of North Carolina Press, 1990), pp. 31–32.

8. The complexity of its referent, Daniel Defoe's *Robinson Crusoe,* as Timothy Dow Adams notes, was anything but "simply" taken as fiction when it was published, pp. 34–35.

9. Gilmore, "Signature," pp. 63-65.

10. Julia Watson, "Unspeakable Differences: The Politics of Gender in Lesbian and Heterosexual Women's Autobiographies," in *De/Colonizing the Subject: The Politics of Gender in Women's Autobiography,* ed. Sidonie Smith and Julia Watson (Minneapolis: Univ. of Minnesota Press, 1992).

11. Ruddick invokes the anthropological notion of sacrifice as a cultural ritual that secures a mind-body dualism, and thus a male-female hierarchization of sexual difference, in her discussion of Stein's most radical experiments, chap. 4 and conclusion.

12. Neuman, pp. 15–17.

13. James E. Breslin, "Gertrude Stein and the Problems of Autobiography," in *Women's Autobiography: Essays in Criticism*, ed. Estelle C. Jelinek (Bloomington: Indiana Univ. Press, 1980), p. 151.

14. Gilmore, "Signature."

15. Philippe Lejeune, "Autobiography in the Third Person," *New Literary History* 9 (1977): 34. Quoted also in Adams, p. 21.

16. The term comes from a paper entitled "Border Culture," delivered by William Nericcio at the American Comparative Literature Association's annual meeting, San Diego, March 1991.

17. See Françoise Lionnet, *Autobiographical Voices: Race, Gender, Self-Portraiture* (Ithaca: Cornell Univ. Press, 1989), pp. 1–30.

18. Ruddick elaborates Stein's use of the word *excreate* as part and parcel of her bodily (excremetal) imagery of filling and emptying, pp. 138–45. I use the term here to connote the idea of self-creation through an externalized perspective.

19. In the *Autobiography,* Stein oscillates between establishing herself as "entity" (the center, the iconic voice) and as embedded in and embedding the times (the mobility of the text, its endless procession of famous and not-so-famous visitors, its historical rootedness). In *A Different Language: Gertrude Stein's Experimental Writing* (Madison: Univ. of Wisconsin Press, 1983), Marianne DeKoven writes that "in her lectures and essays, Stein elaborates two central, contradictory threads of argument: literature must be absolutely pure (serve 'god' rather than 'mammon,' in Stein's terminology), but at the same time it must express and create its time, its 'composition' " (24). DeKoven calls this an oscillation between two concepts of time, the maternal and the paternal, story and art. "Stein's thought offers no synthesis, no answer to that question. Her unwitting theoretical alternation between the norms of artistic purity and of expressing/creating the modern composition in fact resembles the ideal cultural alternation, the permanent dialectic, which Kristeva proposed between the modes of the Mother and the Father" (25–26).

20. Breslin, p. 156.

21. Breslin suggests that "Toklas, no Vallaton proceeding along pre-designed lines, moves by playful, free association—thereby liberating herself from chronological order, while still accepting the reality of chronological time" (160–61).

22. Neuman, p. 23.

23. Marianne DeKoven, in an introductory essay to Gertrude Stein's writings, in *The Gender of Modernism: A Critical Anthology,* ed. Bonnie Kime Scott (Bloomington: Indiana Univ. Press, 1990), pp. 483–84.

24. Catharine Stimpson, "The Somograms of Gertrude Stein," in *The*

Female Body in Western Culture: Contemporary Perspectives, ed. Susan Rubin Suleiman (Cambridge: Harvard Univ. Press, 1986), p. 35.

25. See DeKoven, *A Different Language,* p. 36, and Ruddick, p. 65.

26. See Ruddick, chaps. 1 and 2.

27. Ruddick discusses Stein's use of the term *singular,* p. 64.

28. DeKoven, *A Different Language,* p. 137. See also Catharine Stimpson, "The Mind, the Body and Gertrude Stein," *Critical Inquiry* 3 (Spring 1977): 489–506; and Elizabeth Fifer, "Is Flesh Advisable? The Interior Theater of Gertrude Stein," *Signs* 4 (Spring 1979): 472–83.

29. Stimpson, "Gertrice/Altrude."

30. DeKoven, *A Different Language,* p. 36. See also Shari Benstock, *Women of the Left Bank: Paris, 1900-1940* (Austin: Univ. of Texas Press, 1986), pp. 143–93.

31. Stimpson, "Somograms," p. 35.

32. Ruddick, p. 189.

33. Ibid., p. 212. See also Catharine Stimpson, "Gertrude Stein and the Transposition of Gender," in *The Poetics of Gender,* ed. Nancy K. Miller (New York: Columbia Univ. Press, 1986), pp. 1–18.

34. Stein, *Everybody's Autobiography* (New York: Random House, 1937), pp. 133, 298. Quoted also in Neuman, p. 19.

35. Neuman, p. 20. Newman explores the roots of developmental and impressionistic autobiography and Stein's rejection of both.

36. There are other ways in which Stein resists paternal origins. Her writing generally and the autobiography in particular are devoid of allusions which point to cultural and linguistic inheritances, to paternities of thought and expression, to embeddedness in the pastness of the past. Allusions tie the text to the past, referring backward in a direction against the grain of Stein's conception of "contemporaneity."

37. "Stein exploited," argues Neuman, "that ambiguity [of object and subject] in her repeated attempts to realize a dissociation of the written words from the writer's identity, to make her narrative 'disembodied' " (15).

38. From the Middle English *oste,* the Old French *oiste,* and the Latin *hostia* for sacrifice or victim.

39. For a discussion of the ways in which the language and rhetoric of "Alice" enter Stein's sentences and text, see Adams, p. 23; James R. Mellow, *Charmed Circle: Gertrude Stein and Company* (New York: Avon Books, 1974), p. 524; and Donald Sutherland, *Gertrude Stein: A Biography of Her Work* (New Haven: Yale Univ. Press, 1951), pp. 148–49.

40. See Ruddick, p. 148.

41. See Adams, p. 37.

42. Gilmore, "Signature," p. 64.

43. All three words share the same root.

44. Stimpson, "Somograms," p. 33.

45. For a fascinating analysis, see Ruddick, chap. 4.

46. Judith Butler, *Gender Trouble: Feminism and the Subversion of Identity* (New York: Routledge, 1990), pp. 122–23. Butler also argues that "this purification of homosexuality, a kind of lesbian modernism, is currently contested by numerous lesbian and gay discourses that understand lesbian and gay culture as embedded in the larger structures of heterosexuality even as they are positioned in subversive or resignificatory relationships to heterosexual cultural configurations.... My own conviction is that the radical disjunction posited by Wittig between heterosexuality and homosexuality is simply not true, that there are structures of psychic homosexuality within heterosexual relations, and structures of psychic heterosexuality within gay and lesbian sexuality and relationships. Further, there are other power/discourse centers that construct and structure both gay and straight sexuality; heterosexuality is not the only compulsory display of power that informs sexuality" (121–22).

47. Ibid., p. 335.

48. On the encoding of lesbian experience in Stein's work, see Stimpson, "The Mind" and "Somagrams," pp. 30–43.

49. I invoke here Luce Irigaray, "When Our Lips Speak Together," in *This Sex Which Is Not One*, trans. Catherine Porter (Ithaca: Cornell Univ. Press, 1985), pp. 205–18.

50. For a discussion of Stein's use of the "dirty" and its relationship to the body, writing, and the materiality of language, see Ruddick, chaps. 2 and 3.

51. But this device does much more ideological work, as Timothy Dow Adams suggests. It is evoked for humorous effect, for instance. Its use in the sentence adds a hint of formality to an otherwise informal and often colloquial biographical language. Then too, it spoofs, as Lynn Z. Bloom suggests, "the convention that has persisted in women's biographies throughout the centuries of addressing women subjects by their first names, regardless of their age, rank, or social status," "Gertrude Is Alice Is Everybody: Innovation and Point of View in Gertrude Stein's Autobiographies," *Twentieth-Century Literature* 24 (1978): 83. "Alice" also makes of Stein an oracular voice. Describing her first meeting with Stein, "Alice" recalls, "I was impressed by the coral brooch she wore and by her voice" (5). If "Alice" is the speaking voice, "Gertrude Stein" is the spoken word.

52. Roland Barthes, *The Pleasure of the Text*, trans. Richard Miller (New York: Farrar, Straus, and Giroux, 1975). See also Ruddick, pp. 75–76.

53. Early on she is identified in the text with the moon, the symbol of the female that Stein used throughout her experimental writing practices, when she describes a small blue hat she wore through the streets of Montmartre (14).

54. Ruddick, pp. 151–52.

55. See Teresa de Lauretis, *Technologies of Gender* (Bloomington: Indiana Univ. Press, 1987), p. 17.

5. The Autobiographical Eye/I in Virginia Woolf's "Sketch"

1. Virginia Woolf, "A Sketch of the Past," in *Moments of Being: Unpublished Autobiographical Writings* (New York: Harcourt Brace Jovanovich, 1976), p. 65.

2. Jean Schulkind, Introduction, to Virginia Woolf, *Moments of Being*, p. 11.

3. Woolf indicates in her diary that she read the following autobiographical works: *Journal of Eugene Delacroix*, three volumes; *The Magnificent Rothschilds*; Sir Edward Marsh, *A Number of People*; Andre Gide, *Journal 1885–1939*; F. L. Lucas, *Journal under the Terror*; Elizabeth Robins, *Both Sides of the Curtain*; Robert Francis Kilvert, *Diary*; *The Life and Letters of William Bewick*; Sir Walter Scott, *Journal*; Francis Steegmuller, *Flaubert and Mme Bovary: A Double Portrait*; Emile Blanche, *More Portraits of a Lifetime, 1918–38*; Gerald Heard, *Pain, Sex, and Time*; *Self-Portrait Taken from the Letters and Journals of Charles Ricketts, RA*, compiled by T. Surge Moore; *Letters and Diaries of Henry, Tenth Earl of Pembroke and His Circle, 1734–80*; Gilbert Frankau, *Self-Portrait: A Novel of His Own Life*.

4. Virginia Woolf, "DeQuincey's Autobiography," *Collected Essays*, vol. 4 (New York: Harcourt Brace Jovanovich, 1967), p. 2.

5. See Rachel Blau DuPlessis, *Writing beyond the Ending: Narrative Strategies of Twentieth-Century Women Writers* (Bloomington: Indiana Univ. Press, 1985), p. 162. See also Melba Cuddy-Keane, "The Politics of Comic Modes in Virginia Woolf's *Between the Acts*," *PMLA* 105 (March 1990): 273–85.

6. DuPlessis, p. 162.

7. Ibid., p. 167. The internal quotation is from Virginia Woolf, *The Years* (New York: Harcourt Brace Jovanovich, 1937), p. 296.

8. Woolf, "Sketch," p. 100. All further citations will appear in the text.

9. Madeline Moore argues that during this period Woolf became increasingly dependent upon Leonard for protection and support. See her discussion of the circumstances surrounding the writing of *Between the Acts*, in *The Short Season between Two Silences: The Mystical and the Political in the Novels of Virginia Woolf* (Boston: George Allen & Unwin, 1984), pp. 147–52.

10. See Sue Roe, *Writing and Gender: Virginia Woolf's Writing Practice* (New York: St. Martin's Press, 1990), pp. 41–42. Roe also argues that Woolf "recognized that the external integrity upon which she had always called to counter her sense of inner chaos and fragmentation began instead, with the onset of the Second World War, to *echo* that process of disintegration. . . . the war, and the recent deaths of many of her friends, had effected the removal of her sense of an audience and thus her sense of herself as at once separate from and connected to an external reality" (41).

11. Of course, narcissism and egotism carry different ideological valences for male and female autobiographers.

12. Woolf began to read Freud seriously as she revised the biography of Roger Fry. For a discussion of the significance of her reading of Freud, see Panthea Reid Broughton, " 'Virginia Is Anal': Speculations on Virginia Woolf's Writing *Roger Fry* and Reading Sigmund Freud," *Journal of Modern Literature* 14 (Summer 1987): 151–57. For another analysis that considers the differences in the first two memories, see Shari Benstock, "Authorizing the Autobiographical," in *The Private Self: Theory and Practice of Women's Autobiographical Writings* (Chapel Hill: Univ. of North Carolina Press, 1988), pp. 23–25.

13. See also Mark Spilka, *Virginia Woolf's Quarrel with Grieving* (Lincoln: Univ. of Nebraska Press, 1980), p. 31.

14. Hélène Cixous, "The Laugh of the Medusa," in *New French Feminisms,* ed. Elaine Marks and Isabelle de Courtivron (New York: Schocken Books, 1981), p. 250.

15. John Berger, *Ways of Seeing* (New York: Viking, 1973), p. 47.

16. Julia Kristeva, *The Powers of Horror: An Essay on Abjection* (New York: Columbia Univ. Press, 1982), p. 82.

17. Roe, p. 49. For a different analysis of Woolf's relationship to sensuality, see Phyllis Rose, *Woman of Letters: A Life of Virginia Woolf* (New York: Oxford Univ. Press, 1978). Rose argues that Woolf erases sexuality from the text, even though the opening richly elaborates moments of sensual ecstasy. For Rose the memoirs exude a "well-bred, repressed, but unmistakable eroticism." Despite this "unmistakable" marking of the body, Rose concludes that "Woolf goes out of her way in 'A Sketch of the Past' to prove that she was frigid from birth, telling about Gerald Duckworth's exploration of her and her response to it to assert the myth of her congenital asexuality. She protests, one feels, rather too strongly, and the sensual texture of her recollections belies her point. This was not an anaesthetic childhood" (17–18).

18. For a comparative discussion of this process in Woolf's earlier "Reminiscences" and "Sketch," see LuAnn McCracken, " 'The Synthesis of My Being': Autobiography and the Reproduction of Identity in Virginia Woolf," *Tulsa Studies in Women's Literature* 9 (Spring 1990): 61–67.

19. See Phyllis Rose for another structural understanding of "Sketch." Rose argues that the structure is tripartite. The first "act" takes up the maternal story; the second act the two deaths, of her mother and Stella, and what Rose calls the fatality of mothering; the third act takes up the male ego and egotism and the relationship of the daughter to the father and to the larger social arena.

20. Woolf, *Orlando: A Biography* (New York and London: Harcourt Brace Jovanovich, 1928), pp. 170–71.

21. Peter Stallybrass and Allon White, *The Politics and Poetics of Transgression* (Ithaca: Cornell Univ. Press, 1986), p. 90.

22. See Daniel Albright, "Virginia Woolf as Autobiographer," *Kenyon Review* 6 (Fall 1984): 11.

23. Woolf, "Street Haunting: A London Adventure," in *Collected Essays,* vol. 4 (London: Hogarth Press, 1967), p. 156.

24. Woolf, "On Being Ill," in *Collected Essays,* vol. 4, p. 199.

25. Woolf, "Street Haunting," p. 165.

26. Ibid., p. 161. For a critique of the conservative nature of Woolf's haunting of the London streets, see Susan Merrill Squier, *Virginia Woolf and London: The Sexual Politics of the City* (Chapel Hill: Univ. of North Carolina Press, 1985), pp. 44–51. Squier finds that "description has free reign in this imaginary tour of London, but social criticism is markedly restrained."

27. See McCracken, p. 72.

28. See Roe, pp. 157–58, for references to the linkage Woolf draws between water, petals floating through water and air, fishing, submersion in the stream, all as figurative ways of suggesting a different kind of writing practice, an outsider's, a woman's writing practice.

29. Virginia Woolf, entry for November 1, 1940, *Diary,* p. 335.

30. "The past only comes back," she writes,

> when the present runs so smoothly that it is like the sliding surface of a deep river. Then one sees through the surface to the depths. In those moments I find one of my greatest satisfactions, not that I am thinking of the past; but that it is then that I am living most fully in the present. For the present when backed by the past is a thousand times deeper than the present when it presses so close that you can feel nothing else, when the film on the camera reaches only the eye. But to feel the present sliding over the depths of the past, peace is necessary. The present must be smooth, habitual. For this reason— that it destroys the fullness of life—any break—like that of house moving—causes me extreme distress; it breaks; it shallows; it turns the depth into hard thin splinters. . . . So I write this, taking a morning off from the word filing and fitting that my life of Roger means—I write this partly in order to recover my sense of the present by getting the past to shadow this broken surface. Let me then, like a child advancing with bare feet into a cold river, descend again into that stream. (98)

As past and present moments commingle in a fluid layering of time, time loses its stifling linearity, and death, as part of the ongoingness of time, some of its sting.

31. Benstock, p. 27.

32. Luce Irigaray, *Speculum of the Other Woman,* trans. Gillian C. Gill (Ithaca: Cornell Univ. Press, 1985), p. 145.

33. Roe, chap. 6.

6. Diasporan Subjectivity and Identity Politics in Zora Neale Hurston's *Dust Tracks on a Road*

1. Robert E. Hemenway, "Introduction," to Zora Neale Hurston, *Dust Tracks on a Road* (Urbana: Univ. of Illinois Press, 1984), pp. xii–xiii. See also Hemenway, "Ambiguities of Self, Politics of Race," in *Zora Neale Hurston: A Literary Biography* (Urbana: Univ. of Illinois Press, 1977), pp. 273–318. Hurston's failure to take an unambiguous, hard-edged stand on race relations may have provoked Darwin T. Turner to condemn her as "a blind follower of that social code which approves arrogance toward one's assumed peers and inferiors but requires total psychological commitment to a subservient posture before one's supposed superiors." See Darwin T. Turner, *In a Minor Chord: Three Afro-American Writers and Their Search for Identity* (Carbondale: Southern Illinois Univ. Press, 1971), p. 98.

2. Craig Werner, "On the Ends of Afro-American 'Modernist' Autobiography," *Black American Literature Forum* 24 (Summer 1990): 208. Werner is briefly surveying certain trends in autobiographical texts written in the first half of the twentieth century.

3. Barbara Johnson, *A World of Difference* (Baltimore: Johns Hopkins Univ. Press, 1987), p. 183.

4. Claudine Raynaud, "*Dust Tracks on a Road:* Autobiography as a 'Lying' Session," *Studies in Black American Literature*, vol. 3, ed. Joe Weixlman and Houston A. Baker, Jr. (Greenwood: Penkevill, 1988), pp. 111–38.

5. Nellie Y. McKay, "Race, Gender, and Cultural Context in Zora Neale Hurston's *Dust Tracks on a Road*," in *Life/Lines: Theorizing Women's Autobiography,* ed. Bella Brodzki and Celeste Schenck (Ithaca: Cornell Univ. Press, 1988), pp. 177, 187. McKay identifies the narrator of *Dust Tracks* with "the African *griot,* whose memory preserves the sense of a past culture" rather than the "political activist" who "struggle[s] to improve contemporary black life" (184).

6. Françoise Lionnet, *Autobiographical Voices: Race, Gender, Self-Portraiture* (Ithaca: Cornell Univ. Press, 1989), pp. 97–129.

7. Zora Neale Hurston, *Dust Tracks on a Road,* p. 3. All further citations will appear in the text.

8. Joanne M. Braxton, *Black Women Writing Autobiography: A Tradition within a Tradition* (Philadelphia: Temple Univ. Press, 1989), p. 146.

9. See Raynaud, p. 113. The topics of the second half of the text are research, friendship or kinship ties, love relationships, and religion.

10. Lionnet, p. 100.

11. Raynaud, p. 112.

12. Raynaud, p. 113.

13. Raynaud has revealed the impact of editorial intervention on Hurston's analyses of black employee/white employee relationships in her essay, " 'Rubbing a Paragraph with a Soft Cloth'? Muted Voices and

Editorial Constraints in *Dust Tracks on a Road*," in *De/Colonizing the Subject: The Politics of Gender in Women's Autobiography*, ed. Sidonie Smith and Julia Watson (Minneapolis: Univ. of Minnesota Press, 1992), pp. 34–64. In the deleted passages the critique is much more direct and biting and is informed with an insistent feminist perspective.

14. Ibid., p. 47.

15. Stephen Butterfield, *Black Autobiography in America* (Amherst: Univ. of Massachusetts Press, 1974), pp. 2–3.

16. Alice A. Deck, "Autoethnography: Zora Neale Hurston, Noni Jabavu, and Cross-Disciplinary Discourse," *Black American Literature Forum* 24 (Summer 1990): 237. For additional comparisons of the tradition of women's and men's autobiographical writings in the African-American literary tradition, see William L. Andrews, *To Tell a Free Story: The First One Hundred Years of Afro-American Autobiography* (Urbana: Univ. of Illinois Press, 1986); Braxton; Frances Foster, " 'In Respect to Females . . .': Difference in the Portrayals of Women by Male and Female Narrators," *Black American Literature Forum* 15 (Summer 1981): 66–70; Nellie Y. McKay, "Race, Gender," p. 177.

17. See James Baldwin, "Everybody's Protest Novel," in *Notes of a Native Son* (New York: Dell, 1955), pp. 13–23.

18. See Biddy Martin, "Lesbian Identity and Autobiographical Difference[s]," in Brodzki and Schenck, p. 103. Martin is here theorizing lesbian identities.

19. Johnson, p. 175.

20. Hurston's resistance to identifying according to race invokes strong condemnations of her autobiography. Most recently, Robbie Jean Walker reviewed the problematic because politically "naïve" emphasis Hurston places on individualism as opposed to race solidarity in the autobiography, in "Looking for Zora: Myth and Reality," paper delivered at the Women of Color Conference, Ocean Beach, Maryland, May 28–30, 1991.

21. Elizabeth Fox-Genovese, "My Statue, My Self: Autobiographical Writings of Afro-American Women," in *The Private Self: Theory and Practice of Women's Autobiographical Writings*, ed. Shari Benstock (Chapel Hill: Univ. of North Carolina Press, 1988), p. 81.

22. "In the depiction of Afro-American autonomy in Eatonville and in the young girl's wish for a horse," argues Nellie Y. McKay, "can be seen a deliberately constructed explanation of Hurston's later refusals to conform to the expectations of either the black or the white world. By foregrounding her rejection of certain limitations on her individuality, her childhood rebellion and transcendence, the woman manages to remain within the community identity while asserting the self from it" (186).

23. Critics have pointed again and again to this gap in the text without considering the nature of their (unfulfilled) expectations. For a discussion of the marginalization of heterosexual coupling in *Their Eyes Were Watching God*, see Molly Hite, "Romance, Marginality, and Matrilineage: *The Color Purple* and *Their Eyes Were Watching God*," in *Reading Black*,

Reading Feminist: A Critical Anthology, ed. Henry Louis Gates, Jr. (New York: Meridian Books, 1990), pp. 431–53.

24. For a discussion of the woman-woman or daughter-mother dynamic in Hurston's fiction, see Hite, in Gates, 431–53.

25. See Lionnet, 117–23. The death of the mother is the beginning of the long wandering, the long uncertain journey that becomes a narrative spine to the autobiographical text.

26. I am aware of the implications of dividing the discussion of racial and sexual identities into two separate discussions. The division is artificial, the identities simultaneous and mutually constitutive. For problems of dividing the issues, see Elizabeth V. Spelman, *Inessential Woman: Problems of Exclusion in Feminist Thought* (Boston: Beacon Press, 1988), chaps. 5, 6, 7.

27. See Raynaud, "Rubbing," p. 49. The material comes from MS, folder 14, pp. 212–13.

28. Ibid. The elimination of this passage suggests how editorial intervention moderated and even hushed Hurston's intensely political voice.

29. See Michele Wallace, "Variations on Negation and the Heresy of Black Feminist Creativity," in Gates, *Reading Black,* pp. 52–67; and Barbara Johnson, *A World of Difference,* pp. 166–71.

30. Zora Neale Hurston, *Their Eyes Were Watching God* (Urbana: Univ. of Illinois Press, 1978), p. 29.

31. As Claudine Renaud has remarked, *Dust Tracks on a Road* is sprinkled with moments of female confrontation and female violence.

32. Lionnet, p. 118.

33. Raynaud explores the way in which the pervasiveness and intensity of the sexual voice is mediated through editorial intervention, "Rubbing," pp. 40–43.

34. See Karla F. C. Holloway, *The Character of the Word: The Texts of Zora Neale Hurston* (Westport, Conn.: Greenwood Press, 1987), pp. 114–15.

35. Peter Stallybrass and Allon White, *The Politics and Poetics of Transgression* (Ithaca: Cornell Univ. Press, 1986), p. 199.

36. See Lionnet, p. 102.

37. See, for instance, Johnson.

38. Raynaud discusses the changes in the passage from the typescript to the published version, "Rubbing," pp. 42–43.

39. Johnson, p. 171.

40. See Mae Gwendolyn Henderson, "Speaking in Tongues: Dialogics, Dialectics, and the Black Woman Writer's Literary Tradition," in Gates, *Reading Black,* pp. 116–42.

41. See Holloway, pp. 101–11.

42. I realize that the problem certain critics have with Hurston's position has much to do with the fact that it is played out before the white audience, an audience only too willing to dismiss the grounds for racial pride in the black community.

43. Lionnet discusses the issue of homelessness as it relates to the death of Hurston's mother, p. 166. Hurston's narrative suggests that the psychological restlessness/homelessness emerges earlier than Lionnet suggests.

44. Henderson, p. 137.

7. The Bodies of Contemporary Autobiographical Practice

1. Nancy Fraser, *Unruly Practices: Power, Discourse and Gender in Contemporary Social Theory* (Minneapolis: Univ. of Minnesota Press, 1989), p. 3.

2. Biddy Martin and Chandra Talpade Mohanty, "Feminist Politics: What's Home Got to Do with It?" in *Feminist Studies/Critical Studies,* ed. Teresa de Lauretis (Bloomington: Indiana Univ. Press, 1986), p. 195.

3. Biddy Martin, "Lesbian Identity and Autobiographical Difference[s]," in *Life/Lines: Theorizing Women's Autobiography,* ed. Bella Brodzki and Celeste Schenck (Ithaca: Cornell Univ. Press, 1988), p. 81.

4. Martin and Mohanty, p. 195.

5. See Denise Riley, *"Am I That Name?" Feminism and the Category of "Women" in History* (Minneapolis: Univ. of Minnesota Press, 1988), p. 102.

6. Judith Butler, *Gender Trouble: Feminism and the Subversion of Identity* (New York, Routledge, 1990), pp. 114–15. She adds, "That penis, vagina, breasts, and so forth, are *named* sexual parts is both a restriction of the erogenous body to those parts and a fragmentation of the body as a whole. Indeed, the 'unity' imposed upon the body by the category of sex is a 'disunity,' a fragmentation and compartmentalization, and a reduction of erotogeneity" (114).

7. Mary Douglas, *Purity and Danger* (London: Routledge and Kegan Paul, 1969), p. 115. Quoted in Butler, p. 132.

8. Peter Stallybrass and Allon White, *The Politics and Poetics of Transgression* (Ithaca: Cornell Univ. Press, 1986), p. 192.

9. Ibid., p. 3.

10. Fraser, p. 136.

11. Teresa de Lauretis, *Technologies of Gender: Feminism, Film and Fiction* (Bloomington: Indiana Univ. Press, 1987), pp. 9–10. See also Martin in "Lesbian Identity."

12. "That the gendered body is performative suggests that it has no ontological status apart from the various acts which constitute its reality. This also suggests that if that reality is fabricated as an interior essence, that very interiority is an effect and function of a decidedly public and social discourse, the public regulation of fantasy through the surface politics of the body, the gender border control that differentiates inner from outer, and so institutes the 'integrity' of the subject. In other words, acts and gestures, articulated and enacted desires create the illusion of an interior and organizing gender core, an illusion discursively maintained for the purposes of the regulation of sexuality within the obligatory frame of reproductive heterosexuality" (Butler, p. 136).

13. Nancy K. Miller, "Changing the Subject: Authorship, Writing, and the Reader," in de Lauretis, p. 114.

14. Martin, p. 82.

15. Annie Dillard, *An American Childhood* (New York: Harper & Row, 1987), pp. 102, 103. All further citations will appear in the text.

16. See Janet Varner Gunn, "A Politics of Experience: Leila Khaled's *My People Shall Live: An Autobiography of a Revolutionary,*" in *De/Colonizing the Subject: The Politics of Gender in Women's Autobiography,* ed. Sidonie Smith and Julia Watson (Minneapolis: Univ. of Minnesota Press, 1992), p. 68.

17. See Iris Marion Young, "Abjection and Oppression: Dynamics of Unconscious Racism, Sexism, and Homophobia," in *Crises in Continental Philosophy,* ed. Arleen B. Dallery and Charles E. Scott (Albany: State Univ. of New York Press, 1990), p. 208.

18. Stallybrass and White, p. 25. "The 'carnivalesque,' " they suggest, "mediates between a classical/classificatory body and its negations, its Others, what it excludes to create its identity as such. In this process discourses about the body have a privileged role, for transcodings between different levels and sectors of social and psychic reality are effected through the intensifying grid of the body. It is no accident, then, that transgressions and the attempt to control them obsessively return to somatic symbols, for these are ultimate elements of social classification itself" (p. 26).

19. Gunn, p. 70.

20. While I do not fault Dillard her middle-class childhood, parts of which I share with her, I do question the unselfconsciousness of the normatively white subject she produces through her "adult" retrospective.

21. See Monique Wittig, "The Mark of Gender," in *The Poetics of Gender,* ed. Nancy K. Miller (New York: Columbia Univ. Press, 1986), p. 67: "Each time I say 'I,' I reorganize the world from my point of view and through abstraction I lay claim to universality. This fact holds true for every locutor."

22. Cherríe Moraga, *Loving in the War Years* (Boston: South End Press, 1983), p. 30. All further citations will appear in the text.

23. Lourdes Torres, "The Construction of the Self in U.S. Latina Autobiographies," in *Third World Women and the Politics of Feminism,* ed. Chandra Talpade Mohanty, Ann Russo, and Lourdes Torres (Bloomington: Indiana Univ. Press, 1991), p. 278. See also Yvonne Yarbro-Bejarano, "Chicana Literature from a Chicana Feminist Perspective," in *Feminisms: An Anthology of Literary Theory and Criticism,* ed. Robyn R. Warhol and Diane Price Herndl (New Brunswick: Rutgers Univ. Press, 1991), pp. 732–37.

24. See Mae Gwendolyn Henderson, "Speaking in Tongues: Dialogics, Dialectics, and the Black Woman Writer's Literary Tradition," in *Reading Black, Reading Feminist: A Critical Anthology,* ed. Henry Louis Gates, Jr. (New York: Meridian Press, 1990), p. 120.

25. The phrase is used by Adrienne Rich in "Compulsory Heterosexual-

ity and Lesbian Experience," *Signs* 5 (1980): 631–60; and taken up by Butler in *Gender Trouble*.

26. Butler, p. 136.

27. Susan Rubin Suleiman, "Re/Writing the Body: The Politics and Poetics of Female Eroticism," in *The Female Body in Western Culture: Contemporary Perspectives,* ed. Susan Rubin Suleiman (Cambridge: Harvard Univ. Press, 1986), p. 16.

28. Carroll Smith-Rosenberg, "The Body Politic," in *Coming to Terms: Feminism, Theory, Politics* (New York: Routledge, 1989), p. 102.

29. See Mary Ann Caws's discussion of Lewis Hyde's recent theorizing of the gift, in "Ladies Shot and Painted: Female Embodiment in Surrealist Art," in Suleiman, *Female Body,* p. 285: "To the theories of Mauss, Hyde adds emotion in the place of economics: what cannot be given does not exist as a gift.... A gift, he says, is anarchist property, 'because both anarchism and gift exchange share the assumption that it is not when a part of the self is inhibited and restrained, but when a part of the self is given away, that community appears.' The fragmented self—even a part of us—thus given away uninhibitedly, after Mannerism into Surrealism, and to all observers equally, may redeem—should we acquiesce in it—the sort of communal vision that a more classic holistic tradition was not able to save."

30. Linda Singer, "True Confessions: Cixous and Foucault on Sexuality and Power," in *The Thinking Muse: Feminism and Modern French Philosophy,* ed. Jeffner Allen and Iris Marion Young (Bloomington: Indiana Univ. Press, 1989), p. 139.

31. Ibid., p. 137.

32. Julia Watson, "Unspeakable Differences: The Politics of Gender in Lesbian and Heterosexual Women's Autobiographies," in Smith and Watson, *De/Colonizing the Subject,* p. 160.

33. Jo Spence, *Putting Myself in the Picture* (Seattle: Real Comet Press, 1988), p. 45. All further citations will appear in the text.

34. See Watson, p. 161.

35. See Hélène Cixous, "Castration or Decapitation?" trans. Annette Kuhn, *Signs* 7 (1981): 41–55; Toril Moi, *Sexual/Textual Politics: Feminist Literary Theory* (London: Metheun, 1985), pp. 110–12.

36. We might think of the many female bodies in recent works by women: the father's words written on the back of the woman warrior in Maxine Hong Kingston's *The Woman Warrior,* the scars/signs on Sethe's back in Toni Morrison's *Beloved,* the scars on the body of Dessa Rose in Sherley Anne Williams's novel of the same name.

37. Moi, p. 110.

38. Watson, p. 161.

39. Ibid., p. 162.

8. Autobiographical Manifestos

1. Lourdes Torres, "The Construction of the Self in U. S. Latina Autobiographies," in *Third World Women and the Politics of Feminism,*

ed. Chandra Talpade Mohanty, Ann Russo, and Lourdes Torres (Bloomington: Indiana Univ. Press, 1991), pp. 272–73.

2. Caren Kaplan, "Resisting Autobiography: Out-Law Genres and Transnational Feminist Subjects," in De/Colonizing the Subject: The Politics of Gender in Women's Autobiography, ed. Sidonie Smith and Julia Watson (Minneapolis: Univ. of Minnesota Press, 1992), pp. 115–38.

3. Linda Kintz, "In-Different Criticism: The Deconstructive 'Parole,' " in The Thinking Muse: Feminism and Modern French Philosophy, ed. Jeffner Allen and Iris Marion Young (Bloomington: Indiana University Press, 1989), p. 131.

4. Judith Butler, "Gender Trouble, Feminist Theory, and Psychoanalytic Discourse," in Feminism/Postmodernism, ed. Linda J. Nicholson (New York: Routledge, 1990), p. 327.

5. For a critique of postmodern fragmentation, see Susan Bordo, "Feminism, Postmodernism, and Gender-Scepticism," in Nicholson, pp. 133-56.

6. See Julia Kristeva, "A New Type of Intellectual," in The Kristeva Reader, ed. Toril Moi (Oxford: Basil Blackwell, 1986), pp. 292–300.

7. Judith Butler, Gender Trouble: Feminism and the Subversion of Identity (New York: Routledge, 1990), p. 145.

8. Donna Haraway, "A Manifesto for Cyborgs: Science, Technology, and Socialist Feminism in the 1980s," in Nicholson, p. 191.

9. Robert K. Martin, "Is Anybody There? Critical Practice and Minority Writing," paper delivered at MLA convention, Washington, D.C., December 1989.

10. Nancy Hartsock, "Foucault on Power: A Theory for Women?" in Nicholson, pp. 160–61.

11. Paul Smith, Discerning the Subject (Minneapolis: Univ. of Minnesota Press, 1988), p. 106.

12. The phrase comes from Hartsock, p. 171.

13. Cherríe Moraga, Loving in the War Years (Boston: South End Press, 1983), p. 138.

14. "Knowledge" is "essentially the making visible of material," writes Edward W. Said in Orientalism (New York: Random House, 1979), p. 127. See also Elspeth Probyn, "Travels in the Postmodern: Making Sense of the Local," in Nicholson, p. 178.

15. Hartsock, pp. 171–72.

16. Aida Hurtado, "Relating to Privilege: Seduction and Rejection in the Subordination of White Women and Women of Color," Signs 14 (Summer 1989): 849.

17. Hurtado argues that "for white women, the first step in the search for identity is to confront the ways in which their personal, individual silence endorses the power of white men that has robbed them of their history. For women of Color, the challenge is to use their oral traditions for specific political goals" (pp. 848–49).

18. See also Haraway, p. 205.

19. See Judith Butler's discussion of the relationship of acts to ideas: "Because there is neither an 'essence' that gender expresses or externalizes nor an objective ideal to which gender aspires," Butler says, "and because gender is not a fact, the various acts of gender create the idea of gender, and without those acts, there would be no gender at all. Gender is, thus, a construction that regularly conceals its genesis; the tacitly collective agreement to perform, produce, and sustain discrete and polar genders as cultural fictions is obscured by the credibility of those productions—and the punishments that attend to agreeing to believe in them; the construction 'compels' our belief in its necessity and naturalness. The historical possibilities materialized through various corporeal styles are nothing other than those punitively regulated cultural fictions alternately embodied and deflected under duress" (*Gender Trouble*, p. 140).

20. See Françoise Lionnet, *Autobiographical Voices: Race, Gender, Self-Portraiture* (Ithaca: Cornell Univ. Press, 1989), p. 99.

21. Rita Felski, *Beyond Feminist Aesthetics: Feminist Literature and Social Change* (Cambridge: Harvard Univ. Press, 1989), p. 166.

22. Felski, p. 167. What Felski says of the internal and external dynamics of the feminist counter-public sphere applies to these multiple spheres: "*Internally,* it generates a gender-specific identity grounded in a consciousness of community and solidarity among women; *externally,* it seeks to convince society as a whole of the validity of feminist claims, challenging existing structures of authority through political activity and theoretical critique" (168).

23. Mae Gwendolyn Henderson, "Speaking in Tongues: Dialogics, Dialectics, and the Black Woman's Literary Tradition," in *Reading Black, Reading Feminist: A Critical Anthology,* ed. Henry Louis Gates, Jr. (New York: Meridian, 1990), pp. 118–21.

24. Bernice Johnson Reagon, "Coalition Politics: Turning the Century," in *Home Girls,* ed. Barbara Smith (New York: Kitchen Table Women of Color Press, 1983); quoted in Hartsock, p. 163.

25. Henderson, 121.

26. The collective identification of the manifesto's speaker is perhaps the most problematic aspect of this autobiographical form precisely because the postulation of a counter-public sphere, of "women" for instance, functions yet again as a gesture of universalization, if a universalization whose application is narrower than the hegemonic center's universalization. As recent theorists have argued, community is a problematic utopian ideal. (See Iris Marion Young, "The Ideal of Community and the Politics of Difference," in Nicholson, pp. 300–23; Felski, chap. 5; and Hartsock, p. 171.) Posited on exclusivities, or blindnesses to complex material realities, an idealized community erases differences and contradictory experiences. As Felski notes, "The ideal of a free discursive space that equalizes all participants is an enabling fiction which engenders a sense of collective identity but is achieved only by obscuring actual material inequalities and political antagonisms among its participants" (p. 168). Thus, however

attractive the ideal of "a unified collective subject" might be, we must constantly remind ourselves that the price we pay for celebrating collectivity may be "the actual activities and self-understanding of women, in which gender-based divisions frequently conflict with a whole range of other alliances, such as those based on race or class, and work against any unproblematic notion of harmonious consensus" (Felski, p. 169).

27. Paul de Man, "Autobiography as Defacement," *Modern Language Notes* 94 (1979): 930.

28. Smith, p. 103.

29. Kathleen Woodward, "Simone de Beauvoir: Aging and Its Discontents," in *The Private Self: Theory and Practice of Women's Autobiographical Writings*, ed. Shari Benstock (Chapel Hill: Univ. of North Carolina Press, 1988), pp. 108–109.

30. Hélène Cixous, "The Laugh of the Medusa," in *New French Feminisms: An Anthology*, ed. Elaine Marks and Isabelle de Courtivron (New York: Schocken Books, 1981), p. 249. All further citations will appear in the text.

31. De Lauretis calls these future spaces the "space off"—"those other spaces both discursive and social that exist . . . in the margins . . . of hegemonic discourse and in the interstices of institutions, in counterpractices and new forms of community," in de Lauretis, *The Technologies of Gender: Essays on Theory, Film, and Fiction* (Bloomington: Indiana Univ. Press, 1987), p. 26.

32. Tania Modleski, "Feminism and the Power of Interpretation: Some Critical Readings," in *Feminist Studies/Critical Studies*, ed. Teresa de Lauretis (Bloomington: Indiana Univ. Press, 1986), p. 136.

33. Lionnet, p. 110. As Lionnet has suggested, "Utopian thinking is perhaps the only way out of the impasse created by the neocolonialist strangulation of nations and peoples" (247).

34. Friedrich Nietzsche, *The Will to Power* (New York: Vintage Books, 1968), paragraph 749, p. 396; quoted in Lionnet, p. 74.

35. See Butler, p. 14.

36. Linda Singer argues that for Cixous "the absence of a female-identified discourse adequate to representing women's sexuality in its difference is both a symptom of and instrumental to the continued subjugation of women within the patriarchal order," in "True Confessions: Cixous and Foucault on Sexuality and Power," in Allen and Young, p. 139.

37. Cixous's invocation of "the dark continent" in the midst of this manifesto remains problematic for me. I comment on this in the "Coda."

38. Singer, p. 150.

39. See also Monique Wittig, "The Mark of Gender," in *The Poetics of Gender*, ed. Nancy K. Miller (New York: Columbia Univ. Press, 1986).

40. Gloria Anzaldúa, *Borderlands/La Frontera: The New Mestiza* (San Francisco: Spinsters/Aunt Lute, 1987), p. 80. All further citations will appear in the text.

41. The pastoral speaker is a figure of cultural authority, either con-

ferred or self-identified. Pastoral speakers often refer to previous pastorals, invoking a specifically western genealogy. The speaker joins in that genealogy of artist/intellectuals and assumes generic authority. Over the body of the pastoral, the tug and resistance of generational struggles is played. The pastoral can be invoked to establish genealogy, or it can be invoked to be rejected as an old worn-out form, no longer viable for the new artist. In its embracement and its dismissal it maintains a kind of privileged status.

42. With the romantics, for instance, the pastoral space became the space of an expanding consciousness, forged despite the onslaught of technology, industrialization, urbanization, etc. The pastoral space promised access to a "truer" consciousness.

43. Even in Virgil's *Eclogues,* the authority and power of Rome is pervasive.

44. Roy E. Gridley, "Some Versions of the Primitive and the Pastoral on the Great Plains of America," in *Survivals of Pastoral,* ed. Richard F. Hardin (Lawrence: Univ. of Kansas, 1979), p. 65.

45. See Frederick Garber, "Pastoral Spaces," *Texas Studies in Literature and Language* 30 (Fall 1988): 431–60.

46. With the opening of new territories around the globe, pastoral spaces were identified more with geographical space than with past time, with arcadian and golden ages.

47. See Peter Weston, "The Noble Primitive as Bourgeois Subject," in *The Pastoral Mode,* ed. Bryan Loughrey (London: Macmillan, 1984), pp. 166–80.

48. Lionnet, p. 116.

49. Ibid., p. 189.

50. Ibid., pp. 5–6.

51. Henderson, pp. 122–23.

52. See Edward W. Said, "Yeats and Colonization," in *Nationalism, Colonialism and Literature* (Minneapolis: Univ. of Minnesota Press, 1990), pp. 69–95.

53. Haraway, pp. 190–233. All further citations will appear in the text.

54. Haraway acknowledges the phrase from Rachael Grossman, "Women's Place in the Integrated Circuit," *Radical America* 14 (1980): 29–50.

Coda

1. See Françoise Lionnet, *Autobiographical Voices: Race, Gender, Self-Portraiture* (Ithaca: Cornell University Press, 1989), esp. chap. 1.

2. Donna Haraway, "A Manifesto for Cyborgs: Science, Technology, and Socialist Feminism in the 1980s," in *Postmodernism/Feminism,* ed. Linda J. Nicholson (New York: Routledge, 1990), p. 191.

3. See Monique Wittig, "The Mark of Gender," in *The Poetics of Gender,* ed. Nancy K. Miller (New York: Columbia University Press, 1986), pp. 63–73.

4. See Iris Marion Young, "The Ideal of Community and the Politics of Difference," in *Feminism/Postmodernism,* p. 171.

5. Rita Felski, *Beyond Feminist Aesthetics: Feminist Literature and Social Change* (Cambridge: Harvard University Press, 1989), p. 168.

6. Cherríe Moraga, *Loving in the War Years* (Boston: South End Press, 1983) p. 52.

INDEX

SIDONIE SMITH, professor of English and comparative literature
at the State University of New York at Binghamton, is the author of
*A Poetics of Women's Autobiography: Marginality and the Fictions
of Self-Representation, Where I'm Bound: Patterns of Slavery and
Freedom in Black American Autobiography,* and co-author of *De/
Colonizing the Subject: The Politics of Gender in Women's Autobiography.*